AMERICAN MEDIUM

Cultural Memory in the *Present*

Hent de Vries, Editor

AMERICAN MEDIUM

A New Film Philosophy

Eyal Peretz

STANFORD UNIVERSITY PRESS
Stanford, California

Stanford University Press
Stanford, California

© 2026 by Eyal Peretz. All rights reserved.

No part of this book may be reproduced or transmitted in any form or by any means, electronic or mechanical, including photocopying and recording, or in any information storage or retrieval system, without the prior written permission of Stanford University Press.

Library of Congress Cataloging-in-Publication Data

Names: Peretz, Eyal, author.
Title: American medium : a new film philosophy / Eyal Peretz.
Other titles: Cultural memory in the present.
Description: Stanford, California : Stanford University Press, 2026. | Series: Cultural memory in the present | Includes bibliographical references and index.
Identifiers: LCCN 2025008016 (print) | LCCN 2025008017 (ebook) | ISBN 9781503644229 (cloth) | ISBN 9781503644984 (paperback) | ISBN 9781503644991 (ebook)
Subjects: LCSH: National characteristics, American, in motion pictures. | Motion pictures—United States—History. | Motion pictures—Philosophy. | LCGFT: Film criticism.
Classification: LCC PN1995.9.N34 P37 2025 (print) | LCC PN1995.9.N34 (ebook) | DDC 791.4301—dc23/eng/20250527
LC record available at https://lccn.loc.gov/2025008016
LC ebook record available at https://lccn.loc.gov/2025008017

Cover design: Bob Aufuldish, Aufuldish & Warinner
Cover image: Bob Aufuldish, *Borrowed Landscape #9219*, 2013

The authorized representative in the EU for product safety and compliance is: Mare Nostrum Group B.V. | Mauritskade 21D | 1091 GC Amsterdam | The Netherlands | Email address: gpsr@mare-nostrum.co.uk | KVK chamber of commerce number: 96249943

Contents

INTRODUCTION
The Question of America   1

1   To Be in America   22
    STEVEN SPIELBERG'S *WEST SIDE STORY*

2   The Memory of America   57
    JOHN FORD'S *YOUNG MR. LINCOLN* AND *THE MAN
    WHO SHOT LIBERTY VALANCE*

3   American Tragedy Between Sacred Sacrifice   105
    and Democratic Image
    FRANCIS FORD COPPOLA'S *THE GODFATHER*

4   An American Revolution   150
    SOFIA COPPOLA'S *LOST IN TRANSLATION*
    AND *MARIE ANTOINETTE*

CONCLUSION
The Law and Passion of the Medium   196

Notes   205

Index   229

AMERICAN MEDIUM

INTRODUCTION

The Question of America

What is the secret desire inscribed in American film? Is one even entitled to ask such a general and grandiose question? Shouldn't we instead talk about this or that film, at this or that historical moment, perhaps from this or that region, or as a work created by members of this or that group, or gender, or persuasion? Or, perhaps, we should instead talk of Hollywood versus indie, experimental avant-garde versus commercial, and so on? Are we even entitled to speak of America in the singular rather than of the Americas, "America" being understood—not without good reason—as the name a specific political entity, the United States, has imperially assumed as if it were the sole consequential occupier of an entire region of the world comprising numerous nations and peoples, or as if it were entitled, due to its economic and military might, at the heart of which lies an extraordinary will to power and boundless desire for appropriation, to be one part of a large region, the Americas, that arrogantly assumes the name of the whole?

All of these are undoubtedly valid considerations. Nevertheless, a guiding intuition of this book is that something essential, above and beyond the many problematic issues involved, still resonates and calls to us in the singular name "America" when it is uttered from the context of the specific historical, political, and geographic entity known as the United States, as if expressing something that in, or from within, the United States desires to name something larger, more than, this specific entity. Yet this "more" is of a new kind, a more for which one of the privileged sites of inscription will be the art of film. How is one to think about this more, and can it be distinguished from a will to power and domination that in its essence would like to take over the entirety of the world and even beyond ("to infinity and beyond," to quote a distinguished cinematic character), a will to power for which even the sky is not the limit?

American Exceptionalism

This "more" that the term "America" seems to try to name or express, when used by the United States about itself to name something more than itself, so to speak, can be associated with the oft-used, equally celebrated and critiqued term "exceptionalism." The United States has notoriously laid claim to an American sort of exceptionalism, meaning that there is something in it that is more than any other place, a more that inscribes itself perhaps in the very appropriation of the term "America" to itself, as if it needs this term to express something that the United States, as simply one political-historical entity among many others, cannot. This more inscribed in the use of the term "America," we can say, takes the United States outside (the "ex" prefix, which will interest us, marking always a passage to an outside) or perhaps cuts it out from all the other places and peoples, claiming an apartness that has often and in many cases justly been heavily criticized as an arrogant, power-hungry claim to superiority. Laying claim to "America," something that seems larger, more abstract, and more general than it, the United States appears to want to point to its exceptionality, to its being set apart. The "ex," cutting it out of and separating it from all other places and people, is what the "more" expressed in America, above and beyond the United States, points to. "America" as "more" is that which inscribes the cut severing the United States from every other place and people. In this sense the "more" should be understood not as a quantitative more but as a separating cut.

Of course, there are many ways to understand this cut-out apartness of a group of people, which should not necessarily be reduced to a will to power. One of the most influential models, playing a major role in the conception of an American exception, is that of the Jews of the Old Testament, where exceptionality is articulated through "chosenness," a privileged relation to the divine. This exceptionality seems to indicate both that the divine has a certain preference for this group of people and that this group of people's conception of, or revelation of, the divine is different from that of all other peoples. It is the divine that is different, set apart, from all other understandings and revelations of the divine, and this setting apart also sets apart those who relate to it, who receive their significance from it and through this reception are cut off from everyone else. While we cannot enter here into the question of the Jewish God, we can mention that this God importantly implies a cut in a more fundamental manner. Not only is it different from all the other gods, but it is a cut in that it no longer belongs to any specific time and place but is transcendent with respect to the entire world, governing the world from beyond any specific time and place. Cut out of the actual world, the Jewish divine withdraws from it to a non-place and non-time (rather than occupying this or that specific place, as in the case of the previous gods), introducing into the world an abyssal dimension, that is, an absence one cannot locate. It is in becoming inscribed by the abyss that one is chosen, cut out from the rest. The chosen, then, are witnesses to the cut that sets them apart, outside, but they also, no less importantly, as such witnesses, acquire a responsibility for the whole, for everyone and every place. This is the case since the divine cut by which they are called, because it is cut out of all specific places and times, is that on which all times and places depend.

But the United States, which claims for itself an exceptionality, a being cut out from the rest (a cutting out, I argue, expressed in its claiming for itself the more general and abstract name America), is not a sacred biblical land. It is a political entity that emerged in that historical age usually referred to as modernity, an age associated with what has been called the "death of God," the centuries-long demise of that experience and understanding of the world—a demise whose initial primary site was Christian Europe—as dominated and guided by a transcendent entity from above, from beyond the world. What can, in such a context, legitimate the claim to exceptionality and chosenness, a claim clearly modeled on the logic of biblical Judaism? What is the cut that the United States points to, through its claim for itself the status of being a privileged and chosen witness to such a cut? Despite many of the declarations throughout its history that seem to try, in a revivalist or nostalgic mode, to renew what we can call the theological model of being chosen, with the United States claiming that it has been chosen by the divine to have a privileged destiny, it is clear that the cut by which the

United States is haunted, not unlike Hamlet is by his father's ghost, and paradoxically compelling it to an experience of chosenness, is nothing but *the cut of modernity* itself. By modernity I here mean the death of God that is the cut to the world's theological-metaphysical ordering by a transcendent agent withdrawn from the world. For numerous reasons we cannot get into in this context, including its birth in revolution, its predominantly Protestant provenance, its geographical disconnection from Christian Europe, its becoming a site of numerous groups of people of various origins who do not share a history, language, traditions, and so on, it is clear that the United States has registered, and perhaps is still registering, what we can understand as the modern cut, the death of God (a cut that by now has struck, of course, the entire world), in a uniquely powerful way.

But why should we understand modernity itself, the death of God, as a cut, if we have understood that the revelation of the Jewish divine as uniquely withdrawing from the world, from any specific place and time, is itself a cut that set the Jews, as its witnesses, apart? If the Jewish God, and later the monotheistic God of the other Abrahamic religions, was itself a cut, why should its death also be considered a cut? The answer lies in its death, or withdrawal, deepening rather than erasing the cut made by the revelation of the monotheistic divine.

Drawing on Jean-Luc Nancy's important work on the question of modernity, especially in his *Dis-enclosure: The Deconstruction of Christianity*, I suggest that the death of God inscribed in the birth of the modern was an event with two faces. One face reexposed the primal cut, the cut opened through the revelation of the Jewish God and later amplified in its Christian elaboration (the cut of the divine out of the world, its withdrawal from the world). The cut needed to have been reexposed, or forced itself to reappear as a traumatic irruption, since from the beginning it was immediately sutured and covered over via the withdrawal from the world being substantialized and transformed into that which is occupied by an invisible transcendent agent governing the world from the beyond. From this perspective, the death of God names the elimination of any governing transcendent agency even as the withdrawal itself remains, thus deepening and reexposing humanity to the experience of a cut. Without its suturing by a metaphysical transcendence, the cut, the exposure of all specific times and places to something that *is* not and does not belong to a specific time and place, is revealed in all its unsettling trauma, becoming that which cuts the world, existence, out of any pregiven order, exposing a fundamental abyss. The other face of modernity,[1] thus of the death of God, is forgetting the cut altogether, forgetting the enigmatic dimension of withdrawal—of something not present in the world or in any space-time, yet nevertheless something upon which the whole, indeed the wholeness of, the world depends—and establishing a purely immanent realm made up only of positivities and actualities. From this perspective, then, the death of God is the forgetting of the cut.

One can now begin to see that the history of the United States—as indeed of the entire world, which has been globalized, precisely, by coming to belong to modernity—is a history of being caught up in the tension between the two faces of modernity. On the one hand, furiously embracing complete immanence as the forgetting of the cut, the United States has become the realm par excellence of unbridled modern capitalism (as a system of exchange not grounded in any transcendent origin of value and thus a system where anything can be worth anything at any given moment, since there is nothing beyond the exchange of positivities to give it value) and of technoscientism (which attempts to grasp the entirety of existence via mathematical calculation and technological manipulation of positivities). On the other hand, it obsessively revolves around the traumatic experience of the cut but does so under two main modalities. The first we can call nostalgic and restorative, which itself comes in numerous forms. One, we can say, insists on remembering the cut/withdrawal and does so through the attempt to hold on to, in spite of everything, the substantializing suturing of it involved in the metaphysical-theological tradition and its all-governing transcendent agent. Another is to creatively produce various new revelations, from new religions to alien encounters, that will substantialize and suture the cut in ever-innovative ways. Yet another mode of remembering the cut even as one holds by and large to the theological-metaphysical models is the organization of existence via the narration of various moral melodramas that try to suture the traumatic cut through schemes opposing innocent victims and evil oppressors, thus setting those blamed for the cut (which act as a substantial suturing agent to explain it) against others who suffer it.[2] Of course, in these moral melodramas, in the manner of capitalistic groundless valuation, the sides can constantly be switched, the oppressor becoming the victim, the agent becoming the sufferer.

The second modality of revolving around the traumatic cut—around the attempt to remember a withdrawal that modernity powerfully exposed as well as tried to completely forget and repress—but one that does not take the form of restorative nostalgia, I would call poetic-enigmatic. The poetic in its purest form—though it is unclear if this ever exists—involves, as I will show, the attempt to expose a cut, a withdrawal, on the background of the world, thus a withdrawal upon the relation to which the whole world depends, yet it exposes this cut without instituting a transcendent agent (or, alternatively, a melodramatic logic of agency and victimhood) to suture it. The poetic leaves, in this way, a gaping, enigmatic withdrawal with no appropriation, a withdrawal around which the whole world is now called to gather, in ever-unpredictable ways.

From this poetic perspective "America" becomes a term that tries to draw the consequences of, and name, in excess of the specific entity of the United States, the cut of modernity—a cut to which, for numerous reasons, the United States has become a paradigmatic witness—in its most abyssal aspect. Because the cut in which the dimension of the poetic has interest is a withdrawal (a non-time/place) without a transcendent agent, an atheological withdrawal (the "a" being a subtractive that dispossesses the withdrawing cut from its suturing agent, thus from theology) upon which the whole world, rather than a specific political entity, depends, one needs the term "America," in excess of the United States, to mark the dimension that, from within the experience of the United States as a privileged witness to the modern cut, calls out to the whole world, in a new way.

If the United States is exceptional, it is because it seems to be a paradigmatic witness to ("chosen" by, addressed by in the manner of Hamlet's being addressed by the ghost) the cut of modernity, a cut that took it outside the theological/metaphysical ordering of the world, exposing it to the death of God, and expressing itself in its history in a particularly powerful way according to various trajectories, some of which I pointed to earlier. Even if many of these trajectories involve either a forgetting or, alternatively, a suturing of the cut, the cut nevertheless—and this is true for all aspects of modernity, from capitalism and techno-science to restorative theologies—continues to haunt them. The term "haunting" is justified here to the degree that the cut is what exposes one to that which is out of any time or place, even as it is somehow present. Now, the United States is haunted by the modern cut by which it feels powerfully addressed, unconsciously "chosen," and needing a term, "America," that is "larger" than its political/historical specificity in order to name its inscription of something that, by being withdrawn from any specific place and time, calls the whole world, all places and times. But this does not mean that America, or, for that matter, Americans, knew how to correctly interpret its exceptionality, that is, its being cut out of the existing order, its speaking for a new "divinity." More often than not, as is well-known, it has misread its cut-off dimension as meaning either a divine chosenness of the metaphysical-theological kind or a privilege of power of the imperial kind. In the case of the latter the dimension of exceptionality—a dimension that has to do with becoming cut out from the rest of the world, and this cutting out always implies a certain coming to witness of a dimension of a whole, thus something beyond, in excess of, all specific times and places—is interpreted as a being called, and therefore entitled, to have power over the whole, over all specific places, thus over the entirety of the world.

Yet what I am calling the atheological cut is precisely not the origin of a privilege to have power over the whole (nor, of course, of a theologically inflected destiny) but the origination of what we can call a democratic logic of singularities where none is entitled to have power over the others, even as each is responsible for the whole. Because the modern cut is a cutting out of any pregiven order—implying a dimension withdrawn from any time and place as well as from any ordering of times and places according to a transcendent schema—every specific time and place that emerge from it (be it a specific individual or a social assembly) or in relation to it are to be understood as a singular formation that does not stand in any sort of hierarchical relation to any other in a transcendent ordering schema. This atheological cut—understood as the origination of a truly democratic, thus nonhierarchical and singular distribution of all specific times and places emerging from the cut, a cut that remains in excess of/withdrawn from all of them—is what the United States is a paradigmatic witness to and what is inscribed most profoundly in the call of "America." It is crucial to see that in this sense the term "American democracy" should be understood not as a political concept—if this is understood as referring to a specific political system governing the community of those belonging to the United States—but rather as an ontological concept that describes a logic of the distribution of singular beings in time and place in relation to that which is withdrawn from all times and places but thus opens the possibility that all of them might emerge. Or perhaps we can distinguish between the dimension we can call the ontological-political—understood as that which names the logic of distribution among all the emerging singularities (be they individuals or social groupings, in the formation of states, for example), understood as singularities precisely because they share a cut, the withdrawn, that is in excess of all of them and prevents them from being ordered hierarchically and transcendentally—and the dimension of politics, which refers to the way a specific system, a specific historical community in place and time, organizes itself. In this sense, American democracy refers not to the specific politics of the United States but instead to a whole ontological-political logic (which can be instantiated in many different ways) that the United States, as paradigmatic witness to the modern atheological cut, is as if called to transmit, expressing its responsibility for, that is, the response to the call of, rather than its power over, the whole, the world.

Yet if to become a witness to the cut, a witnessing expressed in the term "America," means to occupy a cut-off site, in this case the United States insofar as it registers the exposure to the enigmatic atheological withdrawal at the heart of a modernity that has suffered the cut of the death of God, a question emerges: How does one transmit, how does one communicate, or even express, the call of the cut? This can be achieved only by bringing about an exceptional site that is itself cut off or cut out of a specific time and place, and that as such inscribes/witnesses the enigmatic dimension of withdrawal and starts to communicate with the question of the whole, of that which is beyond any specific thing and thus can open to all specific things in time and place. The bringing about, and transmitting or communicating, of such cut-off, exceptional sites lies at the heart of the poetic task that, in the context of the United States, will now be understood as communicating the cut of "America."

We can say that all ancient cultures also revolved around the institution of exceptional sites, known as sacred sites, often temples, dedicated to communicating with powers beyond the everyday, be they spirits, gods, or even the Jewish God and his temple, yet it was crucial that these sites, though exceptional, are specific sites, on this mountaintop or in this sacred grove, belonging to a specific land and marking the center of that land. That is, what was essential was still the positive content of these sites. Yet, in the case of what I am calling the poetic, which in many ways belongs to modernity, to the era of the death of God, what was essential in the exceptional sites was that any specificity and positivity of their place and time have been suspended so that the dimension that is withdrawn from any time and place can come into "appearance." These sites were no longer centers of a land but a non-place/non-time out of which a realm with no center (in the sense of that from which a hierarchical order radiates) opens, a realm composed of multiple singularities, each of which is responsible for the whole precisely because they do not stand in any hierarchical order to each other.

To be sure, the emergence of these poetic/enigmatic sites, through which the withdrawn comes to "appear" without being appropriated to any transcendent agency, precedes the birth of the United States by a few centuries. It is first instantiated in such paradigmatic sites as Shakespearean theater and Renaissance painting, a mode of painting that came increasingly to revolve around the question of a pictorial frame that functions, in distinction, for example, from the sort of sacred painting to be found in a church, as a cutting off from any specific locus, and thus is totally mobile.[3] But the United States, itself in many ways a cut-out space that more powerfully registered the modern shock, resonated, I claim, in an exceptional way with the question of these modern poetic cut-off sites to the degree that a political-ontological-poetic question was being raised in a unique way, somewhat different from its other modern counterparts. This question revolves around the relations that open between a logic of distribution of singularities in relation to the cut of the withdrawn-without-transcendent-agent and the coming to be inscribed of the withdrawn in an exceptional poetic site (a site emptying the world of a center from which a hierarchy radiates). This political-ontological-poetic question (which I claim resonates in the term "America," understood from the vantage of a witnessing and a desire to communicate the exceptional call of the modern cut) came to be inscribed in what is perhaps the American poetic site par excellence, American film. To show how film is the response par excellence to the modern cut, also called "America," is the point of this book.

The Meaning of Being

Before getting to the discussion of particular films, I need to say a few words about the question of ontology. To speak somewhat reductively, by ontology I refer here to the question reopened, most importantly, by Martin Heidegger for modern thinking as the question of the meaning of Being, that is, the meaning of that term that is philosophy's unique discovery and sole occupation. Being marks the discovery of a dimension of a Whole, which "includes" everything that is and yet which, as a result, is not itself one more member of this whole. Yet how is one to understand Being, then, and what exactly is the difference between this dimension of the whole and all the regular beings that are "included" in it? According to Heidegger, the history of philosophy—from its very inception, but in particular perhaps from Plato onward—made a "decision" with enormous consequences: It determined the entire history of what came to be called the West and, following it, the entire world, which has been to a greater or lesser degree Westernized. This decision involved the transformation of the "discovery" of Being, philosophy, into what Heidegger calls metaphysics. Due to this decision, Being, which indicates the dimension of a Whole, was itself understood as an underlying, privileged presence and thus as a certain positivity, which is seen as that around which every other positive presence, every other being, revolves. The traditional name for this privileged presence or being was god, or theos, and thus the interpretation of Being as underlying presence, resulting in a history of metaphysics, is what Heidegger refers to as onto-theology.

Jean-Luc Nancy, one of Heidegger's most astute heirs, has added a certain twist to this Heideggerian narrative. For Nancy, the arrival of the Jewish God—an event obviously independent of (even if probably occurring at the same historical moment as) the Greek discovery of Being and its onto-theological interpretation—indicated an excess over metaphysics in that the Jewish God was a revelation of what I referred to as a cut, a withdrawal from any and all positivity, an exit from nature and the world. However, this dimension of pure withdrawal, the emptying out from any positivity, has nevertheless been sutured by the institution of a certain transcendent agent that—following the Christian (and later on, if differently, Muslim) synthesis between the Jewish God and Greek philosophy as onto-theology—has increasingly, even if never fully and always revolving around a troubling excess of emptiness, acquired a metaphysical character of an underlying presence holding the power to order and govern all actual and positive beings from the beginning to the end of time.

What I have referred to as the modern cut or the cut of modernity, the age Nietzsche referred to as that of the death of God, is the age when this onto-theological construction dominating the Christian West has started to tremble (opening a crack that was always in the background between Greek philosophy and Jewish monotheism, which Christianity attempted to synthesize), and the theos has started to die. This death of theos opened in two directions: It exposed the withdrawn cut, the abyss of Being, sutured by the theos, and it completely covered over the abyss that the theos, in its Judeo-Christian formation, even if problematically and as suturing, nevertheless held open. Obviously this complex and ambivalent modern moment, the moment of the death of theos as the organizing principle of everything, can thus also be understood as the moment of the demise of the onto-theological interpretation of Being. Upon this demise two directions open, corresponding to the two sides mentioned previously. On the one hand, from the point of view of the death of theos, understood as the event of the covering over of that abyss of Being opened by the divine cut's revelation, we have a forgetting of the philosophical/Judaic discovery of Being (thus the forgetting of philosophy and/as the forgetting of Being) and the aforementioned rise of capitalism and techno-science, both dealing only with beings or positivities. On the other hand, and this is what Heidegger brought to the fore better than anyone else before him, once Being is no longer or at least not as much under the domination of its onto-theological interpretation, there is a renewed question of Being, or the questioning of the meaning of Being. The death of theos is the birth of the question of Being's meaning.

If "America," as I started to suggest, is the name for the powerful registration of the shock of the modern cut by the United States, then we can see now that "America" is nothing less than a name through which the United States worked out its being inscribed by the modern problem of Being. Thus, "America" will imply, to name only the most oft-discussed aspects, the forgetting of Being and the rise of capitalism and techno-science (as it mainly seems to for Heidegger, for example, and the many European thinkers for whom America represented the worst of the modern, as well as many American thinkers adopting the framework of European thinking). But, a fact seemingly missed by most European and Europeanized thinkers the world over (though not by the world masses, "the great unwashed"), "America" will also stand for the powerful raising of the question of the meaning of Being in a new way. In this sense, though we cannot yet know what this means, "America" is the term that in a way replaces theos, resonating in and as the abyss left open by the death of theos.

We can now understand the "more" inscribed in the term "America" over and above the specific political entity of the United States as being the "more," that is, the question of the meaning of Being in its modern moment, over and above any specific modern entity. The question of Being is of course always "more" than any specific place or time and any specific being, since all things take place in relation to and "within" it. Since the question of Being has the character of a "more" over every specific time and place, every actual content, emerging from it, I will also refer to it with the term "Medium," writ large, for a medium is, by definition, that which names a dimension that is more than, in excess of, any content or "message" emerging from it or with the means of it.

To say that "America" is a name for the question of Being's meaning in its modern age, the age of the demise of onto-theology, thus also means, according to the above, that we can understand the term "America" as a Medium—in the sense of Being-in-excess-of-every-actual- being and in relation to which, with the means of which, all actualities emerge—of modernity (in both senses of the "of"). This does not mean, of course, that "America" is a specific decision, or answers the epochal question, about the meaning of Being but precisely that it is a field of struggle over said meaning. As Heidegger showed, even if modern techno-science involves a forgetting of Being, it is no less a decision about the meaning of Being/the withdrawn, and the same can be said about capitalism. The Medium "America" is an openness in excess of these various decisions, the ones most often associated with the name "America" as far as it is used in relation to the United States.

Film-Philosophy

This book focuses less on the various manifestations of the forgetting of Being implicated in the term/medium "America" (though I occasionally address them as well since they are inevitable, and most aspects of the struggle, all the dramatic tensions, seem to be implicated in anything one examines) and more on that excessive openness that is perhaps the most essential dimension of the modern exposure to the question of Being upon the demise of its onto-theological takeover, an openness implying the remembering of the question of Being as involving a cut, an abyssal withdrawal, before, and in excess of, any appropriation by a transcendent agent. This dimension of the memory-of-a-cut-without-suturing-transcendent-agent (a pure cut, we might say) and in excess of any modern decision regarding its meaning (as capitalism, or technology, etc.) is, I claim, essentially implicated in the term or Medium "America" and is at the background of the opening of the question I call political-ontological-poetic.

The question of this book is how film becomes the poetic or artistic medium par excellence of this poetic dimension, understood as memory-of-the-pure-cut, implied in the Medium "America." A poetic medium, as I understand it, revolves around the memorial "more" implied in the question of Being, thus of the Medium, as it opens in modernity.

The poetic medium is a medium, precisely, in that it is an activation, in a specific modality (say, in the realm of sound, vision, etc.) of the power of the "more," of mediality (Being, the "whole") as such, to function as an excess over any content or message, and out of which a plurality of different contents or messages can emerge. It is poetic to the degree that rather than be mainly interested in these contents, it is fascinated by the memorial "more" itself, by mediality as such (in its modern character as pure cut or pure withdrawal, in excess of its suturing by any transcendent agent). More precisely, we can say, the poetic medium is fascinated by the interplay wherein the contents, or messages, interact with or communicate with and inscribe in themselves, first, the specific medium that enables them (say, a specific content in a film can be understood as a reflection on the very working of the camera). But more deeply they interact with the cutting out, the "more," the Medium (in which case a specific content will be seen as an inscription of the very question of Being, of that excessive "more" at the background of the power of the camera to open to different contents to begin with).

Serving as the means, or the medium, through which the Medium—the withdrawn before any suturing appropriation—comes to be inscribed in actual contents and messages, the poetic medium can be understood as the medium (also in the sense of messenger) of the Medium (of modernity), an essential name for which is "America." As a consequence, the poetic medium, in our case film, which seems to be fascinated by the modern dimension of the "more," insofar as it comes to receive the name "America," will serve as the medium of "America." Of all the artistic media, most paradigmatically American film, so at least goes the guiding intuition of this book, might serve as messenger for the modern Medium (the "more" of Being in its modern emergence under the sign of the death of God) that has come to be activated under the call of "America." This fact certainly has to do with film being the only major artistic medium (in addition to still photography, of which it is a development) whose birth comes after that of the United States and, indeed (jointly with another center of modern revolution, France), happens within it.

The intuition guiding this book regarding the relations between the question of America, the cinematic medium, and American films seem to me to have also informed the important philosophical-poetic project of Stanley Cavell, who, in different ways than attempted here and along lines we cannot get into in this context, has articulated a philosophical meaning for "America" (where at least implicitly, the term "America" has something to do with the question of Being); a philosophical analysis of the medium of film, that is, examining the question of this medium in relation to the Whole, or the world (most importantly in *The World Viewed*); and a critical engagement with specific films (most importantly in *Pursuits of Happiness: The Hollywood Comedy of Remarriage* and *Contesting Tears: The Hollywood Melodrama of the Unknown Woman*), which are examined from the point of view of instantiating the possibilities of the medium of film in general and as an engagement with the philosophical meaning of America.[4]

It is interesting to note that the other major philosophical-cinematic project often mentioned alongside Cavell's as a foundational reference, Gilles Deleuze's books on cinema, though pointing to the essential connection between American film and the question of America—saying in a perceptive aside that basically all American films tell the story of the birth of a nation, the story of the founding of America—has relatively little of deep insight to say, in my opinion, about any actual American films, with the exception of his exciting discussion of Orson Welles. This undoubtedly has to do with Deleuze's choice of giving precedence, especially in the first of his two cinema books, *The Movement Image*, to Sergei Eisenstein's theoretical framework and to Eisenstein's judgment (in my opinion mistaken[5]) regarding the cinema of D. W. Griffith, the limitations of which, as Eisenstein articulates them, Deleuze sees as relevant to much of American cinema. More important though, it has to do with Deleuze's very clear preference, in spite of his pronouncements to the contrary, of a specific European modernist sensibility. The consequences are that despite saying many insightful, at times profound, things about the modernist tradition of European films, Deleuze has little to offer that is essential about American films, which strikes me as surprising, especially considering his insight into the importance of American literature.

In the "More of the World Viewed" section of *The World Viewed*, Cavell points to a certain division for which he himself felt he does not have an adequate name between a cinematic modernist tradition—understanding by "modernist" an art that has lost its trust in the tradition and questions its relation to it through examining, experimenting with, and testing the limits of the medium in which it is created—and another that he sometimes calls "traditional," though clearly he feels dissatisfied with such naming, which seems to guide most of the films he discusses, American films of a particular Hollywood tradition, for which the question of maintaining a continuity with the general artistic tradition is less of a problem.[6] While I do not have a more adequate name for this other tradition that does not fit under the umbrella of modernism, it seems that what is essential about it is that it is, precisely, contrary perhaps to Cavell's point, not more traditional or less modern but modern in a different modality that we might call "American," revolving around the question of "America" as a modern name for the question of the meaning of Being upon the demise of its appropriation by onto-theology.

It is as if there were a fundamental, if difficult to define, distinction between modernist art and another type of art. The first, in many ways emerging out of the European experience of the death of God and the collapse of onto-theological frameworks, is the kind wherein the artistic medium itself—as messenger of a Medium/Being gradually coming under the sign of the crisis of modernity—is increasingly experimented with, its self-evidence put into question, its possibilities explored, though often under the affective modality of disaster, negativity, alienation, and the loss of ground of existence. The second, for which we lack a good definition, is an art in which

16 *Introduction*

a new name, "America," for the question and experience of Being becomes a guide, allowing it to at least have a positive horizon for its aim (which, of course, can also be experienced negatively, as having tragically failed to live up to, etc.). In such art—which, much like "European" modernist art, is not confined to a specific geographical locale but can be created anywhere in the world—the medium becomes the messenger of a new call of Being, the call of "America," and the work of art functions as the attempt to bring about a new world, a new manner of existing, and a new site of "appropriation" or of happy, nonalienated habitation, that of coming to belong to "America."

In some sense, it seems the difference between the cinematic-philosophical projects of Deleuze and Cavell can be attributed to this distinction between the modernist crisis and the new "American" horizon and to their respective privileging of one or the other.[7]

What *is* common to their cinematic-philosophical projects, though in two distinct ways I cannot fully explore in this context, is the insight that in order for art (in this case film) and philosophy (as the thinking of Being) to have something to say to each other, one needs to find a way to connect between the Medium writ large (as the "more," which is Being or the Whole); the specific medium of film itself as being a messenger of this whole; and the actual films that are seen as instantiating, always in ways that cannot be determined in advance, this or that possibility of the medium-as-messenger-of-the-Medium. This guides the distinction between what Cavell understands as an ontological analysis of the medium of film and the critical engagement with specific films, each of which actualizing in unforeseen ways the possibilities of the medium and putting both under the question of the world (i.e., the Whole) viewed. This also guides the relations Deleuze establishes between a philosophical thinking of the Whole (i.e., Being), which itself comes in two forms: the Whole as the open of the movement image—which still to a degree stands under the sign of an onto-theological appropriation[8]—and the Whole as the outside of the time image; an analysis of the general components of the medium of film and how they establish a general relation to the Whole; and a dizzying typology of images as they come into being in the context of some of the most significant films of the tradition.

As brilliant, and indeed essential, as these two philosophical-cinematic projects are, what for me still remains to an extent not fully satisfactory in either, as much as I see myself indebted to both, is the lack of a fully concrete, or even systematic, manner of connecting between the Medium, the specific artistic medium, and the actual films in such a way that every detail and gesture one wants to account for in a specific film is shown from the perspective of engaging with the very logic of the cinematic medium, which itself is shown to inscribe an engagement with the openness that is the Medium. The *systematic* establishing of these connections, meaning a thinking that grounds itself in the whole, which is shown to be that through which everything interrelates, lets us recognize films in their specificity and also, importantly, as allegories (i.e., showings of an Other, the *allos*) of the medium-as-messenger-of-the-Medium, and in our case messenger-of-"America."

The modern work of art understood as allegory is not the display of qualities expressing the relation to a divine or transcendent substance (such as charity or, to the contrary, miserliness) that is Other to the world, as in medieval allegories. Instead, it is the inscription of a specific medium, the "more" at the background of—and is thus Other to—any content emerging from it, a mediumistic "more" that is itself a messenger of the withdrawn, understood as the Medium, which is itself Other than any content as well as Other than any specific medium. Indeed, each of the specific films we examine will be shown to be, as unified wholes, systematic in that they are "about" this engagement with the medium as messenger of the Medium/"America."

It is such a systematic allegorical putting in relation of the gestures of specific films with the poetic medium understood as messenger of the Medium, a putting in relation that I understand as the task of reading, which is the methodological challenge the following discussions try to answer. *To read*, as practiced here, is to trace the way each detail in, and gesture of, the work of art is viewed from the point of view of its engagement with the specific artistic medium as well as with the Medium/question of Being (the Whole, the withdrawn, the cut), as it opens in a new way under the modern sign of the death of God.

We can see from the previous discussion how this book understands the conjunction at its center, that of film-philosophy. This conjunction cannot simply be asserted but is achieved through an act of reading wherein the inscription of the second, understood as the engagement with the meaning of Being, in the first, the specific medium,[9] is traced through following specific gestures of particular works, which are seen as revolving around an allegorical development of singular ways in which such inscriptions happen. Since the question of the meaning of Being this book is interested in is the one that started to gather around the name/Medium "America," film-philosophy as it practices it will be the tracing, through the performance of acts of reading, of the communications of what we might call "American Medium" with the medium of film and the inscriptions of such communications in specific films.

Allegories of America

The films we follow—of Steven Spielberg, John Ford, Francis Ford Coppola, and Sofia Coppola (though other directors could serve as well, which makes these four figures at once emblematic and arbitrary choices)— function, each in its own singular way, as allegories of the way that the call of "America," that is, the demand to ground human life nontheologically, becomes that around which the medium of film starts to circulate.

Thus, in Spielberg's *West Side Story*—at the heart of which is, famously, the question of what "to be in America" means—the call of "America" will be seen as structuring the relations between the logic of the cinematic medium and the possibility of the emergence of a new community, one no longer organized around a theological center but around the cinematic cut, which comes to serve as the messenger of the cut of Being/the withdrawn in excess of its onto-theological suturing. The cinematic cut in this context becomes an abyssal disruption of the metaphysical way of organizing the world, a cutting disruption that nevertheless comes to function, paradoxically, as that which can be shared by a multiplicity of heterogeneous singularities, to be distinguished from a group unification under the power of a grounding, transcendent One, a sharing across the cut that, achieved with the means of song, establishes a new mode of communication.

In the cinema of John Ford, being inscribed by the call of "America," thus suffering an exposure to the cut beyond and before its appropriation by transcendence, is experienced as the opening of a "desert" moment at the heart of cinema (a desert that is seen as a paradigmatic figure for the cinematic screen itself, as a cut-off, decontextualized site), a moment of wavering between the destruction of the old/theologically organized world and the emergence of a new form of life and way of existing in common. This desert/Western/ cut-off screen moment is seen as a site of a haunting memory of something that cannot actually be remembered and is thus withdrawn from all actual memory, a withdrawn that is Being/the Medium-excess-of-any-actuality as a question prior to its theological appropriation. This haunting memory comes to be shared, as a melancholy absence, by the multiplicity of all the displaced people coming to America (thus displaced from having a home in an identitarian community grounded in a theological organization) for all of whom the question is asked: How is coming to belong to America to be achieved; how can we answer this call that has inscribed itself in a memory that haunts all of us, but we don't even know what we remember? In significant ways to be explored, Ford's cinema remains suspended in the desert moment of hearing the call, the moment of being inflicted with an immemorial memory, but feeling one has not yet fully found the way to answer it. We have not yet learned how to exit the desert/the moment of the Western.

In Coppola's great *Godfather* trilogy—which I read as the preeminent tragedy of American cinema, to be thought of alongside the great Greek tragic *Oresteia* and *Oedipus* trilogies—the gap Ford highlighted as the moment of the desert between the call of "America" and the failure to fully arrive in it, is now analyzed as the tragic moment when the belief in America, the declaration of which famously opens *The Godfather*, a belief at the heart of the cut-out cinematic screen as registering a call in excess of transcendence, fails to be fulfilled. In Coppola's films, this tragic failure, as in Greek tragedy, signals the failure of the city to fully open up to the democratic call at its heart. The moment of the cut-out or cut-off screen as Coppola sees it, thus the moment of American cinema, from *The Godfather* to the more optimistic *Megalopolis* (which, in the manner of Shakespearean romance, points the way beyond tragedy), is the moment when the demise of theological organization opens a moment of suspension between two options, which are inscribed in two forms of family, the tragic and the democratic option, and both options now thought of in relation to the experience of America. America as land of the displaced, of immigrants (famously opening *The Godfather II*), thus as subject to the historical cut of modernity signals the collapse of the family as traditionally/metaphysically organized, a family revolving around the central figure of a father seen as representing a theological order, a god-father. Such collapse can result, in the tragic option, in the attempt to form a family that will restore the old order. But in a world no longer organized according to that logic, thus according to the metaphysical interpretation, this attempt results in a criminal family outside the law, the organizing order of the post-theological world. At the heart of the criminal family is a father whose inevitable failure, inevitable since the theological structures that had supported his role are no longer in effect, results in the opening of a tragic world of violence and destruction blocking the possibility of the emergence of the new democratic "city." But such collapse of the old order can also point in the democratic direction beyond tragedy, toward a new family and a new democratic city or polis, a megalopolis. It is the task of the cinematic/democratic image to bring about this new polis and family, as shown by *Megalopolis*'s architect/image maker. It is in and through the image that the tragic blockage can be broken, the new call of Being, that of which "America" consists, can finally be responded to, and the belief restored.

Coppola's daughter, Sofia, takes it upon herself, as it were, to demonstrate the being of the new democratic family achieved via the means of a new image, and a new image maker, in a cinematic project that both deconstructs the work of the poetic father (thus a father who is no longer a theological godfather), as if to free him, and us, from a tragic blockage he has not fully figured a way out of, and extends it by becoming its fulfillment, the demonstration of its viability. The new democratic family, the Coppolas, in distinction from the Corleones, is the one that shares an image or connects through the image rather than through the theological Law of the father. What is most essential for Sofia Coppola in the image, understood as an inscription of the excessive call of "America" beyond its theological, godfatherly/paternal takeover, is the coming into visibility, as a force of transformation, of the dimension of an Eros tied to the being of the feminine. The feminine Eros is seen as a major site through which the excess of Being can be liberated from the theological takeover, a metaphysical framework that itself had found its point of focus in an erotic site in which it is inscribed, the masculine phallus, understood from a metaphysical point of view as the subjection, and grounding, of Eros in a power of an agent, the father, seen as transcendent. The moment of suspension that characterizes the moment of the American screen as inscribing the call of "America," a moment we have associated with the being of the desert and with tragic blockage of democracy, is also a moment, in Coppola's interpretation, of a crisis of the phallus (or, more precisely, of a metaphysical interpretation of the phallus) where the grounding of Eros in the power of an agent is no longer seen as viable. Yet the liberation of Eros, and thus the responding to the call of which Eros is the inscription, has not yet been achieved. This achievement will be possible only if the dimension of Eros expressed in feminine excess will find its place in the world.

From *The Virgin Suicides* to *Priscilla* (though we will focus on two films, *Lost in Translation* and *Marie Antoinette*) Coppola's cinema tells the story of an entrapment in a family compound where the metaphysical regime of phallic Eros has been suspended, yet no way out toward the feminine Eros has yet been achieved. The task of Coppola's major heroines, from Marie Antoinette to Priscilla, will be to become a revolutionary force finding a way out of the compound (thus also out of the tragic compound of the Corleones and toward the new Coppola family), which cinematically means achieving a screen image inscribing feminine Eros beyond the tragic suspension of the phallus and thus fully arriving in an American democracy.

Since all the concepts we are interested in will be investigated from the perspective of the way the medium of film inscribes and activates the Medium, which is the question of Being, this will be true as well for the concept of desire with which we started this Introduction. Desire (as well as the secret, that withdrawal of Being), will now be seen as the way the "more" of Being, its excessive and empty openness, is inscribed in us, an inscription that can be activated via the means of the medium of film. What, then, to return to our opening question, is the secret desire inscribed in, and by, American film? It is the desire To Be, understood anew.

ONE

To Be in America

STEVEN SPIELBERG'S *WEST SIDE STORY*

What does the being of America, or of the United States, as a new and unprecedented way of organizing the shared life of human beings, have to do with the very nature of the cinematic medium, itself in many ways a new and unprecedented way of creating and organizing artistic images? This question, I claim, has implicitly guided a dominant lineage of American filmmakers from D. W. Griffith (with his *Birth of a Nation* and *Intolerance*) onward. Culminating in such filmmakers as John Ford and Howard Hawks, the question, though ever present, has perhaps been less noticeable in the cinematic efforts of the most ambitious American directors of the last few decades. One exception might be the work of Steven Spielberg, who in various ways has continued to investigate the relations between cinema and America, perhaps no more intensely than in *West Side Story*. With this film—so runs the guiding thesis of the following discussion—the director's thinking on this issue has reached its most mature articulation, responding to the current crisis in American cultural politics in surprising and profound ways.[1]

The More-Than-One

> Sorry, but more than one, it is always necessary to be more than one in order to speak, several voices are necessary for that.
>
> JACQUES DERRIDA, *On the Name*

"More than one," a profound and inexhaustible mystery that, Derrida seems to suggest, lies at the heart of the question of speaking and therefore of language. One speaks, there is language—that is, communication and therefore community, all those who share in a communication—only because there is more than one. But what is this "more than one" at the heart of speech, language, and community? Derrida, perhaps too quickly, shifts from "more than one" to "the several," indeed to several voices. Are the two terms equivalent? Might it be that between the one and the several a third option makes its claim, the option of the more-than-one that is neither one nor several? What would that mean? Derrida provides a clue by indicating that in order to speak, it is always necessary *to be* more than one. He does not say that it is always necessary that *there be several* in order to speak. More-than-one thus seems to be a possibility of being, a way to be, that "one" (who is of course not one, at least according to a certain interpretation of the one), indeed, can be, perhaps must be, if one is to be at all, or at least be at all as a speaking, "linguistic" being, subjected to the question of community. One needs to be, one must be, not merely one of several (ones) but more than one(self) in order to speak.

How are we to understand this? The expression "to be" points the way. "To be," according to Martin Heidegger, should not be understood in terms of determinate actuality, be it present, past, or future. Instead, it is a modality of open possibility or potentiality and is before and in excess of anything in particular. The human being, for Heidegger, is the one who, unique of all creatures, is in the modality of "to be," an openness not directed toward any specified determination and having no specific task to accomplish. To live or to be in the modality of the "to be" is, says Heidegger, to live in an openness he calls "world." The human, living in the modality of "to be," lives in, or more accurately as, world. We might understand the term "world" with the help of the term "medium." The world is our medium: not any specific thing, not any content or even the totality of all contents, but a background openness through which we can access any possible, determined content. The world, then, is no-thing, but that pure openness, a background medium, that makes us who we are: those who are in the mode of "to be" rather than those who are determined as this or that.

"To be" is not a power we possess or can will, that is, it is not something at the ground of which we already are; it is what makes us who we are to begin with. As such, it marks the limit, even the absence, of our power and will—a kind of primordial dispossession. We receive the world, the medium through which we are in the mode of "to be," unwillingly and in spite of ourselves, as it were, like a reluctant prophet pained by an unwanted word that in fact causes an emptying and a dispossession, a word burning in the mouth as a wound. Only within the world do we have will and power, with the world itself lying beyond them.

Based on this explanation, we can start sketching a logic of the more-than-one at the heart of speech and community, which is also at the heart of each one of us being more than oneself. The "more" in question is not a quantitative entity and lacks the character of one plus one plus one, and so on (which leads to "several"). Rather, "more" belongs to a completely different order, is Other, than quantity (quantity being what qualifies the "more" in the realm of content), for it is—at least initially and most fundamentally[2]—the no-thing or nothing that is the medium/world, which is more than any worldly content, any thing. Each of us, we can say, is an actuality also "haunted" by its medium/world, which marks the limits of its power even as it inflicts it with an empty and indeterminate "to be." The vocabulary of haunting applies here to the extent that the world itself has no place but is where things take place. The world itself is nothing (actual), yet it is somehow present as a restless persistence that marks both our limits and our obligation, the fact that we must be. To be more than oneself is to live as always inscribed by this restless haunting that remains foreign, or alien, to us, in that it is Other than, more than, our actuality, or any actuality for that matter (and as such not subject to the logic of identity and identification that characterizes determinate actualities in the world, which can become familiar to the extent that we can come to identify and recognize them). If the term "haunting" calls to mind entities such as ghosts, it does so because such entities "embody" or "incarnate" the unplaceable medium/world. Ghosts (and aliens—extraterrestrials[3]) are placeless beings occupying what we can call the limit of the world, which is also the limit of our existence. From this (non-)place, they inflict the foreignness that is the world, rendering us powerless even as we are enjoined "to be."

If to be more than oneself is at the heart of speech and community, then speech, before the utterance of this or that determinate thing, harbors the indeterminate openness of the medium "to be." In this sense, we feel speech itself to be ghostly, foreign, in that it marks the limits of our power, in this case the power to say, confronting us as that which dispossesses us from this power precisely because it is what we receive this power from and what remains in excess of it. The medium-as-speech, we can say, haunts every specific utterance as its imperceptible limit, marking both the site of its extinction, or falling into muteness (where it ceases to be able to say the determinate things it wills to say), and the locus of its opening (the resource enabling it to articulate something that could not have been predicted in advance and is not grounded in any determinate order of things). More-than-one, something in excess of the order of quantity itself, is necessary for any speech to occur, as speech is that no-thing that is the openness beyond any determinate content.

This openness is inscribed in each of us insofar as we are more than ourselves, haunted by the world. Likewise, it defines speech as what is shared by more than one, now understood as several (ones, actualities). Each of the several, insofar as they are beyond themselves—speakers opened to, or being as, world—come to share with one another what dispossesses them all and thus exceeds them all equally: They share the medium/world. Speech is necessarily shared speech to the degree that no one haunted by it can possess it. Consequently, each of the several, haunted by that which is more than them and marks the limit of their power, dispossessing them, is thus forced on the other(s), exposed to one another, beyond their will, forced to share the world, the empty "to be." This sharing of the empty "to be" is the originary form of communication, the forced togetherness, commonality, of all those, the several, who are more than themselves.

All speakers being forced to share a world can be understood as the originary place of the Law that states, "You cannot be the possessor of the whole, or of the world."[4] All who are thus forced by Law to share a world come to occupy the point of dispossession at the heart of the others, each marking, in common shame (the affect of exposure at the limit of willing), the bounds of their world: the joy of its opening and the pain of its extinction, for which each is implicitly responsible in the others' eyes. Love (the attachment to others as bringers of joy) and hate (the blaming of others for one's helplessness) primordially permeate the life-in-common of speaking beings. Forced by the haunting, empty, foreign, and indeterminate "to be," all who share the world in love and hate are therefore forced as well to determine the nature of their communication: how to share the common world by which they are all equally dispossessed, how they are to be.

Art at the Limit of the World

But our immediate context and point of interest is Spielberg and the art of film, specifically the musical *West Side Story*. What place does the question of art, of the arts in general, occupy in the context of the foregoing? I submit that the arts are human activities exploring the enigmatic moments when what I have been calling the limits of the world suddenly flash and come to haunt our lives.[5] At these moments we experience the primordial limit of our power—not this or that limit vis-à-vis a certain power, but the fact of the dimension that is beyond power absolutely—and in joy and pain, love, hate, and shame, we unwillingly receive the gift of the shared world into which we have been forced and in which it is necessary for us "to be."[6]

The arts revolve around haunting inscriptions of the more-than-one, the world or the "to be," whereby a specific element in the world (a person, a thing, a body part, or a geographical place) comes to function so that the world is seen to be at stake in it or to happen through it. Each element occupying the world's limit—which I call the paradoxical element—is characterized by a certain detachment from actuality. By virtue of this decontextualization, it is able to stand at the limit of the world and serve as its place of inscription, becoming something more than itself (as a regular, actual, element of the world; in a traditional vocabulary this more-than-itself would qualify this element as allegorical, inscribing an *allos*, an Other than itself) as well as that through which one in turn experiences what is more-than-oneself, the place of one's own constitutive dispossession. This paradoxical, allegorical element (as it implies an alien/Other addition to worldly content, we can also call it "extraterrestrial") is the site of a complex set of tensions. The extraterrestrial element is a harbinger of our demise, what brings us to our limits and dispossesses us of all we have (as in fantasies of forced alien abductions, such as in *War of the Worlds*, or the all-destroying *Jaws*). It simultaneously is the means through which we receive the gift of the world, the origin of community and communication, calling us to ("phoning") our home (as in the internal alien element to the Nazis, Schindler, who is—almost perversely, for which Spielberg has been heavily criticized—the harbinger, or at least a significant harbinger, of the community of modern Israel; or the internal alien, the communicator with ghosts, Lincoln, at the heart of the American community).

This logic of the alien qua paradoxical/allegorical inscription of the medium, the more-than-one, allows us to sketch a general matrix of Spielbergian cinema. Basically all of Spielberg's films are marked by the following structure: The protagonist (often but not always a child) is someone who is not at home or at least is not fully so (usually as a result of some sort of rift in the well-ordered family due to a divorce, death, etc.); having suffered alienation from the familiar, this figure becomes exceptional, open to the foreign (the presence of the "ex" always marking the presence of the allegorical outside, the Other), encountering an alien, most often from the sky or from on high (though it can come from the water, as with the prophetess of *Minority Report* or *Jaws*) as a post-theological inscription of some indeterminate beyond (it can be the vision of planes by the self-declared atheist child in *Empire of the Sun*, the various Spielbergian aliens, *A.I.*'s Blue Fairy, *West Side Story*'s Maria, miraculously appearing from an elevated balcony, etc.[7]). In their adventure with the alien, the alienated protagonists often undergo an odyssey involving various disasters and hardships (often in the no-man's-land of war, from *Saving Private Ryan* to *War Horse* to the ruins of *West Side Story*'s Manhattan neighborhood as the site of the gang war), during which they, and we with them, reach something we can call a vision of the unbearable (in *Saving Private Ryan*, for example, the movie, exceptionally, opens with the unbearable vision, and in *War Horse* the unbearable becomes the protagonist's actual blindness), a limit vision of Medusa-like horror (often occurring via a viewing of a corpse, from *E.T.* to *West Side Story*) that seems beyond comprehension. Having crossed the unbearable and engaged with the alien—as either friend or enemy—the alienated protagonists come back to, or sometimes reach by going away to (as in *Close Encounters*), a newly configured home; or they become, as in *Schindler's List*, *Lincoln*, or *West*

Side Story's Tony, a figure whose sacrifice allows a new community to be established and to become a home.

The Spielbergian encounter with the paradoxical/allegorical/extraterrestrial element always involves two parties between whom the more-than-one happens in a paradigmatic way: the exceptional, alienated protagonist and the miraculously, and therefore unwillingly and unexpectedly, appearing alien (Tony emphasizes that he did not expect to have the miraculous encounter with Maria on the night of the dance). The structure of the pair—Elliott and E.T., David and the Blue Fairy (in *A.I.*), Tony and Maria, but also, less obviously, Schindler and the (alien Jew) Itzhak Stern, or Celie and the (alien voice, the singer) Shug (in *The Color Purple*)—is made necessary by the logic of the more-than-one as sketched previously. This transpires because the dispossessing/inspiring medium at the limit of the world can never be willed or striven toward, even by one who does not belong (to the family); it can come only unwillingly and unpredictably, as a miracle from elsewhere.[8] Nevertheless, a specific "attitude" characterizes the alienated party to whom the miraculous alien comes as a revelation, the attitude of waiting (as in the Hölderlinian/Heideggerian anticipation of new gods, or in the waiting for Godot). The one who doesn't belong has to wait (exemplars in this regard are Viktor Navorski in *The Terminal* and David, endlessly praying to the fairy, in *A.I.*), that is, to be in the mode of a receptive passivity, the only gate through which the miracle can enter. In *West Side Story* Valentina, describing Tony as being in a state of waiting, calls him "Milagro," the miracle—even if Maria is the real miracle, though in their case they are in some sense aliens/miracles to each other.

West Side Story, a late masterwork, qualifies as one of Spielberg's key "texts," I believe. Indeed, its abstract, almost formalistic nature—without parallel in the filmmaker's corpus, as far as I can tell—makes it ideally suited to the question of the more-than-one. Most likely because it is a musical—the sole meta-genre (genre dealing explicitly with art itself) among the great classical Hollywood genres (the Western, the romantic comedy, the gangster film, etc.)—Spielberg seems to have decided, uncharacteristically, to mount an investigation of the cinematic medium itself, insofar as it revolves around the question of the extraterrestrial more-than-one. Consequently, the film functions almost as a sort of existential algebra where the question of the one, the two, the three, the several, the many, and the more-than-one haunting their various relations is explored.

America Year Zero

The screen is dark. A sound is heard, a whistle. Where exactly are we? We seem to be lost in the emptiness, the nothingness, of the screen. This vacuity colors the sound, the sole "thing" we can hold on to, with a double quality. On the one hand, this detached, decontextualized element seems to inscribe within it, as it were, our dispossession, the loss of the world and the actual context of life. The sound almost seems responsible for our alienation. On the other hand, emerging out of emptiness, it calls to and addresses us in the sense that our identity, the question of who we are, seems to be at stake in it. The very element in which the emptiness seems to be inscribed now gives us this emptiness as a new power: the power "to be." The whistle occupies the intersection between dispossessing loss and the call to—the birth of—the medium/world/speech. We are taken away from ourselves by, and receive ourselves through, the whistle, which inflicts a wound even as it bestows existence, calling us into the empty desert of the screen.

The first shot of the movie, following the disembodied whistle, repeats and amplifies this structure. The camera hovers above, but close to, the ground—like a spaceship either descending or about to take off—exposing us to an indeterminate, completely decontextualized scene: rubble, bricks, stones, and metallic objects that defy identification. Where exactly are we? A foreign planet? Earth? We have no idea. Are we witnessing ruins, fragments of a lost world, or a construction site, a world in the making? It could even be a Jurassic Park, a place where a lost world can be resurrected and start anew, differently (indeed, the very virtual reconstruction by the movie of a lost urban neighborhood participates in this logic of resurrection, so crucial for Spielberg, the ghostly historian, always mourning a lost past yet believing in the miraculous, redeeming power of the image). As the camera continues its hovering trajectory, a sign—our first encounter with any determinate articulation—tells us that we are in New York City, specifically at the site where a slum is being cleared to make way for the shiny new Lincoln Center, a center for the performing arts. Unless, of course, in the manner of the ending of *Planet of the Apes* (or the ruined Manhattan in *A.I.*), we are looking at where the Lincoln Center used to be; has some disaster struck, perhaps even the end of the human race?

As the shot reaches the sign, hung on a metal fence (reminiscent of *Citizen Kane*'s opening upon a No Trespassing zone, indicated by a sign also hung on a fence), declaring that entry is forbidden, the camera rises like an alien spaceship taking off and glides over the border, rendering the fence's powers of delimitation completely irrelevant. This crossing of the border is highly significant in a film dealing with the struggle between rival groups over territory—both the neighborhood's physical limits and the grounds of identity, white versus Hispanic—and with an alien couple (i.e., alien to their respective families/groups, no longer fully belonging), one from each group, whose desire, much like the camera, will disregard the border, too.

We thus arrive at the question of the relation between the alien-camera and the logic of borders. Neither anywhere actually present nor located in any recognizable place, the camera is present only in the mode of a haunting that immediately indicates to us that the camera belongs to the logic of the more-than-one. The camera is the "agent" of the medium/world, the exposing more-than-ourselves in us, which opens us to a realm of content but is itself never part of that sphere and is beyond all quantity/actuality. The camera cannot be limited by any actual, physical border; no no-trespass zone exists for it. The magic of the haunting camera (which was exploited very early in film history) lies in its ability to pass through any wall, any limit, any obstacle, since its openness is not of the order of any actual content. At the same time, the more-than-one is not unrelated to the question of borders and limits. On the contrary, the more-than-one takes place as or at our limits, being precisely what we cannot will and, as such, what marks our irreducible passivity and helplessness, the limit of our world (the camera cannot be, is forbidden from being, seen[9])—both in the sense that it is where we reach the limit of our power (to will) and in the sense of being the medium through which we open up to the world. Though the camera has nothing to do with any actual, physical limitation, it concerns the limit of the world as an open realm. It is this characteristic of the more-than-one to take place at our world's limit, the place of suffering passivity and exposure, that we also associated with a primal Law, an originary interdiction: You cannot be possessor of the whole, the willing ground of the world. At the beginning of *West Side Story* the non-place of the camera, its haunting virtual presence, thus immediately serves as a reminder of our limits, a border our will cannot exceed.

Any actual border or limit will function by reference to this limit of the world; it will remind us of our originary passivity, register a trace of the primal Law. Yet, for this same reason, establishing an actual border can become a means to attempt to overcome the suffering of the Law, a Law marking our constitutive dispossession, by aiming to become those who, paradoxically, try to possess the Law—that is, both metaphorically and actually, to see and control the invisible camera and thus to posit ourselves as the Law's ground. By positing a border we come to control a delimited territory over which we institute our law that we are the possessors and ground of, which counteracts passivity and limitation. Instead of serving as a painful, and shameful, reminder of primordial exposure, the border is now to serve as the means through which we mark our power to impose limits rather than to be exposed to them, our power to possess the Law. In this sense, the positing of the border is where our passivity is transformed into a power of our own will.[10]

The border/limit possesses the paradoxical quality of needing to be simultaneously erased (as the place of our dispossession) and drawn (marking a territory over which we can impose our power of willing) in a dizzying impossibility that makes every border the dream of crossing it in order to further and further erect it, covering ever more territory and thus simultaneously erasing it and constructing it. Thus, as the gang members at the beginning of *West Side Story* march to defend their territory, they kick down a roadblock that declares "Men at Work," marking the simultaneity of needing to construct the border and displaying the power of eliminating it—that simultaneity being the work of men.[11]

We "overcome" the Law, then, by becoming law (possessing a camera) ourselves, bearing a power over territorial expansion that in principle is limitless. But is the camera part of the logic of "men at work," through which the film director, possessor of the camera, kicks down borders in the project of territorial expansion and the imposition of his/her Laws? Or does its border crossing follow a different logic, the logic of alien desire, which also, in a way, "overcomes" or is beyond the Law, but otherwise? I would argue for the latter, or at least would suggest that this is the case for true artist-directors, who, even if using the camera possessively (and Spielberg, undoubtedly aware of the danger here, in fact highlights it), also use it in a more profound way. Opening in a poetic manner to the more-than-one, the haunting alien/medium/world, would mean opening to it not as Law but as passion, as what we receive before and beyond our will. We receive the "to be" passionately.

Passion, as passive reception of the more-than-one, the welcoming of the arrival of the alien, neither cancels the Law nor suspends or overcomes it. Yet it does reach beyond the Law—beyond the Law's setting of limits to our Will—to the degree that in the welcome it is no longer a question of willing. Law and passion are actually not opposed to each other but are equally primordial and fundamental: Even as the Law sets limits to the empire of the will, passion activates a relation to the medium, the more-than-one, the "to be" that calls us, according to a modality that is other than willing. Only by accepting the Law—accepting our fundamental dispossession at the limit of the world—can we exceed it.[12]

The task of art is to open a place for the miraculous arrival (unpredictable and beyond will) of the alien/camera (that detached foreigner to any context in which the limit is inscribed, which becomes in this context the medium of passion, or that through which the medium's passion is activated), in excess of both territorial ambition and the Law's strict limits. Art expresses the place where our acceptance of the Law opens, in excess of the Law, to the passionate welcoming of the medium by means of an alien emissary.

As was clear from at least *Close Encounters of the Third Kind*, the welcoming of the alien in Spielberg happens often, if not always, through music and song. In Spielberg's cinema, music and song have always played a significant part, even if this role was not fully developed until *West Side Story* as perhaps the ultimate expression of the opening of passion in excess of the Law.[13] The medium is inscribed in these passionate, muting musical moments where speech, as willing to say, reaches its imperceptible limit and announces both the possibility of its extinction and the resource, the gift (that which is received beyond the logic of will) of its birth. It is in this sense that we can understand Jean-Jacques Rousseau's famous speculations in *Essay on the Origin of Language* regarding the existence of an original language of humanity, a language expressing the passions, a language of song and music, before the transformation of speech into rational communication. There was no pre-rational, passionate, musical language, as Rousseau's mythical account would have it; rather, language, as a willing to say and as Reason, harbors, as its shadowy limit, the inscription of the medium, which is opened to, received, passionately, as music, beyond and in excess of its reception as Law. Music expresses the passionate side of the origin of language, of the passive reception of a medium that one can never will. The social contract, the common reception of the Law as interdicting the possession of the medium, would be its other side. Needless to say, based on this logic, the social contract cannot be understood in the Rousseauian mythological manner as the coming together of individuals, each of whom had been willing to give up their primordial personal freedom permitted in the state of nature. Rather, the social contract, most essentially, is the recognition that, primordially, there is a common exposure—the common limitation of one's will (giving up the will cannot be willed), the common interdiction of being the ground and origin of the world—that forces the several upon one another in an originary (un-unifiable and un-totalizable since ungroundable in a willful origin) togetherness. In other words, primordially there is Law.

In attempting to sketch the Spielbergian understanding of Law and passion, and of art and music at their intersection (where one comes to be received in excess of the other), and before delving further into *West Side Story*, consider one of Spielberg's most explicitly allegorical figures, Viktor Navorski (Tom Hanks) in *The Terminal*. Navorski waits in that threshold realm, the airport terminal, in hopes of entering America, in order to fulfill a promise to his late father to obtain a jazz musician's autograph (jazz being the American music par excellence and also essential to *West Side Story*) for a collection his father never managed to complete. A man without a country (due to a political revolution), cut off from family, Navorski is unable to leave the terminal and arrive in America—the Promised Land of jazz music and of those who exist in the condition of the promise, awaiting the miraculous alien. He is at the mercy of an agent of the Law, the field commissioner Frank Dixon (Stanley Tucci). Rather than see the airport as the entry to the (messianic) land of musical passion or as the place into which those in the condition of promise can enter,[14] Dixon sees the airport as a territory that allows him to impose his own will and law. Unlike Kafka, one can and does, as Navorski's adventure demonstrates—since he finally enters America with the cooperation of the Law—pass in Spielberg through the gate of the Law and reach the promised, messianic land: America. There is hope for us, in Spielberg (and possibly in Kafka's *Amerika* as well), at the heart of alienation and in its welcome, and in this lies his unique (and perhaps America's) genius.

Spielberg famously—as happens very rarely in movie history—often makes the aliens coming into his films, be they E.T. or Lincoln, redemptive friends rather than destructive enemies. For him, America is that Promised Land that, by establishing a new relation to the alien and the stranger, a new logic of excessive welcoming in passion, announces the possibility of a new intersection of Law and passion. America is a messianic "somewhere" (as Valentina will sing) that, though not exactly actual, can nevertheless—perhaps for the first time in the history of places that come to be inhabited by the several who are originarily together in Law and passion—be glimpsed in and through art, more particularly film, and perhaps especially fundamentally through a musical, particularly a jazz musical.[15] "To be in America," as Anita famously sings (in a dramatic confrontation with Bernardo regarding what exactly this phrase really means), is to raise the possibility of a way of being, thus a possibility of a relation to what we have called the medium, to our passionate necessity "to be," which exceeds all those offered by the various traditions of the human ways of inhabiting the world together, precisely to the degree that the question of "to be" in it is heard differently, in a new and unprecedented manner, in a new song.

"To be in America" means a new way of hearing the "to be" and living according to it. America, it follows, is not a geographical place but a new name for our relation to being; it is a way of living together in common passion in excess of the Law yet also in subjection to it, a passion to which we open ourselves by means of a new song, a song of ourselves as more than ourselves.

In many ways the film works as a mythical narration in the manner of Rousseau or Freud or the Bible,[16] an origin story of human community, starting with the more-than-one/eye of the camera, followed by the arrival of the one (actuality), then moving to several, introducing the traumatizing question of the feminine (and of the birth of woman) and of sexual difference, and asking about the place of an originary war that we might overcome in finally coming to be according to what we are called to be by the necessity of the "to be," by the more-than-one—finally coming to, possibly, be in (or at least have a glimpse of) America.[17]

In the beginning (or at least after the appearance of the mystery of the more-than-one/eye of the camera roaming over a deserted earth) was one (man), not in paradise but in a state of war, immediately opening to other ones in common effort against an unseen enemy threatening to obliterate them and to take away everything they have, their territory. Thus, after surveying that zone devoid of life, suspended between total devastation and possible new creation, with no other presence than the mysterious eye of the more-than-one/the creator, whose agent is the unseen camera, we get a view, in the manner of Roberto Rossellini's great postwar movie *Germany Year Zero* (undoubtedly a key film for Spielberg, evident in the scene of the child's attempted suicide in *A.I.* no less than the opening of *West Side Story*), of a devastated city and some men working among its ruins (in Rossellini we see several people working in a graveyard). The several thus already exist, inhabiting a field between ruin and new creation, before the view we will soon get of one man, in a sense the first human. The musical proper, though, as mythical narration,[18] starts only with him, with his emergence/birth into the sunlight.

He emerges from a womblike enclosure that we soon learn is a storage room; initially, though, this room is presented as a kind of war bunker. A cut follows, this movie's first. Another human appears, also alone on the screen. The second figure receives, via the mediation of a cut, a can of paint from the first, as if he were being handed ammunition. Another cut shows how the can is then passed along to two other men, more precisely adolescents. They occupy the screen together, forming for the first time a group (of men, or want-to-be men).

We thus have the following elements: an unseen eye of the camera/the medium into the exposing power of which—a power of the openness of a nonactual, limitless (since nonactual) more-than-one—someone (actual) emerges, immediately to suffer a cut. The cut also defines the realm we are opened to as a cut realm; the screen is thus not a fully formed, controlled territory but a territory that has suffered a limitation and stands exposed to the medium it cannot will. The screen is a cut territory, thus a territory that has suffered a passivity to the medium. Consequently, the cut signifies the limitation of the power of the individual born into the eye of a medium he can receive only passively and never will. This limitation indicates he is not alone, not a ground or a power over that to which he has opened and surveys, and that there are therefore others upon whom he is forced and who are forced upon him. The question of address to others opens here: a communication the exposed one has been forced into, a world held in common with others. This communicative address at first takes the form of the transmission of ammunition:[19] Having suffered a cut and discovered others, the one seems to want to say to them (if he has overcome the initial desire to kill them so as to eliminate the cut[20]), "Let us make ourselves as one," that is, as one without a cut, a one who is the sovereign ground of all he surveys. "By coming together we will eliminate the cut, a cut that has been perpetrated by an unseen enemy, whom we have to find, and destroy" (a role to be played by the rival group of Hispanics). The exposing, invisible (since nonactual), haunting medium needs to be located in an actuality that can now be eliminated in order to restore the willful sovereignty of the one; a group of warriors thus assembles in pursuit, actualizing the exposure via the finding of an enemy—a role to be played by the rival gang.

As the scene continues, we have a group of four trying to become one by finding an enemy they can eliminate. Yet something else is evidently required: an additional power of unification that can turn these four into one by becoming a power over exposure. Looking to a phallic-shaped instrument of construction, some kind of bulldozer, they lift their gazes as if looking for the appearance of some divinity and whistle as if wordlessly summoning a god. Over and above the address to others in the manner of the transmission of ammunition, then, an additional type of address is required, a prayer, aimed at what we can call an Other, which exceeds all regular actualities. The Leader, as if in answer, appears from above (the bulldozer is shot as towering over the praying group) with a woman at his side who is obviously under the spell of his magnetic power. The one who can unify, the Leader, has to possess a mysterious kind of power: power over the woman or the feminine. It is not enough to look for an enemy together; the group has to be brought together under someone possessing a unique power over exposure, understood to be the power over the feminine. This implies, of course, that the feminine is what the passionate exposing cut is inscribed in, is thus itself a more-than-one, the activator of the medium beyond territorial, possessive power. Woman is the more-than-one,[21] while man, within this logic (though not *tout court*, since there is another logic of sexual difference, complexly inscribing the relations between Law and Passion, which exceeds this division we can call metaphysical/territorial), is the attempt to become one(self), the desire to form a territory one can possess.

This is immediately made evident when the woman takes leave of the Leader, a wounding/cutting Eve ripped from his body (already indicating his future demise and fall), and walks off-screen toward an invisibility that now draws the gazes of the four men. Averting their eyes from the Leader, they look toward the invisible beyond the screen, as if a greater power to which they are subjected has momentarily overcome them. When the dimension of the off-screen—that which is beyond what we can survey and thus marks the cutting moment of our perception reaching its limits and falling into helplessness—becomes an active element in a film (via a character walking to it, disappearing from the screen, or coming onto the screen from it, or when an on-screen character refers, even as is the case here by look, to an invisibility beyond the screen), it is an indication that the medium's dimension has been introduced: the more-than-one, in excess of any actuality and any power of willing. The woman, related here to the invisible off, thus becomes the one in whom the question of the medium is inscribed at the limit of the world.

As she walks off-screen, one of the group whistles after her, as if the whistle has been drawn from his mouth without his willing it, simply by being possessed with the vision of the woman in which the off/medium has been inscribed. The whistle here is erotic, marking the moment of dispossession, which is also the moment when the Leader's power over the dimension of the more-than-one is exhausted and proves to be an illusion. Sensing the demise or limit of his power, the Leader in response utters a call to order (a call aimed to counteract the threat of the erotic whistle), voicing the film's first word: "Jets!" This identifying name (to be distinguished from the passionate name we discuss later) aims to eliminate the threatening limits of meaning (as willing to say) by taking possession of speech. The name is supposed to manifest the Leader's power to take possession of the medium/speech (and of Eros and the feminine) and, by extension, to unify the group in the service of eliminating the primary cut, with the help of an enemy being targeted.

Already in this short drama between the erotic whistle and the identifying call to gather in unity there is inscribed a major tension of the musical, setting the passionate moment of song, where speech reaches its dispossessing limits, against the attempt to counteract this passion, in a sense to forbid it. Indeed, this tension marks the very being of the two gangs' members, wavering as they do between singing/dancing and fighting (often turning the songs into war songs). It even marks the first ammunition used by the Jets: cans of paint. Covering over the Puerto Rican flag rendered as graffiti, the brightly colored paint, in its pure appearance, in excess of its use in destroying enemy symbols, parallels in the visual realm the passion in song. The pure color, at first spread as meaningless spots of beauty, is something we can understand as the appearance of the medium. It is what we can call pure appearance, in a way passionate appearance, to the degree that it expresses, in its meaningless shining, nothing beyond the passivity to the medium itself, which is the condition of its appearance, before and beyond its taking of this or that meaningful form. At the moment of their destruction of the enemy, the singing/dancing gang also luxuriates in the passion of pure appearance (a passion characterizing their being as performers, those who act out the appearance in the light of the medium—often interrupting regular everyday activities with their exuberance—i.e., the activation of the passion of what is outside any actuality and power of willing), a passion they also immediately resist, want to overcome, take possession of via fighting (hence the brilliance of the oft-repeated choreographed gesture where the gang members end a movement of dance in putting their hands in a position of a fighter ready to box). Pure appearance in the passion of the medium (often also associated with the dimension of the feminine), the moment of beauty, is thus often intertwined with combative destruction, something many ancient tribal rituals of paint and war attest to as well.

Law and Passion

Into this unresolved and unresolvable dialectic between performative passion and violence, answering the call to dominate territory, a new element is introduced: the Law.[22] Early in the film, while the gangs are in the midst of a mutually destructive war, the police arrive. The celebrated Officer Krupke calls on the gangs to separate, thus drawing a limit. This is the basic gesture of the Law: "You can't be the possessor of the all; there is a limit to your power and will." Under the logic of the Law we are no longer dealing exactly with territories one possesses in a never-ending dream of territorial expansion but with a logic of the acceptance of limits as an absolute part of one's self-definition. In this sense, one can occupy a place of one's own, but one does so always as a member of a shared world that one's absolute inner limits forbid one from desiring to possess. Within this logic it is essential that the Law not be understood as human-made or as willed by anyone; by definition, it stands beyond the Will. The ultimate Law is the fact that there is a medium, an openness we can never possess, in which everything else is to be grounded.

But since this "ground" is, strictly speaking, no-thing, merely the indeterminate openness of the world, it seems very quickly to be forgotten, and the Law is perverted in the direction of willing. Thus, when Krupke's superior, Lieutenant Schrank, appears, the Law, even as it continues its demand to separate and disperse, starts to come under the sway of the will to power and group identification. Schrank, a white man, seems to take the side of the white tribe or gang in which he still sees himself as belonging, driving the Hispanic gang away.

This corruptibility of the Law, its tendency to be perverted by territorial, group-identity logic, not only points to a failure to live up to its dignity, to what in a way is its "transcendent" demand of the no-thing of the medium, qua limit of our possessive power, beyond any actuality and identity formation. The Law itself has a genuine limitation that makes simply living under its pure demand of limits empty and unsatisfactory; it does not give one any identity or sense of belonging. The corrupt Schrank obviously feels this—hence his effort, against the demand of the Law of which he is the embodiment, to signal his belonging to the group.

Yet belonging and identity do not necessarily have to be understood and achieved through group logic, that is, through the several coming under the power of the Leader to become as one through territorial possession and an enemy's destruction. Belonging means, first and foremost, coming to coincide with that which is most proper to one, that to which one is most fundamentally appropriated, in which consists most deeply who one is, who we are. For we are, indeed, from the ground up, a "we," a primordial togetherness in that the medium that calls us, inflicting us with the necessity to be, also makes it so that we can never be the ground of the world; and the world is necessarily shared. Most deeply, we are inflicted with a necessity to be that we cannot will and in relation to which we are passive and through which we are opened to a realm in which we are irreducibly together. To truly receive the world/our medium, thus to be appropriated to what most fundamentally calls us, requires a different modality than willful appropriation. To acknowledge the world inscribed in us as a common limitation—forbidding any one of us from being the ground and possessor of the world—is to acknowledge a common Law, yet truly receiving the world as world, as an exposing and indeterminate opening, can be done only in passion, or passionately. We share the world in passion, even if we are together in it always as subjected to a Law. The Law alone can never fully give us the medium/world in the way most proper to us, that is, passionately.

40   Chapter One

If the Jets are outside the Law, ignoring its demands as Officer Krupke and Lieutenant Schrank leave the scene, this is not only because they have not yet received the Law of the world, the Law of limits, and still follow a false unifying territorial logic. It is also because they feel that the Law comes empty-handed, does not touch the passion of the world that they share in their togetherness, whose nature is deeper than the tribalism they associate it with and from which they never manage to dissociate it.

In defiance of the demand of the Law—whose unsatisfying and empty nature they feel[23]—both the Sharks and the Jets start to sing the movie's first songs. This is the first manifestation of song as the passion of togetherness in excess of the Law, though they confuse the deeper shared passion of the world with violent, tribal togetherness. Singing together is the ultimate activation of the shared passion of the world in excess of the Law, but the song being sung always risks turning into an anthem of group identity where the many attempt to become one, in unison, possessively claiming a territory. Thus at first, in what is an addition by Spielberg to the original *West Side Story*, the Sharks sing the Puerto Rican anthem "La Borinqueña," a song of a togetherness in freedom but also a song of fighting. Next, there's the "Jet Song," a song of unified togetherness, of the Jets as one family, where "you're never alone, you're never disconnected, you're home with your own, when company's expected, you're well protected." There is no question of transformation or change: You're a Jet from birth to death and can never leave that identity behind.

I have started to suggest that there is a deeper togetherness in sharing the passion of the world. The question of this togetherness is asked through the adventure of Tony, the classic Spielbergian protagonist, whose separateness from the family will lead him to the miraculous encounter with the alien.[24]

Thus, in the next scene, the Leader of the Jets, Riff, unsuccessfully tries to convince Tony—who has returned from jail and, traumatized by the violence he discovered in himself, is taking distance from his "family"—to return to the fold. We then get a conversation between Tony and his employer, Valentina, a feminine presence that he, unlike Riff, is affected by and is opened to, thus passively receives, as she tells him that he was always different; even as an angry little boy there was somehow this promise he couldn't keep hidden, and sometimes she sees him smiling like he's waiting for the Irish Sweepstakes. Keep looking for better, she tells him, calling him "mi

Milagro." Then his song, the first solo song (inspired by the feminine), not of a group (structured on controlling the feminine), begins. Coming to him from Valentina, we can say that what is activated in him is only the capacity for passion, or perhaps more accurately a readiness for passion, not the event of passion. The full arrival of passion itself is yet to come, completely by surprise, without any work of his will. Valentina, his boss, who tells him what to do and thus in a way represents a Law of limits in relation to him, is also the one who, in her inspiring touch (she is more than an employer), allows him to become open to something in excess of the Law. His song, then, the song of the one who no longer belongs to the logic of the unified group, is a song of waiting, the song "Something's Coming."

The song of one who waits—in the manner of waiting for the Hölderlinian/Heideggerian God (we can only wait for a God, can never will God's arrival)—is of course not exactly a song of one person nor of a group but of what is more-than-one in oneself. It is a song (of oneself) coming in passion and in patience (to oneself, and to others), a song that starts to echo, as from an elsewhere, in the one who has been separated from the group, overtaking him from somewhere he cannot will but only receive, occupying the limits of his speech, its origin and possible demise. In this song of Tony, which is beyond him, more than him, the more-than-one in him, is already inscribed his birth and origin as open, in patience and passion, to the world, and his tragic demise, his ultimate dispossession. Every song is both birthday song and swan song. Every song is "Tonight," in which will be inscribed (in its brilliant second iteration), at a culminating moment of the film, all the complexities and contradictions of which a song consists, a togetherness in violence, the birth of the world in passion (when the world becomes a star), and the end of the day in dispossession of life, when "an endless day" becomes "endless night."

The way Spielberg stages Tony's song makes clear that this origin of the song in oneself results from an inner split, from being overtaken by something more-than-oneself, what we can view as an infinity (in the sense of being Other than any finite actuality) in oneself. As Tony looks at the polished floor he worked so hard to clean, he is pleased with his accomplishment; like Narcissus, he sees his reflection, and it is out of this reflection, which doubles him, splitting him from himself, that the song starts to echo. On the one hand, it is as if his reflection were singing to him; on the other hand, it seems that something beyond all reflection, beyond himself, is singing in him, through him.

"Could be. Who knows?" the reflection sings, a song that is thus about the suspension of the actual, the opening to the possible. Through the reflection the more-than-one/medium in oneself is glimpsed, even as it is that which escapes notice and is missed. For after all, what is a reflection? It is the way the relation to oneself (the very fact that there is such a thing as self-relation, by structural necessity) is shown to pass through a dimension of an Other to any actuality, thus through a constitutive alienation (that which inflicts us as something we can never will and is thus an irreducible foreignness in us), a more-than-oneself in oneself we called the world. We come to ourselves through the world, which is the more-than-ourselves in us that calls us, making us who we are as members of a communicative community sharing an open-ended world. To come to ourselves ("something's coming") in reflection, that is, passing through the Other/world, at the same time means leaving ourselves, going out of, beyond, ourselves, toward the more, toward the world. The moment of song, at the threshold of speech, is thus where we are carried out of ourselves even as we are called to ourselves. It is also a moment when we open up a conversation (i.e., a fundamental self-relation through language) with ourselves, activating primordial speech within us. The soul, to speak with Plato, is in dialogue with itself, even as it is a communication with indeterminate others with whom it is forced to share the world. More still, it is communication with that which is Other than any actuality, an address to an Other.

Spielberg directs Tony's singing here as a conversation with himself where Tony discovers himself, in surprise (thus by passing through that which one cannot will but can only receive as a gift, the gift of oneself). Listening to something that starts to sing to him in himself, asking questions and answering them ("Could it be? Yes it could") while also opening to the unknown, the outside, Tony looks off-screen, thus to the dimension by which he is cut, toward which he is passive, as if waiting for the extraterrestrial. Unlike the gang in its earlier singing, which looked away from the cut, as it were, toward territorial togetherness around the Leader, Tony, in his patient waiting for the miracle, sings toward the cut, raising the possibility of a togetherness of a new kind, a togetherness in passion.

As we have noted, the question of narcissism lies open here (famously culminating in Maria's song to the mirror, "I Feel Pretty"). We can define

Narcissus as the human in his/her poetic moment, attached to an excess in oneself (an excess whose presence is manifested as beauty) that is more than oneself, the medium/world in one, through which one comes to oneself. But in being attached to excess (and going out of one's mind, as Maria's coworkers sing in "I Feel Pretty," as they complain she is not the Maria they know, thus not herself but more than herself[25]) one can also, wrongly, come to be attached to one's actual reflection as the excess one is looking for and can find in it, rather than in the medium/world through which one opens up to oneself in reflection, the object of passion. Needless to say, the medium/world itself can never be reflected, since it is through it that one is reflected, opens up to oneself. Passion at its most fundamental is attachment to non-reflection, to the world as inner excess rather than to what is reflected. The singing voice, as what the medium/world is inscribed in at the moment of its activation at the threshold of speech, the birth/death of the world, is of course a major element within the general context of narcissism, to the extent that the excess expressed in the very fact of singing (the surprising discovery of oneself in conversation and the address to the Other in something like a prayer), the excess of the Other/medium over any actuality and over oneself as actual, an excess cutting us in passivity, can mistakenly be seen as inscribed in the actual content, the sound, of the voice, which now becomes an object of passion for itself, an attachment to which any diva, who is born and dies on the stage in passion, is famously at the risk of succumbing.[26]

Spielberg brilliantly orchestrates all these issues in the transition from Tony's song of waiting (which we can describe as messianic) to the next scene, where we first encounter Maria. As Tony looks toward the off, beyond the screen, singing the last line, "maybe tonight" (like "could be," the first line, a suspension of actual being), the camera zooms out, letting the empty street outside the store into the frame. There is then a cut. These three gestures are interrelated. The intrusion of the dimension of the off indicates both the intrusion of the medium as such, thus of the call "to be," beyond and before any actual utterance, and the suffering of a cut, that is, the activation of our passivity to the medium, that which we receive as a gift we cannot will. This suffering of the cut, the origin out of which our world both opens and ends, lets in more of the world (the street, this place of communication of the many without predetermination).

This moment, bringing together the relations among the off, the cut, the medium, and the opening/possible closing of the world, is also the moment of the call: the gifting intrusion of the medium, the place of birth and exhaustion, of our life in language. The call is the gift we can never will, the origin of speech at the heart of speech, in excess of any actual utterance. As per Heidegger's authoritative analysis of the question of the call, we are simultaneously the ones who are calling—the medium as such becomes who we are, is activated in us as who we are—and the ones who are called, the ones who passively receive the gift of the medium. Therefore, when Tony looks toward the off and suffers a cut, which he welcomes, it is unclear whether it is Tony who is calling—addressing, like a prayer (of which he will soon sing), the Other—or whether he is receiving a call that comes to him as a gift from the Other. Likewise, when we see, immediately following the cut, Maria on the balcony looking in an indeterminate direction, we cannot say whether she is the one who receives, like the answer to a prayer, the call from Tony, or whether she is the one who, in unknown passion, is calling. Their manner of initial communication leaves this ambiguity open, indeed unresolvable; neither can be seen as the origin of the call, since the origin can happen only between them, as a sharing of what dispossesses them both: the world.

This common passion is a togetherness very different in kind than the togetherness of the gang, since it is held together by, thanks to, the cut, a cut that indicates their simultaneous separation and connection, their unbridgeable aloneness and jointness. If they will later sing together "make of our hearts one heart . . . make of our lives one life," these words can mean either that the separating cut joining them is precisely what they also dream of eliminating or that their oneness is the oneness of a different kind than is achieved through the attempt to eliminate the cut, the oneness of the connection through the cut itself, which the cut cannot break because it is made of the cut. Both these possibilities are inscribed in their words about death and love: Whereas Tony sings, "even death won't part us now," Maria sings, "only death will part us now." Death/the cut is either at the heart of a connection that is now a oneness of a new kind, in which the cut is included, or is not included in the one, which the one is a defense against.[27]

To continue with the balcony scene: We first hear the name "Maria" when she is called by an unseen feminine voice with a Hispanic accent from off-screen. As Maria enters the room from the balcony, there is a cut in response, a cut through which she would seem to enter, embodying it, as it were. She walks into the room and eyes a large mirror to the side; about to approach it to look at her reflection, she hears her name again. Another cut is made simultaneously with the call; it is as if it cut her at the same time, indicating that her name is itself a cut—a cut that also startles her, as if waking her from a dream. Then she looks to the other side of the room, toward a bed on which a white dress is lying. Is it a wedding dress? She takes the dress, walking with it to the mirror on the other side of the room. Holding it up to see what she would look like in it, she reacts with disappointment, turns away from the mirror, puts the dress against her face, like a shroud, and falls on the bed in hopelessness. Then her name is called for a third time; another cut, and Anita, who has been calling her, enters the room.

This brief scene is awe inspiring in the quasi-biblical simplicity with which Spielberg achieves enormous complexity, a true sign of an Old Master. The first notable element is the sequence on the balcony, which we first saw following the cut from the waiting Tony's messianic song. It is unclear whether Maria receives Tony's call coming to her through the cut, a call she will feel the need to respond to, like a fairy answering a prayer, or whether it is she, in passion, who emits the call. Undoubtedly, it is both. At the same time, there is a fundamental difference, involving sexual difference and the way the call is inscribed in it. Though both Tony and Maria are, like all of Spielberg's protagonists, alienated from their families, waiting for a miracle, Maria is more in the position of the alien miraculously descending from the sky.[28] Maria, or the feminine in its most fundamental aspect,[29] is the cutting call, the place of inscription of the more-than-one. More precisely, she is what we might understand as the allegorical messenger of the call, the extraterrestrial paradoxical inscription of the medium/world as such. While the patient and passionate Tony (who is Christ-like, as the ending makes clear) is susceptible to the cutting call of the world in a way beyond the Law, the world, miraculously, can be delivered to him in, and as, passion (indeed, earlier he sings "deliver to me") only through the cutting call inscribed in, or embodied by, the extraterrestrial Maria.

The feminine, in its foundational passion, is the more essential messenger of the cutting call of the medium/world, or perhaps the call's more essential guardian. It is the task of the guardian to respond to those waiting for the call, to bring them the passionate news of the world, even at the price of being the gift that is also the source of their deaths. The masculine, in its deeper, nonterritorial/defensive aspect, might be more the guardian of the Law of the world, which is the other (if less fundamental) side of the cut. However, both sexes partake in Law and passion, for the call itself is beyond sexual difference yet is inscribed differently in the sexes, and as the sexes, sexuality—not a matter of content but of logic, though a logic with allegorical incarnations—being the dimension of excess, of the more-than-one, as it is inscribed in us (as alien settlements, carriers of the no-thing of the medium, haunting the body), differently.

Sharing the World

Though Maria is the guardian or messenger, the calling of her name from the off, at a moment of a cut, indicates that she is not, of course, the master of the call. The messenger is just a messenger, not the owner of the message. The call strikes her from afar, so dispossessing her that she seems to be in a trance, a dream, as she enters the room. Yet the call "Maria" uttered by Anita not only points to self-loss at the passionate moment of her romantic dreaming; there is also the dimension of possessiveness inscribed in Anita's call, which is partially territorial. Anita is the mistress of the house; her call is also a call against Maria's passion (a dramatic confrontation culminating in the film's final song, the remarkable "A Boy Like That / I Have a Love," where Anita's possessiveness and her attempt to eliminate the love connection is met with Maria's passion of self-loss in response), a call to order and territory not unlike the earlier "Jets!" Anita seems to sense the danger of the balcony, opened in passion to the outside and beyond the gang to which she belongs by association with her boyfriend, Bernardo, the Leader of the Sharks, whose woman she, partially, is (the song "America" will dramatically contest his possession of her: In principle Anita is the one who evenly wavers between the logic of the gang, in which context she belongs to Bernardo, and the logic of passion, in which she exceeds him), and she calls Maria inside. Hence, also, the significance, or an aspect of the significance, of the Hispanic accent, as a marker of the group identity to which she belongs and the drawing of the territory she wants to defend, against Maria, who implicitly threatens to embody its loss, or at least its opening to something beyond the territory.

The accent, of course, in the film (which insists both on the display of accent and on an irreducible linguistic difference between English and

Spanish) and in general is a marker not only of territory. More profoundly, it marks the non-unification of speech/language into one, serving as the place of inscription of an irreducible more-than-one at the heart of speech that makes it so that speech cannot be possessed by any member of the world forced to share it, and thus there is no one way to speak and no single, universally dominant language. In this sense, an accent, when perceived as accent, as if marking a deviation from a unity—accent is of course only a differential, noticed (or basically existing) only as a deviation from territorial unification—is that in which is inscribed an unsettling excess of the dispossessing medium that cannot be owned. The accent is a cut, the threat or wound to territory. At the same time, any such inscription of excess (precisely because it is a dispossessing cut and suffered as such by those marginalized by the power of a territory to which they are perceived as threat) can become the point of attachment for a different territorial desire, such that the accent itself becomes the point around which a call to a new territorial unification is gathered. Rather than remain a trace of an irreducible constitutive dispossession, the accent/wound is transformed into a new center of territorial pride. (The operative logic is similar to the narcissistic attachment to the material of the voice mentioned previously.) Anita's accent when she calls Maria from off-screen (which is also, in this context, the marker of cultural marginalization and the exclusion of those carrying accents[30]) thus inscribes in itself two contradictory aspects: the trace of the call as constitutive non-unification, and the territorial desire invested in the accent/wound that tries to transform the mark of destitution into the center of possessive power.

There is, then, no one language and no one way of speaking: a fact revealed when the excess of the more-than-one/medium/world makes itself noticeable or present as it is inscribed in what cannot be brought into the fold of the one mastering all, inscribed in a wounding, cutting accent. The accent separates the accented from the group, marginalizes one, at the same time that, narcissistically, it becomes the point of gathering for new territorial ambitions. But is there a possibility of gathering around the accent accompanied neither by marginalization nor by territorialization? There is—and it is expressed as music and song. Song, we have started to see, accents language, yet this accenting is transformed into passionate expressivity. The song is the place of inscription, like the accent, of the cut of the medium/language in relation to which we are passive, yet it can transform this cut into a new expressivity of passion, beyond the territorial logic of willing/meaning. In the song the excess of the medium, the place of our absolute passivity, is inscribed in such a way as to allow us to go beyond our desire to eliminate the wound by turning it into territory. In song, the passionate accentuation of language, our passivity to the alien (language/medium), is welcomed,[31] expressed beyond the logic of meaning/willing, and becomes something at the origin of neither exclusion and marginalization nor territorialization but of a new kind of sharing. The song in its profoundest dimension comes to be shared together, separately. It is shared among all those belonging to the community of the medium, insofar as what is common is nothing but irreducible passivity to the medium/world, beyond any positive content. What is common is not any possession but rather dispossession, which needs to be transformed into passionate sharing. Commonality, as the sharing of dispossession, is not a state but a movement outside oneself, passage through the more-than-oneself in oneself, toward others with whom we are forced to share the world. Passionate sharing is creative communication: The world is at stake, is activated as world, as the unpredictable openness of the medium, in the movement between those who share it toward one another. To be dispossessed in the more profound dimension is not simply to lose possession and to be in a state of such loss but to enter the world's unpredictable movement.

Music as passionate accentuation embodies the possibility of being something that does not separate and exclude, that creates no new territoriality but instead connects (which does not mean fusing into one); it is sharing, togetherness, creatively communicative participation in absolute commonality, in the passivity to the medium. Our togetherness can only be an experience of constitutive separateness, the fact that we can never be One, can only be more-than-oneself. This possibility is what the messianic "Something's Coming"—followed by a cutting call—announces. "To be in America": America's song of itself as the possibility of being together in an irreducible multiplicity that does not try to erase itself and create various territories (or one big territory) and without the need to "get rid of your accent."

Hence the profound relevance of the classic question regarding music as some kind of universal language, beyond the babel of linguistic multiplicity. If there is something in music and song that exceeds linguistic divisions, speaking beyond them, it is not because it contains an element of some primordial lost unity but because, inscribing in itself the cut, beyond meaning (as willing to say), it becomes a connecting communicative force, allowing all separate individualities to persist in multiplicity even as they share the world/language as such/the medium. The new "universal" inscribed in music and song means sharing through and via the cut; it is a singing communicated and shared by all accents and languages without canceling them. With music as our creative communicative connector—a new universal exceeding linguistic and cultural divisions that have been reified into territories—it is no longer a question of some pre-Babelian unity but of an American song (of oneself) held and actuated in common. The film *West Side Story* (incidentally or not a work created by at least six major Jewish American artists) is the anti-Wagnerian *Gesamtkunstwerk* or "total work of art." While aiming to bring together all the arts (literature, poetry, music, dance, theater, painting, graffiti, film, etc.), it seeks not to establish a new mythic community but to forge a new logic of creative communication across multiples that can never be unified or totalized; it can thus enter into a new mode of sharing: the popular musical as the world sharing of the people (and not the exclusive, and excluding, sacred temple of art à la Bayreuth[32]).

In this sense, the promise of America is a mode of togetherness grounded not in territory but in Law and Song. The musical exemplifies a new way of understanding the essential significance of art to political life, even as it exceeds this same sphere. Art/musical passion, in excess of the legal framework establishing a togetherness of a place as a series of limits and borders, and in excess of various positive territorial characteristics such as historical customs and habits, is the means to experience togetherness as a conversation—with oneself, with others, and with the Other/medium in a movement of world lived as open sharing.[33]

Song of the Balcony

Let us return to Maria. When we left her, she had suffered the calling cut on/of the balcony, that locus of openness to the movement of the world, to public communicative sharing. We noted that as Maria enters the room, she wavers in her dreamy self-loss between the mirror and the dress. The mirror, the dress, and the cutting call of the world are interrelated because they are inscribed with the question of reflection activated by the call. The wedding dress is simultaneously a potential shroud (the two possibilities of the cut, as passionate connector at the birth of the world in sharing and as absolute disconnector, the end of the world). Both the dress (the inscription of the passion of appearance, thus of passively appearing in the light of the world) and the mirror belong to the double logic of narcissism: passionate attachment to what is more-than-one in oneself (the light of the world, the cutting source of appearance, the origin of passion and death) and the misinterpretation of the "more"/the medium (of reflection) as being inscribed in what appears in the mirror. The mirror, or more exactly the event of mirroring, is the means revealing the surprise of oneself and exposure to the world and, at the same time, is that through which the cut at this revelation's heart is recuperated into actuality that sutures the fissured self.

As we have seen, the "feminine" is paradigmatically the site of the cut: Any encounter across the line of sexual difference, between women and men, immediately participates in both sides of narcissism, the opening of the world's passion and the surprise of oneself, as well as the impulse for territorial unification. This seems to occur more from the point of view of the masculine qua the one who has suffered the cut. The woman, in turn, only ever succumbs partially, if at all, to this masculine desire for appropriation; she remains faithful to the cut of the call inscribed in her and to the passionate side of narcissism as attachment to the more-than-one in oneself as the inscription of the medium/world/infinity.

Spielberg develops this complexity (which in many ways structures the movie as a whole) in a very clear way in the two scenes following Maria's return to her room. A dance is planned for the evening. Bernardo brings Chino, a member of the tribe he thinks will be suitable for her. The next sequence presents the four characters—Anita, Bernardo, Maria, and Chino—in various mirroring arrangements, whose full variety and logics we cannot get into here. The crucial point is that as they leave the apartment to go to the dance, Anita and Bernardo exit the apartment first, leaving Maria and Chino behind. Instead of turning to Chino (as if to reflect him and acquiesce to his possessive desire), Maria turns to the mirror, implicitly wounding him (which will eventually have the consequence of his taking revenge and killing Tony). The turn to the mirror signifies not shallow narcissism but faithfulness to the deeper side of narcissism, the passionate attachment to the cut itself (the inscription of the medium/world), which

Maria refuses to abandon. As she turns to the mirror, the music strikes a menacing tone—indicating the inscription of passion as dangerous cut in it—and her hand opens to reveal red lipstick, which she applies defiantly, looking at the mirror. The vibrant red inscribes the cut to which her narcissism remains faithful, ignoring the possessive logic of Chino and Bernardo's gang (before she goes to the mirror in defiance, Bernardo warns her not to take an interest in any gringo boy). Through this red cut of passion, the open door is glimpsed, leading Maria out into the world, as she follows the call of the balcony away from the territory of the apartment into her story of passion and death.

The dance that follows, another remarkable scene we won't analyze, where she will meet her destiny in Tony, is itself a complex choreography of various mirroring scenes across sexual difference, constantly being territorially appropriated into gang logic, with the exception of the passionate couple (Maria and Tony) who will withdraw, separate themselves, from the logic of gang doubling in order to connect in a different way, through separation and cut, the waiting alienated figure finally meeting the prayer-hearing alien, in passion and, eventually, death.

The structure of the call on the balcony we just traced, leading into the territorial apartment and then, in defiance, out of it (now not into the gang dance but into the democratic streets) is very beautifully echoed, as a liberating doubling (which has to do with the doubling between women, as in Ingmar Bergman's *Persona*, here between Anita and Maria[34]), in Anita's balcony song of liberation from possessive masculine gang logic. "America," an alternative, positive, happy ending to the tragic adventure of the balcony as inscribed in Maria, an alternative embodying the full promise of America, is the one truly happy song in *West Side Story* as Spielberg conceives it (happiness being the full coming home to oneself of the several who share a world and are more than themselves).

As Anita goes out to the balcony, the music starts playing, as if activating this exposed place of the call, and she responds by singing. As she sings, through a series of cuts, other women on other balconies and in windows join her in a new kind of communal togetherness—or at least its possibility.

We can say that the space of the balcony is, in a way, a complement to the excess of the mirror through which the women remain faithful to their deeper narcissism, the attachment to the more-than-one in oneself. This is why Maria goes from the balcony to the mirror. The balcony is the space of women; it is the opening to/of the medium/world through which they escape the masculine territorial desire dominating the apartments and from which they bring another option of togetherness. It is also where they hang their dresses, that is, inscriptions of appearance (exposure to the medium as such), which seem to form a series of screens; it is as if cinematic space (the cutting, or interruption, of territory) opens out of the passion to the call, narcissistically inscribed in the dresses, especially wedding dresses.[35]

This shared, feminine song of the balcony seems to encourage Anita to enter the apartment, dismiss Bernardo, and leave it. She joins, in a series of groups of three (thus not the reflective doubling but the assembly of the several who are at the origin of a new community, of those who sang through the cut of the passionate space of the balcony), other women on the street, that open space of unpredictable encounters of the several as people, thus as those who are gathered not by the demand of masculine territorial unification achieved through the elimination of the feminine cut but instead by the dreams of waiting and of passion activated on the balcony. Those who sing in waiting on the balcony become those who are open to—and who open the possibility of—the unpredictable togetherness of the street, that is, the forced togetherness of those who share a world freely and who make decisions regarding how they are to be. The street is the communal activation of the balcony, of that space through which one receives the call. This means that the people can gather in a street festival only if women intone a new song from the balcony around which a new community can gather. Hence, everyone stops their cars in the scene and rushes to join in.

The song and dance of the street, the festival, suspend all specific daily activities, which yield to the pure experience of sharing the world qua open to decisions about how the many are to be, in a way never given in advance. Like the school dance earlier in the film, the street festival (which has the feeling of a Bruegel peasant dance) revolves around a certain doubling dramatic confrontation. But whereas the school dance revolved around the mirroring confrontation between the two gangs—white and Hispanic, fully dominated by masculine territorial logic—here the dramatic confrontation is not between two gangs but between the sexes. The men (in Bruegel unfailingly armed with knives, and in this scene mainly with their fists) argue in their song for territorial logic (wanting to return to their own territory,

Puerto Rico, from an America that—even though they belong to it to a complex degree due to the legal status of Puerto Rico—they feel rejects them). The women, who have escaped the apartment and have fled to the street, argue for and activate what is beyond gang logic: the dance of cutting passion through which the people can gather in the America where they, and all accents, have a place. The doubling gang logic will end in a fight, a confrontation resulting in death and tragedy. The street fight between the sexes—a double of the later scene of the gang war between the two groups of men—is where the feminine logic is triumphant, and it will end in a new gathering of the people and a passionate embrace across the cut: Anita and Bernardo end the scene with an impassioned kiss. The song "America" is the vision of a place where gang war, grounded in group-identity logic, enters into a confrontation, which it loses, with feminine waiting/world-delivering logic, the logic of the people whose space is the street—amplifying the liberation offered by the balcony. It is as if America were the fulfillment of the balcony dreams of a Juliet—*West Side Story* is famously inspired by Shakespeare—a dream that could never be responded to and could end only in tragedy before America, but also fails to be responded to in an America that has not fully opened to its own possibility.

Maria

I have mainly said what I have wanted to in this attempt to elucidate Spielberg's vision of the relations between the promise of America and the medium of film, understood as the medium of the passionate cut through whose excess over reflection (the world as that which cannot appear in the mirror) the arriving alien can be welcomed. Yet I could not end without paying special attention to perhaps the most beautifully staged song of the movie, "Maria." This song brings together in a particularly profound way the relations among the question of language, the singing voice, the address to the Other in something like a prayer, and the feminine cut as entryway to the opening to a world where others are present in a new way, not as gathered in group identity.

Having left the school dance, the occasion of the miraculous encounter with Maria, Tony roams the empty streets. He leans on a fence; the effect is that he appears to be imprisoned. Music starts to play, to which he would seem to be listening; then he utters the name "Maria." Then, listening to himself uttering the name, he starts to sing "the most beautiful sound I ever heard," then again, repeatedly, "Maria, Maria, Maria." Another cut is made, and he is seen from a slightly greater distance; a bit more of the world is open. The name "Maria" sounds again—this time as an echo, to whose call he responds by opening a door in the fence. Liberated from his imprisonment, as it were, he enters a courtyard and once again sings "Maria." Her name is echoed at the exact moment of another cut (in the same precise way as occurred earlier, in the scene with Anita, when the name was uttered at the moment of a cut). The cutting echo seems to startle him for a moment, very similar to the way Maria had earlier been startled at the moment of her cutting naming, and it is as if he loses direction, only to regain his orientation and, with a new sense of purpose, he finally bursts into full song: "Maria, Maria, Maria...."

This beautiful cinematic moment is itself about beauty: "the most beautiful sound I ever heard." Indeed the moment of beauty—the moment of Tony's encounter with Maria at the dance—that remained imprinted in him as he departed, is what lies at the source of his song; it keeps playing within him, so to speak, after he has received from her the gift of his calling, a gift that allows him to receive the cut and open to it as a passionate song rather than in defensive gang logic. It is the gift of language that he received from Maria at the moment of its origin, a gift to which one is passive, a gift that is thus expressed in a song in excess of anything he could have intended or willed, the song that kept playing within him as he left the dance and that now as if unwillingly has burst out of him and has liberated him from his imprisonment. This song belongs neither to him nor to Maria. She is nevertheless its passionate cutting messenger, who "incarnates" or inscribes the cut in her very being as a woman. The delivery of the medium/world is expressed in her name and in her becoming a call. Her name is that exceptional word that is the name for language/medium as such, at the moment of its being received as an unwilled gift, the moment of its calling. In this sense, it is the place of the possibility of all the "most beautiful sounds in the world in a single word," for it stands for language as such and thus for all the possible utterances that can emerge from it, utterances at whose origin is thus beauty, that which shines at the moment of the cutting gift—inscribed, from the point of view of sexual difference, in the feminine cut—which can only be received as miraculous passion by the one who waits.

Since the call belongs neither to Tony, who passively and passionately receives it, nor to Maria, who is its unintentional messenger, it hauntingly exists or persists as a detached echo belonging to the world at the cutting moment of its origination as an unpredictable opening whose gift we can only unwillingly receive. The echo of the world, the gift of language without a willing origin, inscribed in the haunting refrain "Maria," happens most forcefully in the cut that exposes Tony to the world itself and to others with whom he is forced to share it. Thus, as he continues his song, there is another cut after another mention of "Maria," and then another person appears, a black cleaning person, with whom he now shares the world, both nodding as they pass each other by. Tony continues to sing; another cut, and again "Maria." Now a woman sitting on a bench appears, yet one more person with whom to share a world that one has unwillingly become exposed to through a cut one nevertheless welcomes, with a smile.

As he makes his way, Tony finds himself alone again, singing about the name "Maria" ("say it soft and it's almost like praying"); he looks around, singing to the off, thus to the cut itself, activating the screen as a cut territory in which the singing voice, no longer addressed to anyone specific, is now the praying call to the Other—a pure activation of the medium belonging to no one. Maria, the cut at the origin of the call of language as such, is now something like a prayer, addressed to the Other in yearning waiting, a prayer that will be responded to by the reception of the one who can be the gift's messenger, an actual Maria. Thus, as Tony sings to the off, a young girl appears at a window, as if she herself had felt the call of the outside, followed by an older woman. Neither represents the right response to the prayer. He continues: "I'll never stop saying 'Maria,'" as if it were an eternal refrain, then again: "the most beautiful sound. . . ." Finally, he voices his last "Maria" as he exits the screen, his voice continuing briefly to resonate from the "off," now a pure voice without origin (like the earlier echo), which is also in a way the pure prayer, the more-than-one in oneself having become detached from oneself as the pure activation of the medium. It is this having become a pure prayer inscribed in the echo that simultaneously brings, as a miracle, Maria—the one who answers prayers—to the balcony and, at the same time, announces that the prayer's answer, a truly passionate activation of one's acceptance of the cut, implies the actual Tony's disappearance, thus his eventual demise and dispossession, and his remaining in the world as inscribing in and for the world the world's pure echo, an echo signifying both Tony's death and his gift to the world. The refrain of his voice, his more-than-himself in himself, will remain beyond him in the world and will deliver his message to the world, the message of the world as a realm of cutting that one can receive as passion, opening to others in their accents, and to the Other in something like a prayer. This message to the world—at the moment of his death, and with Maria as the witness to this message, which she herself first unknowingly and unintentionally delivered—becomes the origin around which a new community, beyond the division into the warring gangs, gathers, as members of both gangs carry Tony's body in mourning at the end of the film.

"Maria, Maria, Maria, Maria. . . ." The haunting refrain that is Tony's praying message now becomes the center of a new community and a new way of being. "Maria" is now the word for this way of being, the song/name keeping guard over the message of the "to be" in a newly born America.

TWO

The Memory of America

JOHN FORD'S *YOUNG MR. LINCOLN* AND
THE MAN WHO SHOT LIBERTY VALANCE

The guiding question we have been following concerns the relations between the being of America, in its instantiation as the United States, understood as the project of bringing about a new and unprecedented way of organizing the life that human beings share in common—and the very nature of the cinematic medium. There is perhaps no filmmaker who has dedicated his efforts to the examination and development of this question more extensively than John Ford, who basically made it the unavoidable center of his entire cinematic corpus. As such he merits consideration, as has been suggested,[1] occupying for American film the place that Walt Whitman holds for American poetry: the central figure attempting to think together the being of the nation with that of an artistic medium, which itself has to be marked by the novelty characterizing the newness of America.

It is important to remember the context within which such a question of the relations between the being of America and the being of an artistic medium, specifically film, is asked and holds essential stakes. The context is the attempt—which starts in the late eighteenth century and reaches perhaps its first paradigmatic formulations in nineteenth-century Germany with the writings of Richard Wagner—to resist relegating art (itself in a way a modern phenomenon, something that begins with the European Renaissance) to being understood within the framework of aesthetics. Even if aesthetics itself was formulated in a conceptually rigorous way only in the writings of Kant toward the end of the eighteenth century, we can say that these writings, for the first time, managed to bring into its most fully developed philosophical formulation the position that art increasingly came to occupy in human life within the context of its post-religious age, that is, from the end of medieval Christianity and the beginning of the European Renaissance, and thus of European modernity. In fact we can say that art itself—if we regard art as something increasingly understood within a framework not sacred or religious but of what eventually came to be called aesthetics—is, in a way, something that emerged only with modernity. Yet something has been lost in this transition from a sacred to an aesthetic framework, with the work of art being understood as an autonomous, detached object meant to provoke an experience of beauty, a loss famously expressed in Hegel's formulation regarding the end of art: "In all these aspects art, considered in its highest vocation, is and remains for us a thing of the past. Thereby it has lost for us genuine truth and life, and has rather been transferred into our ideas instead of maintaining its earlier necessity in reality and occupying its higher place."[2]

What has thus been lost in modernity, in the aesthetic era initiated in the Renaissance and characterizing the ages after it (at least in its theoretical thought, if not necessarily in the practice of the artists themselves[3]), is art's (if we still choose to use the same name for phenomena happening within the context of the sacred world and within the new context of modernity) relation to truth and life, its necessity in reality. Briefly, we can thus say, art for Hegel is no longer essential or originary, that is, it no longer connects us to what most fundamentally makes human life what it is: that by which human life is to be guided and from which it is to draw its resources.

Even if for Hegel himself this loss inscribed in modern art does not imply a need to reconceive art, to think in a new way about its place and practice in modern life—since art for Hegel, after the demise of Christianity, where it still held an essential function, has indeed finished its historical task and is to be overcome by philosophy, which will now be that through which the highest in human vocation is achieved, that which fundamentally connects humanity to its origin in the sense of essence—there is nevertheless, if only negatively, a challenge implied in his articulation of the end of art, a challenge to understand and to create an art in a new framework, a challenge that most likely signifies as well a need to exceed and dismantle Hegel's own understanding of the task of thinking. Such art (if that which exceeds aesthetics, yet is not a return to the sacred, is still to assume that name, and it probably needs another[4]) will have the task of occupying in modern, call it post-theological, human life and reality a place equally essential to the place occupied by premodern art within its own sacred or religious context. It is such a challenge to give art a newly conceived, essential place, that is, a newly conceived relation to the origin of humanity's way of life, which animated some of the fundamental artistic efforts—most of them, within the European context, in Germany, for an essential reason we will look into—of the nineteenth and twentieth centuries, from the Wagnerian so-called *Gesamtkunstwerk*, the total work of art ("total" also in the sense that it has to do with the totality or whole of human life) revolving around the construction of a new sacred temple of the arts in Bayreuth, to Joseph Beuys's so-called social sculpture (where the creativity implicit in society as such, as society, or common life, is what comes to occupy the artist). What characterizes all these efforts, as different in their logics as they are, is indeed the need to transform art from its definition via aesthetics to an art in which the very ground of life and reality is at stake, albeit in a new way, in the sense that what is to be reconceived is the very ground or origin of human life.

The dangers of such efforts, especially in the case of Wagner (though not, in my view, in the case of Beuys, who in fact achieves a complex deconstruction of Wagnerian logic) and a certain line of "artists" following him (culminating in the fascistic work of propaganda that is Leni Riefenstahl's *Triumph of the Will*) are well-known. These dangers have to do with the way the newly conceived function of art in life and reality is to supply a unifying ground, through which the dispersal of modern political life, which can no longer ground itself in the religious divine, manages to gather itself into a new whole, or new totality, achieving the status of a functioning organism. The function thus conceived of art, or of something beyond (aesthetic) art— an art often conceived of as a new mythology—is then to serve as a substitute for the missing divine (this is why this new mythology is not exactly a return to sacred art, since it assumes the loss of the divine) as that in which modern political life (i.e., the formation and organization of life in common) can be grounded and through which it can be unified. It is quite clear that such efforts took place first and foremost in Germany—within the European context, and we will get to the similar yet very different American context soon—precisely because, as Jean-Luc Nancy and Philippe Lacoue-Labarthe have pointed out in a slightly different context, discussing the question of what they call the Nazi Myth, Germany itself as a political entity has been, historically, particularly fragmented and dispersed, without the unifying identity characterizing, at least to some degree, many of its European counterparts (though perhaps Italy, and the adjoining question of Italian opera, most significantly with Verdi, stands as another paradigmatic case study in the context of these questions). Thus, Germany was in greater need to identify itself, to come to be as a unity, and the newly conceived work of art, as a grounding mythology, came to be one of the main resources used in such efforts.

Nevertheless, what is crucial for our purposes in these efforts—as misguided as they are, at least partially—is that the very thinking and to some extent the practice of art began to be transformed, accompanied by a quest for a new, post-aesthetic place for art in life, a place where art is to occupy an essential, irreducible site for human life in its post-religious age to connect to its ground, or in other words to its origin, to what makes it what it is.

The whole question though, of course, consists in these sub-questions: What does this mean? How are we to understand the origin of human life in which art is supposed to ground us? For in the differences among various possible answers to such questions lie the differences among a premodern religious or sacred work, a modern fascistic work, and a post-aesthetic nonfascistic one.

A New Mythology?

Rather than embark on a general discussion of this question, I propose looking at the case of Ford, who perhaps more than any other American filmmaker, is an heir to this by and large Germanic tradition in his, at least implicit, understanding of the status of the work of art, no longer seeing in it an autonomous object for aesthetic contemplation, nor of course mere entertainment, but regarding it as an event through which the origin of human life is activated in such a way as to bring about a new way of life, a new world, call it America. Film, for Ford (who appropriately always rejected the designation of "artist"), is a medium whose task is to activate the origin or essence of human life in a new way, as America or as the United States. America for Ford, in other words, is not exclusively a name for a specific political entity but a name for a new opening of human life, one no longer grounded in the divine or in any gods, and film is the medium through which the origin is to be activated, and thus that through which a new world comes to be. To see the relevance of his work to the questions mentioned previously, it is enough to think that Ford's establishment of the Western as the genre dedicated to creating a so-called American mythology is at the same time the genre investigating, but thus also aiming to stand at, the threshold of the constitution of a new world, occupying the moment of transitioning, or of the attempt to transition, between the desert and organized, or unified, communal life, if of a historically new kind. We can also think of Ford's complex investigations of the European world that the white part of America left behind, or from which it was violently cut off, destined as a result to attempt to create a new way of being, as in his *How Green Was My Valley* (where old Europe has been left behind as a memory) or *The Quiet Man* (where the new way of being seems to have failed, and Europe is returned to).

Yet what, precisely, does "origin" mean for Ford or in Ford's films? Is it the establishment of a unifying ground that is to serve as an anchor, in the manner of the German fascistic myths,[5] to a dispersed common existence, or to a common existence dispersed in post-religious modernity, which cannot otherwise find itself, identify itself? There is undoubtedly a certain proximity between the American problem and the Germanic problem, as Nancy and Lacoue-Labarthe have articulated it. Not unlike Germany, we can say, but even more radically, there is no given tradition, no common history, religion, or even language, and no established common political system to bring together and unify, to identify, the dispersed multiplicity of inhabitants of what came to be America or, as an ideal goal, the *United* States. In this sense, it would seem, forging a common myth of origins—in the manner of the Western, narrating, as it supposedly does, a heroic overcoming of desert dispersion, where one is seen as being exposed to various enemies from without, and for which the main figures are the Indians (taking the implicit place of the Jews of Germany), and from within, in the form of lawless criminals (though the Jews for the Germans were simultaneously outside and inside, thus uncanny enemies[6])—will be what allows the dispersed multiplicity (irrespective of its indigenous inhabitants) to unify. It is as if each one of the dispersed—no matter their historical origin, religion, language, and so on—is now seen; or each dispersed person is to see him- or herself, identify him- or herself (an identification to be experienced as a heroic self-overcoming of one's own dispersive excess over identificatory unity), as the historical offspring of that originary, heroic achievement of self-unification, belonging to the story of America's emergence out of the lawless, enemy-filled desert (the enemy being that which threatens unity, or self-unification). To be an American, in such an understanding, would be to relate oneself to, to belong to, this heroic myth of origin.

It might seem needless to say, or perhaps not, considering some of the misreadings of Ford's work,[7] that this is very far from the director's cinematic project and his attempts to inscribe the origin, or to activate an origination, of an America in which the dispersed can share and through which they can come to be American. For Ford, to be American, to come to belong to America as a new way of life or a new mode of being (and it remains an open question for him whether this has ever been achieved or whether we are still roaming the desert), would not be the becoming unified around a common myth of origins that will give those lacking it a grounding identity or a mechanism of self-identification, but coming to share in a common, and new, event and logic of origination, to be activated by the cinematic screen and through the mediation of "mythical" (i.e., originary) figures who function in a new way. America is, at least as a call not yet fulfilled but powerfully heard, a new, common way of experiencing the origin of the world—in excess of the various historical logics of origination around which human life came to organize itself—and activated most paradigmatically perhaps by film.

Suffice it to think of *The Man Who Shot Liberty Valance*, Ford's last fully achieved masterwork—where the so-called mythical, in the sense of heroically inscribing a unifying origin and overcoming the desert, is itself shown to be a myth (in the sense of a misleading cover-up)—to realize that Ford, and not only in his late, critical (and self-critical?) phase (a phase distinguished perhaps by his increasing realization of the not-yet-achieved nature of America, but not by a new understanding of the logic of origination announced by America and film in their interrelations) is after something very different than the creation of an identificatory, heroic myth of origins.

To the contrary: By exposing the truth behind the shooting of Liberty Valance (not unlike Freud, in his *Moses and Monotheism*, exposing the truth behind the Mosaic myth and its narration of the way out of the desert and into organized common life—and we can say perhaps that the late work *The Man Who Shot Liberty Valance* is Ford's *Moses and Monotheism*, which was Freud's last masterwork[8]), the myth, understood in this heroic way, is shown to ground a failed, empty, political reality, a reality devoid of the truly political, that is, devoid of an organization where the life in common is grounded in the essence, or origin. If Ford is indeed interested in creating mythic, exceptional figures through which the origin of America is effected or through whom it is activated, the mythic logic of these figures will be very different, if myth (which always stood for that exceptional moment of inscribing the origin) is even the right name for it (in the sense that though inscribing the origin, the origin inscribed is of a very different kind, and as such a new name might be required for the event of its inscription).[9]

We will get to these questions, and to *Liberty Valance*, soon enough, but I would like us to begin our investigation of Ford's conception of the work of art's task as the event of a new activation of the origination of the world, as America, with some of his earlier works.

It is in 1939, which could be considered his *annus mirabilis*, when Ford's understanding of the relation between the question of the origins of America (in both senses of the "of") and the cinematic medium reaches perhaps its first fully thought-out realization and when the two sides of the "mythic" or paradigmatic, in some sense more-than-human figures[10]—who for Ford are to stand at the origin of the new community of America—come into full view in two films: *Young Mr. Lincoln* and what is often considered the first great Western, *Stagecoach*.[11] These two films each revolve around a central figure, Lincoln and John Wayne, respectively, each incarnating in different degrees four main "elements"—and each of Ford's paradigmatic figures will be a different distribution of the relations among these four elements, even if we might also see his characters as falling into two main types (who often occupy the same movie in dramatic tension), having to do with the more powerful pull of one of these elements—the Law; memory and/as mourning; the desert (or its equivalent, the open sea in some of the war movies); and love. By and large the Lincoln type (whose last great iteration will be the James Stewart of *Liberty Valance*) will be the one revolving more around the question of the Law, and the John Wayne type (usually played by Wayne himself, its last great iteration being the John Wayne of *Liberty Valance*) revolving more around the mystery inscribed in the pull of the desert. Together they form the two main sides or two faces of Ford's Moses, the founder of a new community, Law and the desert (which are not opposed but do not yet coincide, for reasons we need to look into), who in his Wayne aspect will often be doomed not to reach the Promised Land, the announcement of which he nevertheless inscribes, as if there has not yet been found a new Law, one that will truly transform the desert (and thus end the Western), allowing one to exit it.

Yet there is a third face of Moses or a third face required for the foundation of a new community (three faces whose complexity of interaction will be most fundamentally investigated via the three main characters of *Liberty Valance*), and around this face the two types mentioned earlier will revolve to different degrees: the feminine and the dimension of love at its core. This dimension of feminine love is itself classically presented in Ford under one or the other of its two aspects, the maternal and the erotic, even if, in one of Ford's countertraditional, though possibly highly Christian, moves, most explicitly exemplified in the prostitute of *Stagecoach* who heroically cares for a newborn, the erotic and the maternal are not necessarily seen in exclusionary opposition but, to the contrary, are called to be brought together and seen in their interrelation.

The Gift of Law

Let us then start our investigation of Ford's development of film as a site for the inscription of the origin of America—which implies an understanding of America as a name for a new relation to the origin, an origin exposed and activated by film—by looking at the opening of *Young Mr. Lincoln* since, like all major directors, Ford fully establishes the rules of the game via his films' opening scenes.

"If Nancy Hanks came back as a ghost, seeking news of what she loved most, she'd ask first 'Where's my son? What's happened to Abe? What's he done?'"

Even before the first image, the film presents us with these words from Rosemary Benét's poem "Nancy Hanks," etched on what looks like a tombstone. Our eyes, then, poetically open to the image—which is not a regular opening of perception—through a tombstone, through an experience of loss (of a beloved). It is memory, inscribed in and as poetic speech of the one who has been lost, which is the ghost through which we see an image, open up to it. This means that the image is inscribed by something that withdraws, is missing, from what we perceive, a withdrawal nevertheless somehow present as a haunting memory.

Though while we see these words etched on stone—which occupies the entire screen, making the screen itself seem, and perhaps be, a tombstone, a resting place sheltering a memory continuing to speak to us (memory is a speech: speak, memory)—we are not yet confronted with the visual image; there is nevertheless already an indication of how the question of the screen image is to be thought in relation to these problems. For, though we do not yet see any positive visual content—besides the etched stone, and it is not even clear that it *is* a stone and hence is not really presented as such as an object for perception—negative "content" is nevertheless presented to us in the form of the shadows of leaves and tree branches spread across the screen. These shadows point to something missing from the screen, outside the screen, off-screen, that leaves its trace on-screen. We can associate the off-screen here with that withdrawal, the loss, a dimension that exists only as ghostly memory, as an inscription of what is not actually there. The poetic cinematic image, then, is the relation between what we see on-screen as an actuality and a ghostly memory, the trace of a loss, which by definition remains off-screen (i.e., is not actual) but is somehow nevertheless inscribed on it or in it as a shadow. The screen, in this sense, as Ford interprets it, if it is not itself a tombstone (though it might also be that, the rectangular shape of both being often highlighted in Ford's films[12]), is the relation between a tombstone and some actual content of perception upon which the tombstone casts its shadows and haunts with its speech. It is as if every screen image has an attached double that is not apparent on it but is off it, a tombstone (in the sense of the place for that which has no place, the non-actual) whose ghostly shadows are inscribed on-screen as a constant reminder of loss.[13] Those who will come on-screen, in this sense—that is, come to occupy it as actualities—will be those who are inscribed with, and open a negotiation with, a haunting loss, often having the character of an inaudible memory speaking. If, in Ford, most essentially, those who come on-screen are those whose question is what it means to belong to America, this means that being an American is first and foremost, for Ford, an experience of being haunted by an irrecuperable loss (loss of God, of Europe, of an America of their ancestors for the Indians, of Africa for black people, of Mexico for the Mexicans, etc., of a beloved home, of a beloved person, etc.), an off-screen, which continues to speak to them, even as they are called to bring about a new place in negotiation with that loss, in negotiation with the shadows cast upon them.[14] What first of all seems to define the Americans coming on-screen for Ford is the sharing of mourning, a mourning that is their one commonality, precisely because each is inscribed by a loss. The specific loss itself is, however, not common to them and in many ways is the reason for their hostility toward each other, each seeing in the other, unconsciously and at times consciously, the cause of loss.

Thus, as we open our eyes to the visual image after first having been inflicted with the shadowy, ghostly memorial in *Young Mr. Lincoln*, what we see is the following: a dispersed group of people standing in some kind of field surrounded by trees. The presence of an isolated, unassuming-looking house, toward which most of the group, from their dispersed and unordered place, direct their gaze, indicates that we are not simply in an open field in the middle of a forest, nor are we in some organized, defined public space—instead, we find ourselves in something in between the two, as if what is precisely at stake is the question of the transition from the one to the other. To the left of the screen stands a partially seen wagon, part of it on-screen, the rest outside it. On the right, a wagon led by horses is making its way onto the screen, arriving from the off-screen, from what is withdrawn from perception, as if carrying with it the burden of this withdrawal (we will soon discover that the wagon's occupants have been displaced and are on their way to a new home).

On the steps of the house, still seen from a distance, an elevated character dressed in black seems to be addressing the dispersed assembly. A cut, and we get a closer look. Dressed in formal black attire—which separates him from his audience, dressed in working clothes—the man seems to be a politician who has arrived from Washington, railing against the corruption of Andrew Jackson in inflated, artificial, and overdramatic rhetoric, always a sign in Ford of the false organization of public space, thus the failure of real politics, that is, a real engagement with the human ground or origin insofar as the question of the sharing of the world constitutes one of its fundamental aspects.

Addressing the people, urging them to send him again to Washington, the speaker calls upon someone whom we still do not see, who is thus offscreen, as a witness to the incorruptible Whig Party. As he turns to the side, lifting his hand toward the off, we experience a cut and see a figure who appears as if from the off and through the cut. Voilà Lincoln! Who arrives as one in whom a new possibility of the sharing of the world is inscribed.

Appearing from the off-screen, from the dimension of withdrawal and memory, thus of an emptying of the actual world of perception, Lincoln will be the one who carries with him, and is carried by, a dimension of absence and loss through which he will become the recipient and transmitter of a new calling (and he is called to appear on-screen by the first speaker). The dimension of withdrawal, or loss, cinematically inscribed as what is off-screen, will thus become for Lincoln a new principle of calling. The calling will not be the calling to erase, to heal from, this absence or loss, to have it be a source of redemption, as would traditionally be the case, but rather to see in this loss—a loss marking America as the realm of the displaced—the essence of the call itself, which one needs to transmit. Something new is heard from the direction of the off, the dimension of memory, mourning, and withdrawal, which will be not only a calling but a new way of understanding what is at stake in being called.

To be called, most fundamentally, is to come to be inscribed by the origin of the world (however that is understood, which is precisely our question), to open up to the significance of such inscription and, as a consequence, to become the one who serves as mediator between that origin, say, the classical gods or the Christian divine, and all those who occupy the actual world and who are to receive the world, the message of the world, in the most originary way through the one who has been called. The one who is called thus comes to serve as what we can call the messenger of, and to, the world. Yet the origin to which Lincoln is a witness (from which he will receive the call), which is also the origin around which the medium of film circulates—as a medium constituted on the relations between on-screen actualities and a haunting of something that is withdrawn and can never appear—is not some inaccessible, say, transcendent, plenitude to which he, like the classical mythic and religious hero (even Christ), will have exceptional access, a plenitude whose word (which can be experienced as pain by the one who receives it, as with the biblical prophets) she or he will bring to the inhabitants of a realm who are called to organize around the mythical figure who gives them access to the origin. Rather, the origin is now itself, to begin with, a constitutive, absolute loss (in the sense of being something that can never be actual but by which we are nevertheless inscribed and that makes itself present in our lives)—a constitutive loss that all those who have suffered a concrete fundamental loss (of love and home, thus of that which grounded them in the world, serving as what we can call the medium through which they had a world), thus all Americans (or the American people as a whole) as Ford sees them have been exposed to. We can say that America, for Ford, is perhaps the first place whose mode of togetherness is understood not as grounded in a primary togetherness of some kind—of religion, or ethnic identity, common history, etc.—but as "grounded" in common displacement and constitutive loss, as a land of immigrants.[15] This dimension of absolute loss can exist only as memory, yet not as a discrete memory of any actual this or that but memory understood as the inscription, the coming into a certain presence, of an absence that was never anything actual, and in this sense it is, strictly speaking, a memory of no-thing. A memory before any (actual) memory.

Before and beyond every specific memory of loss (most fundamentally of love and home) there is absolute memory (memory as primordial "loss"), understood as the trace of a constitutive nothing. To remember any actual loss is to remember it through, via, the originary, primordial memory of nothing. Lincoln, as the one who is called, will be he who, through coming to be inscribed by memory and loss and opening up to the significance of such inscription, becomes a new kind of messenger, like a modern Moses, to a new type of world, one "grounded" in absolute loss (in the sense of something we never had, could never possess, since it is nothing). In such capacity can Lincoln be described as the memory of America, that is, as the one carrying (for America) the trace of an absolute loss, as well as learning to accept this memory as a calling, around which a new community is called to gather and to establish a new way of organizing human life. The memory of America can also be understood in the sense of it being the kind of memory of which America, as a new kind of habitation, is a guardian.

But what, then, is this nothing, the memory of which Lincoln will become an exceptional witness to and carrier of? We can perhaps learn about it in a fundamental way by looking at the question of the cinematic medium. For the screen's very structure and the basic tenets of the cinematic medium are in fact organized around this dimension of absolute loss, and for this reason the filmic "hero" or paradigmatic ("mythical") figure, in our case Lincoln, the one who can be described as the messenger of the medium of film, will be the one in whom is inscribed a new logic of origination, an origination out of, or from, nothing. It is because of this that Lincoln and cinema have been seen as belonging to each other basically from the very beginning, and up to our own day, thus from what is often considered the first feature-length film, Griffith's *Birth of a Nation*, to Spielberg. Lincoln stands at the intersection of the relations between the question of America's coming-to-be and the significance of the cinematic medium for such an enterprise. It is as if Lincoln had to wait for the birth of the cinematic medium before his full import could finally come into view and America could connect in a deeper way to the promise of which he was the herald.

The Off-Screen

We have started to see that the screen itself is constituted on the relations between what is on-screen, actual and visible, and a dimension of an off-screen, which in many ways is a withdrawal that can become present only through leaving shadowy traces on-screen. Of course, in a literal sense, we can say that what is off-screen can always be made present, if we just turn the camera toward it and bring it on-screen. However, no matter what we do with the camera and however much more we bring into view, we will never eliminate the dimension of the off: Whatever we see, we will always be driven by the question, "What is beyond what we currently see on-screen and which is unavailable to us?" The reason for such a constitutive question is that the photographic medium that film is, a medium passive to a reality that preexists it, always shows us only a slice or a fragment of the world. Thus, there is always more to see that we feel is left outside of what is currently accessible to us. However, there are always two aspects of this more:[16] One is the dimension of more actuality, which we can indeed get by simply turning the camera; and the other, a more mysterious one, the dimension of more-than-actuality. This dimension of the more-than is empty of actuality, and is in fact nothing, in a way, but the potentiality to show, or a potentiality through which, by means of which, things can be given us to see. Each on-screen cinematic image thus points simultaneously to more actuality existing off-screen but also, and in a way more essentially, points to something that is more-than-actuality and that haunts the on-screen, something that is nothing but the potentiality to show and see, or in other words the medium of showing and seeing, medium being that which is always more-than this or that content it can make available. It is the medium of film, as potentiality to show, that haunts every actual image, a medium brought to a mysterious kind of presence through the dimension of the off-screen, to which we are inevitably drawn due to the camera's passive nature that forces us to ask for more, for something beyond the screen. We can use the language of haunting here to the degree that the more-than-actuality is only present as nothing (actual), thus as that which can have no precise place or time but only accompanies every actual (on-screen) place or time as a restless, shadowy disturbance.

The medium of film, the specific way in which filmic content is created, is then what is constituted on the relations between the showing of an actual slice of the world and the potential "more-than" that unfailingly haunts every such actuality and drives film forward to show more. Every actual image we see, accompanied as all such images are by the disturbing presence of nothing, is thus also a place of the memory of this nothing, since, we said, this nothing in a way can exist only as memory—that is, as a trace of loss (of actuality[17])—since it has no actual presence. A ghost can only be remembered,[18] as Hamlet *père*'s "Remember me" reminds us, coming as he does from the dimension of the "off" himself, this time the off-stage.[19] In a way, every viewing of an actual cinematic image carries with it a memory of the nothing at the ground, or origin, of film (a ground and origin we can thus understand as the filmic medium itself, thus not any actual thing), and thus it is also, we can say, a memory of the medium. The origin of film (in both senses of the "of"), then, is the nothing that is the medium (the potentiality to see and show), and in this sense to be called by the origin is, in the case of Lincoln (who is a witness to film), to be inscribed by or with the memory of that which never was (actual) and to become the one around whose message, the message of the nothing/medium, a new community is called to gather.

The memory of that which never was, the more-than-actuality, which film as a medium is haunted by in a particularly powerful way (due to its photographic, thus passive nature), and which the paradigmatic figures of cinema—figures inscribing the origin/medium—such as Lincoln stand as witnesses to, is also that which is at the ground of an essential aspect of film that became clear at least as far back as the development of Griffithian montage. For what this montage demonstrated is that the progression of images, driven as they are by the cuts between them—cuts that are nothing but the intrusion of the medium itself as nothing, that is, as more-than-actuality that is nothing but the potentiality to show, to give us more to see—is not guided by any pre-given or transcendent order of things but is rather a potential openness without any given end and with no pre-given reason directing it. What we will see next, what our vision is about to open us to, is never given in advance: hence the fundamental excitement of film, inextricably connected to its being a medium of foundational loss. For the "ex" in excitement, the "ex" denoting an outside (as in exit, exteriority, etc.), refers to this outside-any-actuality, the dimension of the more-than, which haunts the screen as the shadow of the "off." The screen is a place of fundamental excitement to the extent that what appears on it emerges in relation to the "ex" inscribed on it, the more-than, the medium haunting it, and doing so not only as a ghostly memory but as an unpredictable openness, a non-givenness in advance at the heart of a world characterized by adventure, the exploration of the unknown. Ford is undoubtedly one of the more profound directors who has known how to connect, in a fundamental way, cinema as a medium of mourning, of the memory of absolute loss (i.e., loss as the inscription of a dimension that was never actual) with which every actual loss communicates, and cinema as the unparalleled medium of excitement, the adventurous exploration of the unknown.

Going back to our opening scene: Coming out of a cut, and from the dimension of the off, it is as if young Mr. Lincoln (who we later learn has lost his mother, a burden he always carries with him)—who is the first person in the film summoned onto the screen, and as such it is as if he immediately becomes the focus of what coming on-screen, from the dimension of the "off," most fundamentally means—carries with him, and is carried by, this unique memory, the memory of the medium. Such memory implies both a painful loss (of actuality, as well as of traditional ways of grounding actuality in some kind of transcendent order) and a new kind of openness, the origination of the world in a haunting more-than-actuality without any pre-given order or direction. America, I argue, whose messenger of the origin is here shown to be Lincoln, will be a world that needs to establish itself in relation to a painful cut—inscribed as a haunting and collective memory of an irretrievable loss seemingly shared by all its inhabitants, irrespective of the actual losses they have suffered—and in relation to an unprecedented, and exciting, openness (expressed in the oft-repeated injunction in Ford's films, "Go West, young man") that is the other side of this painful cut.

Thus, as he comes on-screen, the question highlighted is that of Lincoln as the one who addresses the as-yet-undetermined-in-its-mode-of-togetherness public, a public that can emerge only in relation to the message of a new origin.[20] Filmed as coming out of the shadows into visibility, yet still remaining partially shadowed—thus as if being shadowed, carrying the trace, the memory, of the nothing/medium of which he is the messenger, is the essence of his occupying the open realm of the screen—Lincoln starts to speak. Only one person from the public is shown sharing the screen with him, and even this person occupies the edge of the screen, partially outside it, the rest of the screen remaining quite open. This emphasizes that the public Lincoln addresses is in the futural mode of the "to come," and to come from the "off," where we the audience also are. For the public to come (and after a cut we see Lincoln in close-up alone on-screen, emphasizing that the public is not the actual one there with him) is composed of all those, us included (whose relation to the screen indicates the condition of our exposure to loss), who are inscribed by the "off," thus by the dimension of a fundamental loss of a determined place—of home and love—from which they have been cut, exposed to an open potentiality they simultaneously experience in common mourning and shared excitement. The words of Lincoln, his address as a new kind of message coming from the direction of the medium of film, is what will allow the public to be transformed in such a way that their common loss (as well as excitement) will come to signify the possibility of a new mode of togetherness and a new kind of home, a new way of inhabiting the world, of organizing around the experience of its origination.

Yet, at this initial stage, as he comes to occupy the screen out of the shadowy "off," out of the cut, Lincoln—though carrying the cut in such a way that he already sees such a burden as implying an obligation to address the public, thus to carry to a world to come the revelatory message of its origin—has not yet fully opened up to what comes from the cut, to what is implied in it. Thus, as he finishes his speech, a call from off-screen is heard: "Hey Abe, somebody wants to do business with you." This call will mark the first essential step in his initiation—an initiation that is the preoccupation of the entire movie (and indeed of Ford's entire oeuvre, for there is something in this initiation that will never be fulfilled, a failure that will lie at the heart of America's nonfulfillment)—into the question of what it is that comes from the off (an "off" of which he is at the moment only a beginning messenger, still mostly an unwitting recipient).

What precisely, then, comes from the off here? Not business, as the one who called Lincoln seemed to think—as if operating under the assumption that the most basic concept guiding the togetherness of people, their being called to interact with one another in their (American, i.e., fully modern) condition of being exposed to the off, thus to an open potentiality that prevents determining in advance the terms of their interaction, is bargaining about the value of that interaction—but a gift of a book whose "message" we forgot how to read and probably never fully knew how to. Who gifts this book? A paradigmatic (i.e., inscribed by the exposure to the origin) American family, having lost its home and on its way to hopefully find a new one, a finding that will be possible only if a new public, a new mode of togetherness, is created for those occupying the condition of being exposed to the open potentiality of the "off."

The gifting family of the opening scene—the one riding in the coach, coming from the off onto the screen—is a family on its way, on the road. For to be on its way to . . . having been severed by the cut of the screen from any recognizable past orientation, either temporally or spatially, as well as having no determined-in-advance future one, is the mournful and exciting condition of those who occupy the screen, or who live as exposed to the new origin activated by the screen—simply put, the condition of being in America. Basically, all of Ford's films open with those who are on their way to . . . : those who have lost their place and, in mourning and excitement, are in search of a new destination.

The cut-off family in our scene—which is even cut off from itself, as emphasized by the editing cut separating the mother who rides in the coach from the father walking alongside it (a father whose death we learn of later, but it is already announced by this cut)—is the carrier of a new kind of call (whose interpretation as a call to a business transaction is an error), the recipient of which will be Lincoln. It will be Lincoln's task to become the messenger of this call, to interpret its full significance and transmit it to a public that is to gather around it—a public that in the movie most importantly will be created (or at least undergoes the beginning of its true creation as a public of a new origin) through the court of Law as Lincoln will come to activate it. For it is the trial of one of this family's members, a few years later, unjustly accused and whom Lincoln will defend, that will occupy the center of the film, as if it were a call for a new kind of justice (namely, a just response to a call coming from the origin) that this family-cut-from-its-past, its home, and its paternal figure (as a traditional way of inscribing the origin, and speaking in the name of its authority) emits and that Lincoln already here vaguely hears.

Thus, as it has become clear that the dispossessed family has nothing to offer (which also means that what it does offer is the nothing, an absolute loss as memory of that which never was) in terms of business bargaining, it is mentioned that they have certain things that might have a different value: books. Startled by the mention of books, which is immediately followed by a cut (the introduction of nothing), leaving him alone on-screen, Lincoln—as if the mention of books echoes something deep within him, a silent call he almost did not know was inscribed in him—looks toward the off-screen, uttering, in yearning and marvel, "Books?" It is the books, as it were—books the family can no longer read, having received them as an inheritance from a past (since they belonged to the grandfather, who perhaps still knew how to read)—that come to him as a gift from the off, indeed, the gift of the off. Most importantly it is one book, *the* book, a Book of Law, which is the one he receives and aims to learn how to read, as if to read anew for the new world. The Law, then, is the gift received from the off as a calling, via the dispossessed (American) family on its way to....[21]

The first scene ends with this reception of the gift of Law—the first main aspect implied in the calling from, and of, the off, which Lincoln here starts to open up to. A second scene in that primary initiation to the call of the off, to which we now turn, will be needed, in order both to expound upon what the Law implied in the call is and to open up to the other essential aspects of the call: love and a mysterious speaking memory. All these aspects, law, love, speaking memory, as gifts of nothing implied in the call coming from the off, will also have to be brought into closer contact with the question of the medium of the screen.

The American Landscape

We next see Lincoln, having received the Book of Law, in a new setting. We are in the midst of woods and a river, an open landscape whose sole occupant is Lincoln. Lying down or sitting (hard to decide what to call his posture), his legs elevated, supported by a tree, his head on the ground, Lincoln is reading the book. His legs being up, it is as if he is grounded in the openness of the river, which serves as the background to his legs, rather than being grounded in the static and stable ground, thinkingly translating the river's message, bringing it to the earth. The screen is divided into two: the shady part, mostly grass, where Lincoln is; and in front, in the sunlight, the river that extends to a mostly open horizon. Our eyes seem to waver between being drawn by the open book he is reading, the most illuminated object in the shady part, and by the illuminated open horizon, a distance that would seem to lead to an indeterminate infinity, as we follow the river. Also present is a sole trace of an organized human world: a fragment of a fence, now mostly destroyed, toward the bank of the river, as if to emphasize that, in being drawn toward the infinity of the horizon, we are exceeding a border. What is the relation between the Book of Law and this border-exceeding movement to infinity that has drawn our gaze? This seems to be a fundamental question posed by this scene's composition.

The key to answering this question seemingly lies in understanding the role here of the landscape, obviously a major preoccupation for Ford, perhaps the paradigmatic landscapist of American cinema. What is a landscape? Most fundamentally, we can say, the landscape is a new kind of open realm—emerging most fully within the context of the West with Renaissance art—that is cut off from a determined horizon, from a set of coordinates within the context of which everything that appears has a recognizable and determined place. The landscape thus first of all takes the form of a question: "Where are we?" "Who are we?" For once the recognizable coordinates are cut, we are unmoored.

If the task of a border (a figure of law) is to demarcate the proper place and measure of things—say, the original fence in the scene, whose function was to separate land from river, clearly demarcating what belongs to each and where each belongs—then the opening of the landscape as such signifies the breaking, or overflowing, or exceeding, of the border, the putting into question of the determination of everything that appears. Everything can now be viewed as being suspended between the ruin of an organized world where things all had their place and belonging, and the call for the birth of a new world where things might find their place, if possibly according to a new way of demarcating where they belong. In this sense each thing now appearing, say, the river, is inscribed both with the sign of a world's ruin and with a call to bring about a new world, the call to originate a new existence. The river thus carries the question of the world with it: Where is the river going? What is its place?

Once the border (here represented by the fragment of the fence) is broken, then we are no longer in an organized world but in a landscape, exposed to the question of the world, suspended between the old world's ruin and a possible new formation to come. In this sense, we can say, each landscape is, in a way, a desert, both in the sense of an abandoned realm deserted by the organized and ordered world and in the biblical sense of a site of inscription of the call for a world to come (a call perhaps most powerfully inscribed in our scene in the river), thus of a possible new world's origination. In a way the desert (hence the significance of the paradigmatic Fordian space, the desert of Monument Valley) is what exposes the very essence of the question of the landscape as a deserted realm between ruin and birth, abandoned by the old Law of the world (in the sense of that which gives proper place and measure to things) but where a call, a voice crying in the desert, is heard (and a new Law received).[22]

But there is of course another dimension of the landscape beyond its desert aspect. Each landscape, while serving as a desert in which an originary call is inscribed, is also always accompanied by displaying a possibility of paradise, of the pastoral return to the garden, paradise being understood as the space where a life emerges that has achieved a full coincidence with the call of its origin, with the new Law, and thus has managed to respond to the call in a fully appropriate way, and as a consequence to fully come home, home being the coming to coincide with one's calling, thus with what is most proper to one, finally being oneself. Such a space has not been reached in Ford's American films, which never fully manage to leave the desert (thus never managed to overcome the moment of the Western), clearly signifying that the transition from the desert to paradise, from the calling to one's coinciding with it, has not yet been complete. It is only in his film about the return of an

American to Ireland (itself a place that belongs and does not exactly belong to Europe), as if achieving some synthesis of America and Europe in excess of either, *The Quiet Man*, in which a certain view of paradise is given.²³ Such a view of paradise is clearly not a real solution for Ford—seeing as the film's genre is the fairy tale, and the Irish world depicted is a pastoral fairyland out of time in the manner of *Brigadoon*—yet it is something that should serve as a certain guide for the place to seek.²⁴

The moment of the landscape, then, the moment when the fence/border is broken, is the moment of being cut from a determining organization of the world. Such a cut is shown here to coincide with the very being of the screen as a cut-off space, unmoored from any determined order. In this sense we can say that every cinematic image, being an image achieved by cutting the world out of its determined and determining context, exposing it to the open potentiality of the off, is in essence a landscape, and every landscape, now understood in relation to the very being of the screen, is inscribed by the call characterizing the medium of the screen, the call we have associated with the dimension of the off, the dimension of the more-than. If the desert is a realm cut off from an existing ordering of the world and serving as the site of a call for a new world, and if this call is now understood as the call of the off, of the more-than, then the Fordian project—the bringing about, by means of the screen, of a way of life called "America"—is both that which exposes us to a new, screen, desert as well as that which points to a new paradise, the coming to coincide with the call of the screen.

Needless to say, the paradisiacal life has not yet been achieved in America, though it is America, the call heard in and as America—as that which has been cut off from Western, European ordering, as well as from the traditional ordering of the indigenous people, a cutting off finding its most appropriate expression in the very medium of film—that newly opens in human history a place of habitation suspended between the desert and the image of a paradise.²⁵

It is in our opening scene's river, we said, where, from the point of view of the components of the landscape, the call at the origin of the new world is inscribed most powerfully, and it is inscribed in the way the river extends to the off-screen, its cutting off from actuality infusing it with the dimension of the call of the more-than, a dimension we can also call infinity (in the sense of its being more than any finite actuality). Our eyes, following the river toward the off, are now infused with this infinity, inscribed by its call. But it is of course not only us who become inscribed, through the landscape, with the call of the origin as the call of a new infinity, but Lincoln, who serves in this scene as what we can call the witness to the landscape, inscribed with its call and tasked with being its messenger: first and foremost under the aspect of the message of Law.

Though, as we saw, the landscape's opening implies the breaking and exceeding of the border, thus the putting into question of the reigning Law of appropriation, this implies not the abandonment of the very idea of borders and limits but, to the contrary, a reconception of what these might mean, serving as a call to their refinding and refounding, hence the significance of Lincoln's reading the Book of Law. It is the Law, a new Law so to speak, a Law to which the very dimension of infinity is henceforth immanent, that is implied in the newly discovered open infinity of the landscape. For if, on the one hand, the landscape, as a deserted realm—meaning deserted vis-à-vis the borders and laws of an existing order, outside them—can be seen as a no-man's-land, a lawless realm, it is, on the other hand, being the place of inscription of an infinity outside the old law, the site of a call that itself implies a new Law, a law of infinity. It is as if the old, historical laws were laws grounded not in the idea of infinity but, we can say, in a logic of metaphysical transcendence. Such transcendence can be conceived of through the prism of eternity, understood as a constant present—to be distinguished from infinity, understood as the unpredictable openness of the more-than—that determines and hence legislates in advance the world's borders and limits, as if there were a determined order of things.

A world with a fully open horizon, though, a world exposed to the infinite dimension of the off, cannot be ordered, cannot be bordered or fenced, transcendentally; yet it is not without a new kind of Law, meaning a new way of marking limitations and appropriations. What is called for is a Law grounded in infinity rather than in transcendence, taking the form of a call emitted through the desert of the screen and its paradigmatic recipient, Lincoln.

As a desert space where a call for a new Law is emitted, or where a new Law is received, the screen is that space through whose passage might lead to a Promised Land, an America to come, a land that, as in the biblical logic, can emerge only when the Law received in the desert by the American Moses, Lincoln, finds a place to be informed and guided by it.

Even before looking at the precise trajectory taken by Lincoln in this scene to interpret the call coming from the off (from the infinity activated by screen and landscape) as a new Law, and before we examine the questions of love and memory implicated with the call, we can look at the very structure of the call of the origin activated by the screen as we have defined it and see how its very structure implies the question of the Law in a new way. For the medium of film—defined as the photographic projection on a screen that gives us a fragment of reality forcing us to look for more than what we see due to the camera's passivity—immediately implies the experience of a limitation (forced upon us by the desire to see the more-than activated in us), a fencing off, which can even be seen as an interdiction: You cannot see the whole; indeed, you are "forbidden" from seeing it. This is not because the screen is physically limited—this limitation can easily be overcome by turning the camera in the direction of what lies beyond our current purview—but because the physical, actual limits of the screen point to (in fact are the means for the mysterious experience of our being exposed to) a more fundamental limitation and cut, that between actuality and potentiality, the dimension of the more-than.

The inability to see the whole, the limitation of our power by the logic of the off, implies not that there is a whole we are forbidden from, or even are just incapable of, seeing, thus of appropriating as a visual experience—a whole available to some transcendent agency that can have in its purview what we, poor limited beings that we are, cannot—but rather that there is no whole (understood as total actuality). Rather, there is a potential openness without predetermination,[26] an openness that is the source of, the medium of, our seeing (we see with the means of a potentiality) yet is itself nothing, and therefore it can never become the object of our seeing. What we are "forbidden" from seeing is the medium, that which lies at the source of our seeing but can never turn into an object of experience for our appropriation: This is the source of Law. The Law is the Law of the excess of the medium over any actuality, an excess that the unique nature of the limitation of the screen forces us to be exposed to, and it indicates that there is an absolute border, a "fence," between the on-screen and the off, which can never be crossed (the screen in this sense is a no trespassing zone, as the opening of *Citizen Kane* famously indicates). Actuality is always haunted by the dimension of the more-than, preventing it from being totalized and appropriated by any transcendent agent.

80 Chapter Two

The breaking of the fence in our scene, to be jointly thought with our opening to the infinity of the landscape, eliminates a wrong understanding of borders (which has characterized the various historical ways of organizing human life) either as originating in the separation of distinct actualities, each having its determined place in a cosmic ordering of existence, say, the land and the river here, or as grounded in a metaphysical transcendence thought along the lines of an eternity, yet an eternity that is itself conceived on the basis of actuality, one that never ends (from the transcendent point of view everything is as if it were given in advance), a never-ending actuality that is unavailable, thus forbidden, to us mortals, who would seemingly need to be subjected to the Law of our limitation (thus wrongly understood as eternity's inaccessibility) in the manner of God's scolding of Job: "Where were you when I laid the foundation of the earth?"

The infinity of the landscape, or the infinity that the opening of the world as landscape is the inscription of, exceeds, and in this sense breaks any conception of the border as actual, be this actuality finite or eternal. At the same time, the landscape's infinity implies the emergence of an absolute border/fence, a new Law, the one between finitude and infinity, an absolute border now marked for us by the limits of the screen, correctly understood. The question would now be—the question that modernity (and America as a certain privileged witness to the abyss opening in modernity) has not ceased struggling with—how to bring about a world grounded in the new Law of infinity (rather than any determined order of things, or an unknown decree issued from the point of view of eternity[27]), a Law transmitted in the age of film (the age when technological modernity has brought about a new image, an image proper to it—image to be understood as the inscriber of infinity[28]) by the call of the off as the screen, and its messenger Lincoln.

Two Faces of the Law

Let us continue to follow Lincoln's reception of the gift of the call of the screen, starting with his first interpretation of the Law. Having read his book, Lincoln sits and says to himself: "Law. That's the rights of persons and the rights of things. The rights of life, reputation, and liberty. The rights to acquire and hold property. Wrongs are violations of those rights. By Jing, that's all there is to it. Right and Wrong. Maybe I ought to begin to take this up serious." At the moment he says this, the moment he thinks he has grasped all there is to the Law, a surprising call comes from the off-screen, interrupting Lincoln's thinking: "Hello, Mr. Lincoln." Following a cut, Ann Rutledge, Lincoln's beloved, appears, and when he sees her, he closes the book and stands up. A power stronger than the Law, a power before which the Book of Law closes, the power of the gift of Love and Beauty, now strikes in the call of the off (gift being that which is received unexpectedly, as an interruptive surprise, thus from the off, as the gifted book was received earlier). Lincoln stands up, they start to talk, and then, following a cut, they begin walking, moving along the river, as does the camera. "River's sure pretty today," Lincoln comments as they begin moving, as if highlighting that their movement, as well as the camera's, is attached to the flowing of the river—reaching as it does toward the open of the off, we saw, flowing beyond the limits of the screen, toward infinity—and that the river's prettiness, or beauty (a quality Lincoln is emphasized as being susceptible to, also as a reader of poetry and Shakespeare, in addition to the Book of Law, which Ann soon comments about), is the inscription of the off/infinity of the medium in it. Beauty is the surprising reception of the open in movement. Such a movement, we can say, is a movement belonging to the screen as a realm exposed to the off. Real movement is not a transition between one actual place and another but the adventurous and exciting passage through the undetermined, the passage through the off/medium. Love, in this sense, is the surprising reception of the call—that is, reception of the gift coming from the off—shining as beauty and inscribed as one's being moved, meaning moved beyond oneself, moved in a sort of self-transcendence by having received the dimension of the more-than, of infinity, which now becomes the medium of one's passage. Beyond the Law, then (at least as initially conceived), a power greater than the Law, is the reception of infinity in/as self-transcending movement expressed as Love. The object of love, Ann in this case, is the one who serves as the messenger of infinity, the one in whom the call of the off/origin is inscribed.

Yet if the reception of infinity in movement through becoming attached to infinity's messenger—embarking on a passage by means of the medium—is a power greater than the Law (we will soon inquire into why that is in greater detail), this does not mean that it is separate from the Law nor that its arrival means the cancellation of the Law, its overcoming. To the contrary, it is the understanding of their inextricable relation that Lincoln still needs to open up to (and that will lead him to an understanding of an even higher Law) as he progresses along the road of his initiation to being a witness to the call of the off, first expressed in the reception of the Book of Law, then in the reception of the poetic gift of love and beauty, and finally as haunting memory, the gift of a time that never was (actual).[29]

Thus, after he comments on Ann's beauty in an implicit declaration of love, Ann exits the screen toward the off, never to return. Lincoln is left alone; a cut, he looks backward, gazing toward the off—it is as if his eyes are becoming infused with the power of the off (which we saw is the medium as nothing) as agent of the gift but also of annihilation—and he turns away from the disappearing Ann and walks toward the moving river. He throws a stone onto its surface, looking at the ripples; then he himself disappears from the screen, and after another cut all we see is the river that, time having passed in the invisible cut, has now frozen over and is mostly covered in ice. The cut is shown here to be the pure power of time, the becoming-present of the off as the empty opening of a passage (a time tunnel through which one passes/moves in such a way as to be inscribed with its nothingness), in excess of, more-than, any actual specific thing happening or passing/moving in time.

If earlier the experience of time (the nothing that is the medium as unpredictable openness) had been mediated by the flow of the river, time's messenger qua a specific actuality passing in time's tunnel, now, with the introduction of the cut between the two states of the river, summer-water and winter-ice, it is as if we experience the power of time as the medium of passage—the medium of being on one's way or on the road—more directly. We do so because the transition from water to ice is made to happen unpredictably, thus in a way miraculously (rather than causally or through the gradual progression of so-called natural order of the seasons), by means of the passage through the cut/nothing/time tunnel, and thus it is as if we detach ourselves from the actuality of the river and experience the medium enabling this unexpected transformation.[30]

It is now that Lincoln reappears. It is as if he has passed through the nothing, undergoing something we might understand as a metamorphosis (the final step in his personal initiation—for the rest of the movie will have the nature of a communal initiation), having suffered a direct inscription by the pure power of time rather than having experienced time indirectly, through the transporting movement of love (mediated by the flowing river and Ann) by which he was earlier carried.[31] This metamorphosis, the result of his passage through pure time, is also linked to Ann, yet no longer as only the object of love but now as the object of love having been lost in death, as we soon realize when we see Lincoln standing alongside a grave, Ann's grave.

Having been the mediating messenger of the off as moving, poetic love, Ann has now been inscribed with the off's pure power of annihilation. This annihilating power had of course already been operating, unseen, in the gift of love, since that gift was the gift of nothing, of the off/medium as such, thus of the world as unpredictable open realm, received in a movement of self-transcendence, an opening beyond oneself. Jacques Lacan famously described love as the giving of what one does not have, and this gift, we can now see, is the gift of the nothing understood as the medium opening the world, the giving of pure time. One does not have the medium/time, since one cannot have it, cannot possess it, since it is nothing, a pure openness of potentiality/the more-than/infinity without any specific end. In love, then, one gives what cannot be had, what is beyond the order of possessions, the medium/infinity/pure time. Because the medium is a nothing that can never be possessed, it can only be something that is either given, transmitted by a messenger—who is merely a messenger, not the proprietor of the message—or received as a gift, that is, that which is outside the circulation of possessions. A gift, as gift, can never be possessed, only received, in surprise, or given, unwillingly. The gift of love is thus higher than the Law (at least in its initial understanding by Lincoln), for the Law is that which forbids our possession of infinity, since being infinity, or nothing, it cannot be possessed. Yet, though forbidden from being possessed, infinity or the nothing can still be received, as well as given, through the movement of love, to begin with, and thus we can have access to it, yet not as property but as the gift of the medium opening us to the world. In other words, while we cannot have infinity, which is what the Law forbids, we can nevertheless be in the mode of openness to the world through infinity's reception as a gift, which is what love allows (having and being constituting our two fundamental positions).

When attached to an actual messenger, through the attachment to which one is moved, embarking on a passage through the medium, the gift is in the realm of love, or in the relation to a love "object," to speak as Freud does, but when the actual object/messenger of infinity as giver of love (a love calling for a self-transcending movement) is lost, one is exposed to the gift through mourning, which is the opening to a memory of the pure power of time, thus a memory of that which never was, even beyond any specific messenger.

Yet there is an intermediary stage that lies between the memory of pure time and the gift of love transmitted by an actual messenger, the stage of the ghost and, more precisely, of the speech of the ghost, the moment when the actual love object has been inscribed, in annihilation, by pure time and acquires the strange quality of time not to belong anywhere, since it is nothing actual but only the opening to any and every actuality. The nothing already inscribed in the actual love object now comes to the fore more powerfully, yet at the same time still remains attached to something that is neither actual nor pure nothing. The screen, as Ford understands it, circulates most profoundly around this ghostly moment between lost love and nothing, a ghostly moment characterizing everyone who comes on-screen as, in some way, a speaking memory hovering between lost actuality and the medium's pure inscription.[32]

Having suffered a metamorphosis, the inscription by the pure power of time that one nevertheless survives in some manner, Lincoln, as he approaches Ann's grave (the icy river moving to the off behind him, crossing a broken fence, a sign of the exposure to infinity, and bringing with him pretty flowers, in his words, the gift of beauty), opens a conversation with her inaudible, ghostly speech. Speech in general, we can say, is that which the medium enables as pure, unpredictable openness. The medium, as pure potentiality, which we can also understand as the pure potentiality to say and to see, more-than any specific actuality, in this sense becomes the possibility of opening to (the possibility of saying, of seeing, etc.) any actuality, and unpredictably so. The ghost, as inscription of the medium at the moment of the loss of actuality, is in this sense a speech, a voice, "Remember me" (i.e., remember the medium before any actuality—and that which is beyond actuality can only be remembered—remember speech before any specific saying, remember vision before any specific view). This ghostly speech is situated at the closest proximity to the pure medium, before its attachment to any actual speaker; yet it still functions as the echo to an actual source of speech that has been lost. Both actual speech and what we can call pure speech, the very activation of the empty medium as such, are thus equally present in ghostly echo speech, the gift of which Lincoln receives at the grave, the gift of speaking memory.

And how does Lincoln, like a Saul going to the witch of Endor, approach this ghostly speech? With a meta-life question, thus not any specific question about life, but a question about the very medium that is to guide one's life in general. Should I study the Law, Lincoln asks Ann's ghostly speech, addressing himself to the off-screen, or stay where I am? "Study the Law," responds the ghost/off, as messenger of an infinity-even-beyond-love, the infinity of pure memory, and this is its ultimate saying. This means that the Law now received is to be the Law prescribed by infinity/the medium as the very relation to infinity that one should follow. This Law is infinity's Law, a Law beyond the earlier formulation of the Law Lincoln gave us, as the distinguishing of right from wrong regarding life, freedom, and property.

Infinity's Law, obligation (to receive infinity) as well as forbidding and limitation (from possessing it), derived from the very fact of our exposure to infinity/the medium, is the ground for the earlier Law. For what does Infinity's Law say? You must receive the gift of infinity (or you must open yourself to the gift in receptivity), because infinity or the medium can only be received (being a nothing one can neither possess nor will) and is thus that which in fact one is forbidden from possessing. The medium can only be received as a gift, expressed most profoundly as the memory of what never was, and it must be received since one can neither want nor not want it, for it lies at the source of our capacity to want, meaning always wanting this or that. The nothing cannot be wanted (though it can be expressed in or as pure, empty desire) since it is nothing, but it is that which we receive as the origin of wanting. The gift of the infinite is thus both our obligation—we cannot will or decide not to receive it—and the originary source of our limitation, for the same reason, that is, it limits what we can will, marking a point of our fundamental passivity/receptivity. We can call this Law the Law of our finitude. Our finitude is not the simple fact of life coming to an end in death. It is the irreducible limitation of our will and power, the fact that we are inscribed by an infinity/the medium/pure time, an infinity that is our very essence, that we are obligated to receive, passively, and are forbidden from possessing.[33] This is the gift of Law that Lincoln receives at the grave as the site of ghostly speech and memory. This Law of infinity is a Law more powerful even than love (earlier love had been more powerful than the book of

Law), for love, we saw, was the reception of the gift as movement-beyond-oneself through a specific love object, while the Law received at the grave is that of a memorial speech already connected to pure time, beyond any specific love object.

From this moment of the grave—where Lincoln receives, alone in the open landscape (not a biblical mountain, proximate to a transcendence, which is perhaps the difference of democracy), the Law of finitude and infinity as memory of that which never was—to the film's conclusion, when following the proceedings of a trial, Lincoln brings justice to a community, namely, he enables the community to gather around the reception of the Law whose messenger he is, it will be necessary to follow a whole trajectory of initiation. This tale of initiation is the story of the paradigmatic/"mythical," exceptional figure (the one inscribed by the origin—through being exposed to the infinity of the landscape, to the call of love from the off, and to the call of ghostly memory speech through love's loss) as he is integrated into the life of a community into which he is to bring the Law, a community tempted, as we see in the film, be it in a Platonic or biblical manner, by false idols and violent mass gatherings.

We will not get into the precise details of Lincoln's communal initiation in the film, that is, into the question of how the life in common, the life of an America to come, is to be informed, or formed, by the unique Law that he brings, by means of the cinematic medium, from the dimension of the off. I will just say that though *Young Mr. Lincoln* traces an initial way of delivering Lincoln's message to a community taking its first steps in organizing itself around this message, it is no accident that Ford chose this youthful moment of the delivery of Lincoln's message. The film ends with an enigmatic moment showing the solitary Lincoln, walking in a deserted rainy landscape, leaving the screen toward the off, as if pointing to the mythic or perhaps messianic future (i.e., a future informed by a relation to the origin of which Lincoln is the messenger) when Lincoln's full message to the community will be delivered. Yet this successful delivery is to be understood as that which happened in the latter part of Lincoln's life but, clearly for Ford, is yet to happen. Lincoln's, and thus Ford's, full message has not yet been delivered, Lincoln/cinema is still in his/its young moment, and a community, America, which is to gather around his message, to be mediated by it, has not yet been achieved. The moment of Fordian cinema is the moment of

The Memory of America 87

the *young* Lincoln, the moment between the reception of the call—as Book of Law, as open landscape/desert, as gift of love and its loss, as ghostly echo speech, as memory and suspended watching—and the coming down from the mountain/modern landscape to deliver this message to a community not yet informed/mediated by the Law of infinity and finitude, and thus in this sense a community still in its idolatrous stage (i.e., the stage of injustice toward the medium, not receiving it in the way it demands). This makes the moment of Fordian cinema most essentially the moment of the desert, thus of the Western, the moment between the call that can be heard only in the desert—that is, in a landscape open to infinity, a landscape that is a realm in excess of, and deserted by, any of the known historical laws of culture—and what it is on its way to, a community informed by this desert call, a community not yet historically achieved. It is also because of this that Ford's second key film of 1939, *Stagecoach*, is the first great Western, the first appearance of the man of the desert, John Wayne, a Western that ends with Wayne (who, exceptionally, *did* find love) rejecting civilization, the community of the city, which he views as false, and leaving with his beloved to return to the desert, being thus unable to leave the genre of the Western.

It is clear that Ford himself (as well as America)—and hence the split mentioned previously between the man of the Law and the man of the desert characterizing his films and their paradigmatic figures—is caught in this desert moment, casting one eye toward the call's demand to bring the Law uttered in the desert/landscape to a community that is still to come, with the other eye seeing in the desert moment (and the open screen, the desert's embodiment) the only authentic place one can occupy in the context of a reality where the Law to come (or the coincidence of the community to come with a Law that calls it) has not yet arrived, a place of excessive life to be saved from, in the final words of stagecoach, the "blessing" of civilization, a community formed not according to the Law of infinity and finitude but according to the false and empty (in the sense of ungrounded in the true Law) codes of society.

The problem for Ford, the problem for America, the problem for modernity, and a problem that, I think, remains unresolved, is how the moment of the screen (as a paradigmatic space of modern art in general), the moment of its infinite calling heard at first in its desert modality, in its abandoned landscapes, can become a Law of infinity and finitude mediating a new community. Though Ford, or we, never managed to find the way out of this problem, his last great film, *The Man Who Shot Liberty Valance*, brings its contours into clearest visibility, analyzing in a particularly profound manner the various deadlocks preventing the problem's solution. It is this bringing into visibility of the problem involved in the transition from the desert moment (a space where the call of an excessive life—i.e., a life informed by the more-than—is heard, yet it is as if the Law it implies still remains inaccessible) to the community to come that is America, an America we have not yet figured out how to bring about, which makes *Liberty Valance*, I suggest, to adopt Richard Brody's judgment (which I tend to accept) "the greatest American political movie."[34]

The Return to the Desert

I now turn to *Liberty Valance*, examining how the Fordian discovery of the Law and the call implied in the very being of the cinematic screen, and the community to come that this call is to be at the ground of, confronts a deadlock we have yet to figure out how to resolve. We have not yet learned how to coincide with the call implied in the being of the screen, how to become appropriated to its inaudible Law and thus to turn the desert into a garden, the Western into a pastoral.[35]

The events and plot of the film are as follows. Senator Ranse (James Stewart) and his wife, Hallie (Vera Miles), arrive in the Western town of Shinbone to attend the funeral of an old friend, Tom Doniphon (John Wayne). When asked by a reporter attracted by the august company, Senator Ranse narrates, in a flashback, thus in a memorial speech, the story of his coming into town as a young Eastern city lawyer seeking adventure in the West (thus as one whose restlessness implies that the city's Law, of which he is the embodiment, is lacking, that it does not fully answer to a deeper call, the call of the desert, he somehow feels addressed by). When he is shown arriving, we see his carriage attacked by a desert outlaw, Liberty Valance (Lee Marvin), who robs him of all he has, and thus here the encounter with the desert, the outside of ordered civilized life, signifies the violent emptying of the current world. This violent outlaw is also someone in the service of local landowners at the historic moment when the region is being called upon to vote about whether it will fully join the United States or remain in its current autonomous, territorial, desert being, not part of the common social contract and general Law of the land. Ranse becomes the leading force of the attempt to become part of the United States, while Tom Doniphon—the desert man who is not an outlaw but is not one of those who desire to join the Union, an individual friendly to Ranse yet ambivalent about abandoning the desert— helps Ranse in his legal efforts, even if he is never willing to fully join him. On top of that, the desert man, Tom, is particularly attached to the question of the gun, seeing in it an essential component of the self-sufficient logic of the desert and seeing himself also as a teacher of the desert. Tom insists on helping Ranse learn to shoot so that the latter will be able to defend himself against Liberty Valance, who, being the emissary of the territorial refusal to join the Union, needs to kill Ranse to put a stop to his efforts. Having learned, a bit, to shoot, Ranse finally faces Liberty in a gunfight, in which he, or so at first he thinks, kills Liberty. In addition, the townspeople vote to join the Union, and Ranse is chosen to be the region's representative to Washington, an honor that Tom has refused. Ranse is also reluctant at first, because he believes himself guilty of killing Liberty; yet, at the film's most crucial moment, Tom reveals to him, in an enigmatic flashback, that it was in fact he who killed Liberty, unbeknown to Ranse. Having thus been cleared, Ranse agrees to go to Washington, becoming known there as the heroic, mythic figure who shot Liberty Valance. Ranse leaves for Washington with his beloved, Hallie, who used to be Tom's beloved. At the end of the film, after publicly telling his story for the first time, revealing the falsity of his heroic reputation, Ranse, in agreement with Hallie (who he finally realizes has never stopped loving Tom, her heart unfulfilled by her Washington existence and still belonging to the desert), decides to leave Washington and come back to Shinbone to practice the Law again, thus, like Wayne's character in *Stagecoach*, indicating that the organized social contract as it stands, the life of the city, thus of common human civilization, has failed to fulfill the call of the desert, and thus the desert, and indeed the Western, must be returned to, as if we are to try to hear the call anew, getting it right the next time.

This fact of needing to return to the desert, we can say, marks *The Man Who Shot Liberty Valance*, a Western now understood no longer as belonging to the first age of Westerns (those narrating the moment of the desert before the transition to the United States) but a Western understood as a necessary return, as if indicating the failure of all attempts to get out of the desert to the United States. This late return as acknowledgment of a failure also seems to announce a sort of the birth of the neo-Westerns of the next generation, from Sam Peckinpah's films onward, all of them seemingly symptomatic of the failure to leave the desert, thus the Western, for good, the social contract having been called by the Law discovered in the desert never having really arrived. It is as if the Western, and this is the reason for the ceaseless returns to it as a genre, has not ended, since a successful way out of it, toward the United States, has not yet been achieved.

What needs to be emphasized right away is that one of the main features making *The Man Who Shot Liberty Valance* such a profound late statement by Ford is that it revolves around a single enigmatic event (perhaps the most fundamental cinematic enigma since Rosebud): the shooting of Liberty Valance, the very enigma of which is shown to be tied to the enigma of the screen as such (which is precisely what makes it a *cinematic* enigma), thus the enigma of its call as a medium, insofar as the screen is understood to be shadowily inscribed by that which does not appear on it, the off, the dimension of the more-than.

This is the case, since the film's central event, the shooting of the outlaw Liberty Valance, is shown in a flashback reconstruction (opening with Tom Doniphon asking Ranse, "Remember?") to be not what we thought it was based on, what we saw on-screen, that is, Ranse's shooting of Liberty, but actually to have come from the direction of what is off-screen, which Doniphon, the real shooter, unbeknown to Ranse, and invisible to us, occupies. This off dimension in fact consists of multiple offs, since Doniphon himself receives the gun from his black helper Pompey (Woody Strode), who occupies the off-screen vis-à-vis him, and of course all of them refer to another off, occupied by Ford the director who is the shooter of the scene.

The becoming-present of the off in this scene when it is retold, due to the camera now showing us more than we saw on first view, is not just what supplies us with an additional piece of information to transform our knowledge and understanding of the event; it is the becoming-exposed of everyone involved in the event (us included) to that more mysterious side of the "more," the non-actual more-than, or the more-than-actuality that, as we saw, is one of the off's two fundamental dimensions. The exposure to this more-than-actuality, to the cinematic medium itself, to the call it transmits, becomes the enigmatic crisis (in the original sense of the term, the moment of decision, a fundamental existential choice) around which (in the manner of Oedipus's and the city's exposure to the plague coming from some indeterminate outside) the entire, to a large degree tragic destinies of (at least) all the film's main characters revolve. Each character, in a different way, fails, we can say, the test of the exposure to the off, fails their screen test, so to speak, never managing to coincide with the demands of, the call of, the medium they inhabit, by which they are nevertheless inscribed. This analysis of the failure to appropriately respond to the call is at the heart of Ford's understanding of the as-yet unaccomplished arrival of America.

Thus Doniphon himself, when first shown coming on-screen from the dimension of the off in the memorial reconstructive flashback, is a fully dark figure emerging from a shadow (and we saw that the shadow is the very inscription of the off on-screen, the emptying presence of that which has no actuality). His having had to occupy the shadow, thus to have become inscribed by the dimension of the off, will become a burden that Doniphon will never escape, and it will result in his relegation to a sort of erasure. For this shadow that he is forced to occupy so that he can kill Liberty and in so doing not shame Ranse will now come to define his own action as shadowy: it is a shadowy killing that from the point of view of the heroic desert code that guides him (demanding a pure visibility, forbidding any secretive obscurity) is cowardly, dishonorable, and unforgivable, in fact signifying the loss of who he is. The moment he commits the shooting is essentially the moment of his death, even if (like Lear after his abdication, existing between two deaths) he will actually die many years later, in a death with which the movie begins. On the other hand, Ranse, the man of Law—at first racked with guilt, thinking he has killed Liberty and so has blood on his hands, and is therefore unworthy to be the people's representative in Washington— has been unburdened by Doniphon's confession and, cleared of the blood of crime and the accompanying guilt, can embark on a political career. Yet the politics he is now able to practice, as is made immediately clear in his hollow way of speaking, proves empty, that is, it is without any ground (in the Law of finitude and infinity, in the call of the desert), since it has lost touch both with the dimension of the off and with the heroic desert code (itself grounded, even if problematically, in the experience of the call of the off, thus in the call) by which he, for a moment, when confronting Liberty, even if ambivalently, had been guided. As a man of Washington "politics," that is, not real politics (for the true political—a necessary condition for the real coming of America—is a relation to the ground, i.e., the medium), he will be neither the heroic man of the desert (even if the false belief of others in his mythical heroism is that which sustains his place in politics, allowing it to have a kind of ground) nor truly a man of Law. The dimension of the off in which he was at least partially grounded qua a man of Law (for the Law, we have seen, is grounded in the off and legislates that the off cannot be possessed) has been, so to speak, taken away from him by Doniphon's having come to occupy it, as a sacrificial scapegoat relieving him of his guilt. Doniphon's self-sacrificial consumption by the shadow allows Ranse to become shadowless, but it also renders him groundless and thus, in a way, without real connection to the source of Law.

Both the mythical-heroic and the legal, then, are destroyed in this scene when the off intrudes, the former because, constituted in its very being upon a rejection of the off and the attempt to master it the mythical-heroic suffers an unwilling exposure to the off and as a result is consumed by the shadowy dimension the very existence of which it cannot bear and under the obscure "light" of which it dissolves; Law, for its part, is destroyed because it is deprived of the off by a sacrificer taking the off upon himself. This double destruction of heroism and Law revolves in this scene around that other fundamental dimension that was, we saw, associated with the off, love, understood as the gift (as transmission and reception) of the infinite more-than, transmitted by the feminine. For it is as answering the call of love that Doniphon enters the shadowy, Hades-like off—since he protects Ranse in response to Hallie's wishes, and it is for her sake he abandons his code—even if at the price of his heroism's dissolution. This self-sacrificial burning in the fire of love (he will later indeed set fire to the home he built for himself and his beloved) simultaneously results in (1) his own destruction and the loss of his beloved to whom, upon the loss of his heroic manhood, he will no longer feel entitled; (2) his maintaining, despite or even because of his sacrifice, a never-broken bond of love with the one he has lost; and (3) the dooming of Ranse—who has lost both his heroism and the Law—to a life without love, as the film's ending makes clear.

It is for the sake of his beloved, Hallie, who is fearful for Ranse's safety, that Doniphon decides to protect him from Liberty, yet protect him, precisely, by placing himself in the shadows, by occupying the off. This shadowy protection is undertaken to allow Ranse to preserve his manly heroism, with which Doniphon identifies, love and heroism being the two forces guiding him, their irreconcilability (an irreconcilability that has constantly prevented him from actually declaring his love) ultimately destroying him.

Why are love and desert heroism irreconcilable, even as the opening to the call of the desert in all its implications signifies a true reception of love, as we saw in Lincoln's case, where the landscape and its openness are also the site of the gift of love? To understand this, we need to gather the various aspects of the desert as we have been discussing it. First of all the desert, a figuration of the being of the screen itself as a decontextualized space, is the site where the hitherto organized, ordered world is emptied of all its determinations. As a result, it becomes both a space—since it is devoid of any specificity and determination—with no specified function in the world and a space that is lawless, outside the law, since it is not subjected to any order of things. Being decontextualized and exorcised from the world's order, no longer belonging anywhere in the world, the desert has the potential to become the site where one communicates with the very medium that makes the world a world, what we can understand as the call of its origin. When the being of the desert comes to be associated with the being of the screen, the medium of the world, now understood through the logic of the cinematic medium, is shown to involve a dimension that exceeds any of the traditional, metaphysical interpretations of said medium, say, the eternal divine, and is now seen as having to do with an infinite more-than, an open indeterminacy to which one becomes exposed unwillingly. This infinite more-than at the heart of the call of the desert/screen, we saw, involves three main dimensions: a Law forbidding any and all attempts to possess the whole, or the medium; love, which is the unwilled, passive, and passionate reception, beyond this Law, of the gift of infinity via the mediation of a love "object"; and the higher Law, the Law of finitude and infinity, which we must receive.

The desert, then, is what we can understand as a threshold realm, in the sense of a realm that is not part of the world, or not exactly in the world, but an exceptional site where one experiences the relation to the world as such, as a medium. The desert, not being part of the world, is also the site, negatively, of criminals, those who are outside the world and the order governing it. The *figures*, or *types*, who come to populate the screen/desert as Ford interprets it in *Liberty Valance* are thus, respectively, the criminal (Liberty Valance); the man of law (in its first aspect, as the law of forbidding—Ranse); the messenger of love, or the woman (Hallie); and, perhaps most fundamentally, as in the case of Lincoln (a figure for which there is no exact parallel in *Liberty Valance*), the prophetic Lawgiver, the one who is the witness to the higher Law, that of finitude and infinity, and who needs to be the recipient, simultaneously, of Law, of love, and of the higher Law uttered by a ghostly speech that one reaches through the loss of love, mourning, and the pure memory of the Medium/nothing, a Lawgiver who is tasked with bringing all of the above to a community that is to gather around it, that is to be informed by it.

There is another crucial desert/screen figure in Ford: the desert hero, represented here by Wayne. This figure is like an uncanny double of the Lawgiver in that he is a true witness to the call of the desert in all its dimensions, thus an exceptional figure (the "ex" marking being outside the world, thus being inscribed by the medium of the world as such), yet one who partially misinterprets his witnessing and becomes a defensive figure, one who in fact eliminates the very call whose witness he is by being one who tries to take possession of the call (a call that by definition one cannot possess and that one experiences passively and passionately), tries to master it, a mastery that, by definition, is also a defense against love as the passionate, passive reception of infinity. Such a defensive response to the call (call it "phallic") aims to transform the dispossessive place of being inscribed by the call into a source of power and possession. Such heroic possessiveness is most importantly inscribed in the gun, as well as, at least partially so (since it will also have a nonheroic function), in the camera.

Gun and Camera

Both gun and camera—held by Ford occupying the off in the key scene we are in the midst of examining, who is, from this perspective, Wayne's double, most essentially in his cowardly aspect, avoiding, withdrawing from, visibility—are instruments of shooting and of possessive power over the visible, aiming to transform exposure to the medium, which characterizes everyone occupying the visible realm opened by the medium, into mastery over it. If the heroic "code" of the gun, in Wayne's hands, is that of occupying a fully illuminated realm, with nothing to hide, no shadows (shadows being the traces of the passivity to the medium which, by definition, cannot be included in the visible realm since it is that which opens this realm), the camera's "cowardly" position is that of, in principle, pure invisibility. Such cowardly position, though, is not the camera's alone but also, potentially, that of the gun, first, the gun of Liberty, who shoots from the direction of the off and hides himself, and then the gun of Doniphon as he shoots from the off.

Both gun and camera, then, at least in one of their main aspects in the film, share the similar aims of mastering the visible and avoiding being inflicted with the shadow. While Wayne's heroic gun (until his shadowy shooting of Liberty) is premised on the demand that within a realm of pure exposure, meaning exposure to the dimension of the off that signifies one's originary helplessness and failure of will, it can dominate exposure (and thus eliminate the off), taking full possession of it in spite of its potentially destructive menace, the "cowardly," invisible position of the camera (and of Liberty's gun, as well as Wayne's shadowy shot) equally aims to dominate exposure, by becoming a fully unseen seer, thus a seer completely protected from exposure. Desert heroism and cowardice, both inscribed by the excessive off, thus finally converge in their aim to dominate exposure, even if the hero is the one who faces exposure head-on, in order to overcome it, while the shadowy coward overcomes exposure by withdrawing completely from it. Absolute visibility and absolute invisibility meet at the same place, the domination of the visible.

That the desert hero (Wayne), as master and possessor of exposure, as pure creature of the daylight, is actually implicitly a coward (and thus not unlike Liberty, as well as Ford/the filmmaker in one of his fundamental aspects), in the sense of trying to avoid an exposure he cannot tolerate, inscribed as he is by an intense anxiety of the shadows, is most paradigmatically emphasized in Ford's cinema in the character of Ethan Edwards (again, John Wayne) in *The Searchers*, where the desert hero Wayne is also the racist Wayne, the one who cannot tolerate any "contamination" of white purity by Indian blood, a contamination that Wayne sees as worse than death. This contamination can be understood as that which exposes white people to an off, a shadowy realm of uncontrolled eroticism, an eroticism signifying the failure to maintain racial continuity, the maintenance of self-sameness. This relation of the shadowy dimension of the off with racial exposure and transformation is displayed through the mixed member of the family, the partially American Indian Martin Pawley (Jeffrey Hunter), who is, it is constantly emphasized, someone inscribed by shadows, but beyond that, he is someone whose exposure to the shadows is not a weakening but, to the contrary, the source of a new mysterious power, a different kind of heroism. Martin is unafraid, or is friendly, with the shadows, not qua dominating them but precisely qua allowing himself to be informed by them, most spectacularly toward the movie's end when he uses his knowledge of the shadowy night to infiltrate, under cover, the Indian camp and save his sister. This aspect of Martin as one who is always in relation to a principle of shadowy self-covering, a covering that is nevertheless neither cowardice nor an attempt to control the visible, is also emphasized in a comical moment when Martin unwittingly gets himself an Indian wife while thinking he has bought a blanket, as if his very essence (as well as the essence of erotism and love, which he, unlike Wayne, successfully achieves) is to be one attached to the principle of blanketing or shadowy self-covering (and, indeed, he is constantly shown in the movie as covering himself with blankets).

In *The Man Who Shot Liberty Valance* it is the black man Pompey, Wayne's helper, who is also emphasized as being in the shadow (the nonwhite races being relegated to the shadows precisely to the degree that they implicitly threaten the clarity of the sunlit day understood as domination of the visible) and in the off, always arriving from beyond the screen, often, as we saw, to help Wayne, as in the case of the shooting scene. He is a shadow, though, that Wayne can tolerate (perhaps even love) precisely because he is a shadow that Wayne can master, being his boss. The one scene where Wayne shows the possibility of introducing the shadowy Pompey into the world in a way that exceeds his mastery over Pompey (and racism is understood in Ford as the attempt to master those who are seen as inscribing a shadowy off, be they Indian or black, thus those who threaten the pure visibility of whiteness, or the fantasy of whiteness) occurs after the shooting scene, thus after he himself was swallowed by the shadow, when Pompey enters the bar to fetch him and Wayne forces the barman to give Pompey, who is usually not allowed to drink with the white townspeople, a drink.

The desert-mythic hero as inscribed in the Wayne type, then, at least from one of its main perspectives—since he is also to be understood as the one remaining faithful to the excessive call of the desert beyond its falsification in the codes of civilization, thus keeping the call alive, and this is the Wayne of, for example, *She Wore a Yellow Ribbon*, who, in a somewhat untypical way, is one who is open to, thus friendly with, the shadowy realm, in that, like Lincoln, he is in memorial conversation with his dead beloved—is the one who aims to possess a unique and exceptional power, the power over the fundamental place of dispossession, thus that over which we in principle have no power, the medium/origin. This defines him as, in principle, a desire to eliminate the off, since the off, the non-actual infinity of the medium, is precisely that which cannot be possessed and to which one is exposed.

We can also see that the hero is one who is essentially isolated, for two fundamental, though not coinciding, reasons. First, most crucially, the hero is by definition exceptional, the exceptional person being one who is inscribed by the call of the origin/medium (that which is "ex," thus outside, any actuality), becoming responsible for the call rather than simply being a participant in a world informed by the medium. As exceptional, the hero partakes in that which characterizes any essential or paradigmatic place—a place such as the cinematic screen, inscribed by the origin/open potentiality of the off—the being cut off from any determined continuity of the world, since inscribing the ground of the world, its empty openness, thus not being part of any determined context.

Second, more negatively, the hero is isolated and alone, not only as an exceptional respondent to the call but as one who aims to take possession of the call. If to be called is to be exposed to the medium/world, that which one cannot will, it implies that to truly be in the world is to be exposed. It follows that the hero, as one who attempts to take possession of the call, rejecting exposure, refuses to be part of a world, of the common, exposed (to the off), realm, thus sentencing himself to an apartness from civilization, understood in this context as the realm commonly shared, an apartness that is another aspect of the non-civilized desert.

This is, of course, the reason for the well-known characterization of the hero as basically silent, as a man of few words. To speak would be to partake in the medium, thus to be exposed. Silence, from this perspective, is what expresses one's externality to, and refusal of, speech. The desert is not only the exceptional, and paradigmatic, place where the call of the world is received—an exceptional place by definition not exactly part of the world, outside it—but it is also the place to which the one who refuses the exposure of the world withdraws.

Returning to the question of love and to Doniphon's relation to it, we can see how his very conflicted position is inscribed in the complexity of his desert-being, thus of his exceptionality due to his being the inscriber of the call, both as true witness to it and as defensive attempt to possess it and exclude himself from the open exposure that is the world. For, as true witness to the desert call, Doniphon is also particularly susceptible to that aspect of the call that is the reception of infinity through love; yet, since he is heroic resister to the call, thus someone attempting in a defensive way to take possession of the call, love is precisely that which he cannot bear, that which signals the limit and extinction of his heroism. In the scene under discussion, Doniphon is willing to follow love into occupying the shadows, for the truth of love in a way is accepting the passion of the shadows, the passivity to the infinite off, yet the shadows, the inscription by the off, whose very being is the failure of heroism, ends up destroying him.

Hallie herself, the messenger of love, fails her screen test as well for the same reasons, unable as she is to fully grasp the incompatibility of love, understood as the gift of infinity, with desert heroism qua attempt to possess the off via the mastery of the gun. For even as she is in love with Doniphon, it is Ranse's heroic, "phallic" killing of Liberty (Hallie is of course unaware of who really shot Liberty)—especially in its juxtaposition with Doniphon's absence at the time of the killing, which she implicitly seems to see as a neglect of duty on the border of cowardice—that lies at the root of her abandoning Doniphon and replacing him with Ranse. The trajectory she thus follows is the preference of heroism over love, a choice that dooms her.

It is, then, in the relations among the desert as a site of the (American and cinematic) call, the question of the shot, the exposure to the off, and the message of love that the film's tragedy as well as the nonachievement of America lies. America, for the tragic reasons indicated in this scene, has not yet fulfilled the transition from the cinematic/desert call to the new form of life called America (and remember that the movie's entire plot concerns the moment of a decision regarding the transition from the desert to the coming to belong to a newly formed political entity).

In many ways it is the shot—emerging out of that threshold moment between the call of the desert and the establishment of the United States as a new political way of life (whose task is to turn the desert into a garden), between visibility and invisibility, between law and lawlessness—that occupies the heart of the American tragedy. For the shot, Ford shows (in the cases of the gun and of the camera), is a paradigmatic witness to the American call. The shot inscribes in its very being the renewed intrusion of the empty desert—the resonance of its newly conceived call (qua the activation of a new, empty infinity, finding one of its most fundamental expressions in the screen)—that marks the interruptive place of America at the heart of Western modernity.

Thus, in its gun aspect (hence the unparalleled psychic place of the gun in American life, that is, in a life exposed to the desert call in a unique way), the shot marks simultaneously the witnessing to a new source of Law (for the one carrying the gun often implies "I bring the Law with me, a Law of which I am an exceptional witness"); the excess over the traditional ways of ordering marking the history of the metaphysical West; the criminal occupation of a lawless realm, a realm abandoned by the traditional laws, manifesting a criminality tied in its essence to an attempt to block any new legal-political realm from being founded; and the heroic (mis)interpretation of the dispossessing call to which one has become a witness, trying to declare one's possession over it, avoiding passivity to the Law by declaring oneself a Law of one's own.

Overall, then, we can say that the gunshot as an inscription of the threshold is simultaneously that through which one can declare oneself a witness to the call of America; that through which one can announce oneself outside of America, not fully seeing oneself as belonging to it, since the call exceeds it as political entity, at least as it has been so far (Wayne's character seems to waver between these two positions); and that through which one actually declares one's opposition to the emergence of the United States (as do the territorial ranchers or the criminal Liberty), for as a political entity it implies a dispossession that the gun holder is unwilling to accept. We can also say that in all the abovementioned aspects, the gunshot, even as it is inscribed with the exceptional call of the off/medium, remains a defensive figure, trying to transform passivity to the call into property and possession.

Nevertheless, it is also clear that for Ford there is a passionate excess attached to the being of the gun that is lacking in what we can understand as the man of formal Law—that is, Law only in its aspect of forbidding possession of the Whole, not the more profound Law of finitude and infinity in which the dimension of the passion of existence, the passivity to infinity, is inscribed—as represented by Ranse. This passionate excess has to do with the gun, though a defensive inscriber of the witnessing to the call, still somehow holding the passionate excess over the Law (the first, formal law, that is) implied in the call itself, and in the love dimension and memorial dimension it brings as the gift of an infinity beyond the (first) Law. The man of the gun is still closer to the call for Ford than the man of formal Law, since the man of the gun is grounded in love and passion, thus probably also in beauty (hence the desert rose Wayne gives Hallie, which is emphasized), dimensions superior to and more powerful than formal Law.

Yet there is a need to go beyond the gun (and thus beyond the phallus?) if one is to open to the desert call in a way that will truly bring about a new political form of life, America, and turn the desert into a garden. For, we can say, the tragedy of America lies in the problem of the gun (shot) precisely to the degree that even as it can be that which inscribes, in its American, desert modality, a new relation to the call of infinity, it indicates at the same time a blockage to what is truly implied in the call, a passionate, thus shadowy memory of infinity/the off, a new Law (of finitude and infinity) one cannot possess but must receive, around which the dispersed members of a new community need to gather.

It is here that the question of that other shot, that of the camera, comes into focus. For, even as the apparatus of the camera, no less than the "phallic" gun, is a technology of inscription of the call at the threshold moment of the desert/screen—the moment of abandonment by the constituted, established world and its orders, and the emergence of a decontextualized, "lawless" space—and even as the camera can be said to be implicated in the attempt to master and control the visible (characterized by an often cowardly avoidance of exposure), there is nevertheless an excessive passion, a shadow, which the camera can inscribe and activate, that goes beyond the defensive, controlling passion of the gun. For the camera, in its relation to the being of the screen, in its passive registration of a reality cut off from any continuity and thus exposed to, and hence exposing us to, the infinite dimension of the off, exceeds any directorial attempt to take possession of it, and in fact is the instrument of dispossession for anyone holding it. Though, from one perspective, the holder of the camera is one who withdraws from visibility in order to be able to control it, from another perspective the camera holder is one suspended from the world of action, thus from any capacity to do anything and becomes (like James Stewart as L. B. Jeffries, the photographer in Hitchcock's *Rear Window*) a paralyzed and passive watcher (though *Rear Window* of course also emphasizes the cowardly desire not to be seen by the one who uses the camera as an instrument of power), thus one who passionately receives the world beyond having any control over it. In this sense, the camera and screen are those that register one's being caught in the passion of watching, a passion that by definition goes beyond the gun, to the degree that the gun is precisely that whose task is to transform the passionate witnessing of the world into something one can dominate.

In this sense, in the scene we are investigating that forms the enigmatic center of *The Man Who Shot Liberty Valance*, the intrusion of the shadowy off qua marking the position of the camera (and of Ford, the shooting man behind it) is what marks this shot as going beyond the gun that Wayne holds. The man who shot..., and we the witnesses to the shot, are now the passive and passionate watchers of a scene beyond his and our control, which exceeds the shooting of the gun. Beyond the gun there is the camera, through whose passivity we become the passionate receivers of an existence, witnesses to the call of the screen in its profoundest aspect.

Only if we manage to overcome the gun and receive the camera, receive the message it transmits, becoming passionate watchers, can it be said that we are truly inscribed by the call of the off, in a nondefensive manner, and have thus come to participate in a new opening of a community, call it America, that receives the world in a new mode. It is only this shot—the shot of the camera, the coming to the fore of the being of the medium of film, through which we start to receive the world passionately, thus receive the Law of infinity and finitude, in a memory that goes even beyond love (and recall that at the beginning of the flashback to our scene, Wayne says, "Remember"), and open up to the call delivered to us by the screen—that Liberty Valance, and the gun logic he stands for, can truly be exceeded and surpassed, in fact eliminated.

To receive the off through the shot is thus to receive the passion opening us to the world, beyond our will, the world understood as a potentiality to open up to that which we receive. It is in this reception that we truly receive the Law of finitude and infinity, a Law around which the community of moviegoers, at the heart of America, is now supposed to gather, each losing, as they watch the screen from which they receive the passionate off, any determined place they had in the world, all becoming homeless exiles who begin to share the world as the sharing of its passion, thus sharing the reception of it as an indeterminate opening, the source of a new world to be created together among all its passionate witnesses.

The Ford film that treats, in the most explicit and paradigmatic way, this transition from the gunshot to the camera shot—to becoming, through the medium of film, passionate watchers opening us to the new community of America—is also one of Ford's most visually beautiful films (since it is the film about beauty that turns us into passionate watchers, witnesses to the call of the screen, through our receiving it): *She Wore a Yellow Ribbon*. Its plot is basically structured upon the transition from shooting the gun to watching, in that it deals with the moment when its main character, Captain Nathan Brittles (again Wayne, this time in his aspect most like Lincoln, a figure inscribed by mourning and loss), is about to retire from his army service and thus will lay down his gun. And at this moment of Brittles's imminent withdrawal a grave conflict with the Indians is about to erupt, a new war that Nathan then manages to prevent, bringing peace without a single gunshot.

I will not go into the details of the film's conception of the moment when the gun is laid down, but I will mention that the entire film revolves around numerous occasions when, instead of acting and shooting, characters are called upon to watch, to passively and passionately receive the world they no longer dominate through their shooting action. In fact, in an allegorical moment, upon his retirement Captain Nathan receives from his troops a watch, on which is inscribed a "sentiment," as Nathan calls it, "Lest we forget," thus connecting to the question of watching, time, and memory, which is at the heart of Fordian cinema. The moment of film in *She Wore a Yellow Ribbon* thus becomes the moment of retirement from action and domination, the moment of transition into watching, a memorial watching through which peace arrives. And more than that: It is implied that this transition into watching, and into the memorial reception of beauty (and love, for one of the film's subplots is a love story involving a young officer), is at the heart of the final arriving at America, that which is needed for the full birth of the United States. For the final words of the movie, though forging a relation that links the emergence of the United States with guns and fighting—"wherever they rode, and whatever they fought for, this place became the United States"—also indicate that we are now in the age of memory, no longer that of guns, and that our watchful memory is brought about by film, on which the final transition to the United States depends.

The central scene of *Liberty Valance* that we have been concentrating on, itself a memory scene (opening with Doniphon's "Remember"), structured around the complex intrusion of the off/medium, is thus one with the ultimate aim of opening in us, beyond the gun, through the reception of the off, the passion of watching, which we can also understand as the ultimate moment of the reception of the Law of finitude and Infinity, transmitted to us by the call of the screen. And as this scene becomes one through which we receive the Law beyond the gun, passionately, memorially, we can also be said to become part of another fundamental space occupying the heart of *The Man Who Shot Liberty Valance*, and of Ford's cinema in general, the classroom (the parallel to *Young Mr. Lincoln*'s court of Law, which functions as the classroom that educates the people into the Law).

Learning to Read

The classroom scene in *The Man Who Shot Liberty Valance* (a full elaboration of its complexity would have taken us twenty more pages!), perhaps its most moving scene, serves as an allegory for the task of film as Ford understands it, becoming the site through which everyone, all the dispersed, are introduced into the call of the Law. Thus Ford stages the classroom scene as a dedicated space in which an "audience"—composed of the dispersed people, each coming from some kind of loss, black people, mixed-race Mexican-white children, immigrants, thus all of us (and all looking at a board in the manner of looking at a screen)—gathers to learn the Declaration of Independence and the Constitution, thus the Law of the unique land they are called to inhabit.

This introduction into the Law in the folds of which everyone, all the dispersed, are to equally gather is also understood, in a crucial move by Ford, as a learning to read (the context of the class is teaching those who are currently illiterate to read). To learn to read most fundamentally—hence the use in this lesson of the Declaration of Independence and the Constitution—is to learn to receive the Law (of infinity and finitude) that is to serve as the ultimate Law of a new kind of human gathering, the United States. This learning to read, thus to receive the Law (of infinity and finitude), is also understood in this classroom scene as that through which we can exceed the gun. For the gun, as this scene emphasizes, is the interruption of the classroom. Thus Doniphon enters the classroom, interrupting the lesson and calling the men to the gun while declaring, "Your schooling is over."

"Votes," he says, which is the form of speech of those who learned to open up to the American Law through finally learning to read, "won't stand up against guns." Following which the teacher, Ranse, forsakes, indeed betrays, his teaching mission by deserting the class and going to a shooting practice. Yet as Ranse leaves, abandoning the classroom, Hallie, who served as the teacher's helper, remains alone in the classroom, signaling that her passion, and the message of love accompanying it, is what the classroom's future beyond the gun depends on. (In a way it is this interrupted class that we, the audience, are called upon to return to and complete through the memorial scene of *Liberty Valance*'s shooting, where the gun taken up by Ranse and Doniphon, having been shown to betray the true calling of the Law [of the off/medium/infinity and finitude], is exceeded.)

This filmic classroom scene, giving us the task of film as the site through which we learn to read and thus to open up—in passionate, memorial watching—to the Law, brings us back to the gift of the book received by Lincoln with which we started. For the book, understood in essence as the Book of Law, a book that, it was hinted, we forgot how to read, if indeed we ever fully learned how to, is a "Bible," understood in the most fundamental way as what enables us—through learning to read it—to open up to the Law of the world. Perhaps we never learned to read it, or forgot how to, because we never fully learned how to remember, thus never knew how to open up to that trace of nothing/the off, the site of the Law's true call.

It is the cinematic screen, in general, and Ford's cinema, in particular, that thus sees itself (and this is its "mythic" function, which is thus in fact an interruption, to use a term from Jean-Luc Nancy,[36] of the German type of myth as unifying ground) as aiming to serve both as The Book (to speak like Mallarmé or Blanchot) and as the classroom through which we, the people/audience/dispersed migrants, learn how to read and thus to open to the Law of the world, and to arrive, through memorization, at a historically new place of belonging, thus of appropriation to the Law of the call: America.

THREE

American Tragedy Between Sacred Sacrifice and Democratic Image

FRANCIS FORD COPPOLA'S *THE GODFATHER*

"I believe in America," says a voice whose source we cannot yet see or identify, and hence strikes us with anxiety, opening what has undoubtedly become one of the paradigmatic works of American cinema, *The Godfather*. If it is indeed a paradigmatic work of American cinema, a work inscribing the very question of the meaning of Being in America (or perhaps of America as a new name for the meaning of Being) in a fundamental way, it is so as a tragedy; that is, it belongs to that genre that emerged simultaneously with Greek democracy and through which the members of the city, of the polis, thus of the being together of the people (the demos), experienced in nightmarish visions the possibility of the dissolution of their common life, of their world. Such a world, a democratic world (if of course not fully so), is no longer grounded in any guaranteed and regulated metaphysical order and is thus open to new possibilities of existence (partially brought about through the free and open debate of the Athenian agora, as well as through the philosophical dialogues of the Platonic academy), but at the same time it is haunted by the other side of that openness, the flip side of freedom, a bottomless abyss, in the sense of a lack of any metaphysical ordering ground (an abyss expressed in the dramatic nightmares of the amphitheater, as well as in its fundamental accompaniment, the flourishing of artistic creativity).

105

If indeed tragedy, as Aristotle says, originated out of (and was a transformation of) sacred rituals of sacrifice, and if tragedy, in many ways, marks the birth of the work of art (as distinct from sacred artifacts and performative rituals, thus artifacts—such as ritualistic masks, statues of divinities, etc.—and rituals belonging to a sacred world and having the precise function of communicating with the world's sacrality),[1] then we can say that art, and this is at the heart of its mystery, aspires to replace sacrifice, even as it might continue to bear something of its function, and of its structural position in human life, a position we might call that of occupying the world's limit, its place of birth and death.

In art (and it is an open question whether we have ever fully reached the condition of art, that is, whether we have fully overcome sacrifice), we watch sacrifice as it is transformed into a poetic image (a concept we will keep returning to) or fiction. This birth of the poetic image/fictionality occupies a fundamental place within the context of the emergence of democracy, thus of a common life not grounded in any given order or regulated in advance and thus not controlled by an idea of an unchanging center from which a destiny emanates, or of a cyclical, cosmic repetitiveness. The very being of democracy and that of the artistic, fictional image are thus inextricably tied, as if you cannot have one without the other. We can even push this further and say that there cannot be a fully democratic life in an age that has not achieved the condition of art, thus an age when sacrifice has not been overcome and been replaced by the creation of images (hence the Schillerian idea that an aesthetic education of man is a precondition for the achievement of democracy). Tragedy, we might further suggest, is the name for a moment of blockage (a moment in many ways still ours) when an age of democracy and art (an age that, historically, was never fully achieved, it is clear) has not yet emerged, and we are still in the transition (which might never run its course) from sacrifice to art (or more precisely the Image, in a new sense we are still far from grasping), failing to have fully transformed from one to the other, remaining in suspension between them. In such an age the tragedy is expressed not only in tragic works of art, works that register the failure to fully be art, but also in violent and horrific worldly events, often resulting from being stuck in the tragic blockage.

If sacred communities were communities (a sharing of a life in common) gathered around sacrifice, a sacrifice through which they experienced their

American Tragedy Between Sacred Sacrifice and Democratic Image 107

commonness, then we might thus also say that democratic communities (and it is an open question whether such communities have ever fully emerged) are those called to be gathered around a poetic image (hence the logic of this present book) rather than around sacred rituals, and the sharing and transmission of the image become a new kind of experience of commonality, serving as the ground out of which this commonality is to draw its resources. America, in its instantiation in and as the United States, as Coppola sees it, is a privileged site for the expression, in a particularly powerful way, of, on the one hand, the tragic moment of suspension between art and sacrifice at the threshold of a not-yet fully arrived democracy and, on the other hand, a privileged site from which the call to a new community is heard, the call to a mode of togetherness (a megalo*polis*?[2]), that is to go beyond sacred community (sacred community being structured in many ways around the figure of God the father and his inextricable accompaniment, the sacrificed son), as well as beyond the tragic blockage.

Perhaps no cinematic image allegorically invokes the mysterious transitional realm between sacrifice and artistic image as much as the celebrated image from *The Godfather* (perhaps the fundamental image around which the entirety of Coppola's cinema revolves) of the movie producer, the image maker, waking up from a nightmare, finding a bloodied horse's head in his bed, as if having to confront the sacrificial rituals from which his art distanced him (to the degree of forgetting) even as it has always tied him to them: sacrificial rituals in fact unconsciously inscribed in the pseudo-Roman villa he inhabits, the horses he raises, and so on.

The power of Coppola's cinema, I suggest, and perhaps especially of his two masterworks, *The Godfather* trilogy (echoing great tragic cycles such as the *Oresteia* and the *Oedipus* trilogies) and *Apocalypse Now*, has to do with their attempt to locate themselves in this mysterious relation and transition between sacred sacrifice and poetic image/fictionality (as if going back to the moment of the birth of tragedy out of the spirit of democracy), desiring to endow the poetic image with something like the foundational force of the sacred (and thus to go beyond the aesthetic function assigned the work of art in the modern era), even as they try to distance the image, indeed to liberate it, from the general logic of sacrifice (as well as of religion). Indeed, there is perhaps no other American film, neither *Citizen Kane* nor *Vertigo* nor *Psycho* (though perhaps, in a different register, *It's a Wonderful Life*?), that has come to function in the popular imaginary (thus in the imagination that the democratic people share as a people) as an almost sacred work to be ritualistically returned to again and again, for reasons I suggest are far from accidental, as much as *The Godfather*.[3]

We will return to these questions and to the paradigmatic cinematic image of the horse's head (i.e., an image in which cinema's very being seems to be at stake), but for now let us examine the film's astonishingly complex opening scene and follow the way it ties the question of America to that of the emergence of images, that seems to repeat the eruption of a new type of image at the founding moment of Greek democracy, thus at the tragic moment of the threshold between the logic of sacrifice and that of art. America, as the United States, one of the paradigmatic birthplaces of modern democracy, is, among other historical repetitions, the site of repetition of Attic Greece,[4] the birthplace of the idea of democracy; and film is the art that repeats, perhaps more so than in the other arts, the birth of art as the shadowy aspect of the spirit of democracy, in a tragic mode but also as aiming beyond tragedy, toward the death, or overcoming, of tragedy.

Between Two Fathers

"I believe in America," says an unseen voice on the background of a fully dark screen. This decontextualized sentence provides no indication of how we are to take it, hence our anxiety. Is it, for example, uttered by someone who still believes in America? Or by someone for whom America has not lived up to his belief in it, and if so, why? Or perhaps by someone whose belief in America is conditional, depending on an action that will or will not be taken? We could go on and on, of course. And beyond this, what is the relation of the question of America to such a sentence, hovering in suspension and striking us with anxiety? Is the question of America itself the question of belief rather than that of a determined existence, and is this belief colored (as belief perhaps most fundamentally must be) by the anxiety of the sentence in indeterminate suspension? And even beyond that, what is the relation of this decontextualized sentence to the medium within which it is uttered, the medium of film? Does the question of the relations between America and belief have, as a privileged site for its occurrence, the cinematic medium?

American Tragedy Between Sacred Sacrifice and Democratic Image 109

Next we see a face, the source of the sentence's utterance, but itself still completely decontextualized, against a dark background and only partially illuminated, hence undetermined (thus already containing a certain nightmarish quality, nightmare being that which emerges when the "head"—already foreshadowing the horse's head—is decontextualized and cut, thus when the organizing center no longer holds and suffers a decapitation). Since the face seems to be directed at someone, though it is not yet clear at whom, we are in the midst of a situation of address rather than of simply the utterance of a statement. Yet who is the addressee? Us? Or perhaps someone with whom the utterer shares a space, whom we cannot yet see? Whatever the case, the lack of a determined addressee makes each of us an addressee, implying that in each of us what is at stake, as we open up to the cinematic image, is the question of the belief in America and how we are to position ourselves in relation to it. Since we do not yet know who is the one who addresses, nor to whom the sentence is addressed, we indeed become addressees, but addressees whose identity is itself suspended, since we do not know as what, or as whom, we are addressed. Who are we, those who are responsible (in the sense of those from whom a response is demanded) for this indeterminate address of which the question of America, as a subject of belief, lies at its heart? It is as if not knowing who we are is essentially implicated with the question of the belief in America so that a decision about the one depends on a decision about the other.

Let us look further into the address, which continues, following the speech uttered by the face. "America has made my fortune," continues the face, "and I raised my daughter in the American fashion. I gave her freedom, but I taught her never to dishonor her family. She found a boyfriend, not an Italian. She went to the movies with him." All this is followed by the description of an attempted rape scene: The daughter escapes her attacker but is deeply wounded. As the father is speaking, addressing an unknown speaker with his crisis, the camera slowly withdraws from him, increasingly exposing him (the dark space surrounding him growing more prominent) in alignment with his pain's ever-heightening expressiveness as he narrates the damaging of his daughter's beauty—until, finally, a hand seems to enter the frame from off-screen, first as an almost unrecognizable, shadowy stain on the edge of the frame and then, vaguely, a head, shot from the back, thus undetermined. The wounded father continues to narrate the failure of the Law to deal with his case. As the presence of the listener, still unrecognizable, grows more prominent, the father says that for Justice, beyond what the Law accomplished, they need to come to Don Corleone. What does he want? asks the Don. The wounded father approaches, whispering in the Don's ear, "I want them dead," a request that the Don, whose answer accompanies the appearance of his (Brando's) face, finally becoming fully part of the scene, says he cannot fulfill.

What is going on in this remarkable scene? We can, first, indicate that it narrates the event of coming to America as signifying the event of fortune (both economic—the economy of life as a whole changes—and destinal—if destiny signifies the way we are inscribed in the whole of existence, this modality of inscription changes with the coming to America); of freedom; of the liberation of a sexuality not guided by paternal order, as well as female sexuality; of the dissolution of the traditional family and of paternal authority; of the crossing of identity lines (the boyfriend is not Italian); of the emergence of film (she goes with the boyfriend to the cinema) as the site of the crossing of these traditional identity lines; and of the irruption of a horrifying violence inscribed in the possibility of these crossings (not unlike the case of Oedipus crossing the incest lines, the lines demarcating the Law of existence). This narration by the traditional father, whose coming to America signifies the failure of his position as a father (failing to protect the daughter whose sexual freedom, on its own, already signifies his loss of power), the dissolution of the authority of his ordering, is shown to be linked to the very nature of the cinematic medium itself, by showing us the traditional father's exposure, so to speak, to film. For in the camera's withdrawal from his face—exposing him, until the arrival of the Godfather on-screen, to an ever-increasing opening without any ordered determination of where it is leading—is inscribed the very essence of the medium of film (as we have seen in the previous chapters) as structured upon the relations between what appears on-screen and a dimension of an off-screen, a dimension that is nothing but the exposure of what appears on-screen to a potential opening and transformation without any predetermination or willed ordering. This indeterminate opening, the movement of the camera expressing an exposure to the dimension of an off-screen, is itself, in this sense, the very undermining of the traditional father, whose nature was premised on the capacity to serve as an ordering mechanism (or as the privileged agent of such a mechanism) that safeguards against any indeterminate excess.

American Tragedy Between Sacred Sacrifice and Democratic Image 111

This dizzying and abyssal moment of exposure to the open, or the off, an exposure expressed by the camera movement, is inscribed in the disturbing stain penetrating the frame as the camera moves, a stain that slowly comes to take the shape of the Godfather, as if he is a figure who will come to be projected onto the stain, the final appearance of Brando's face completing this transformation. In fact, we can say (reading this moment as an allegory of the very being of the medium of film) that the appearance of the disturbing stain is, first of all, the appearance of the medium of film itself—understood as an indeterminate exposure to the off, a dimension that is nothing but the empty potentiality of indeterminate opening—as it becomes present within the field of perception. It is as if the exposing camera movement, beyond giving us ever-expanding content, leaves a strange, disturbing trace of itself. Because the medium is nothing but the potentiality for indeterminate opening that allows various cinematic contents to emerge (or is the "condition" for their appearance), it cannot itself appear as content but only as the content's disturbance, a negative appearance of what is not a manifestation of content and thus, in principle, cannot exactly appear. This disturbance is the stain. Art, as that which revolves around the activation and investigation of the medium (of appearance), is also always that which circles around a stain, the disturbing showing of the very (invisible, by definition) medium it activates.

The figure of the Godfather comes to crystallize around the stain qua the place of inscription, in the world or as part of on-screen content, of that medium that is the potentiality enabling this content's appearance or enabling the world itself. In this sense the figure of the Godfather, in distinction from other figures in the filmic world, is one the medium itself is inscribed in or is a specific critical modality of the medium's inscription. We can call such privileged figures in whom the medium itself is inscribed sovereign figures, that is, grounding figures in relation to which (as in relation to a medium that is the source of all appearances) all other figures appear.

Since the sovereign figure is the figure inscribing the medium itself, and since the medium can be understood as the power (power implying a potentiality for . . .) on which depends the very appearance, thus being, of any content, we can say that the sovereign figure is the one in whom the very power of the medium comes to be inscribed, a power that can be (mis)interpreted as the power to give, as well as to take away, being/life. And it is indeed as holding this power that the decontextualized face addressed the Godfather, asking him to kill those responsible for the wounding of the daughter, and it is as holding the other side of the power that Michael, the new Godfather, will be approached toward the end of the film, asked as he is to participate in a baptism and bless the birth of his sister Connie's child (a baptism during which the consignment of all his enemies to death will also be carried out).

Yet it is in the transformation of the medium's power "appearing" in the stain—a power that is in a way nothing but the potentiality for things to appear (that is, to come to show themselves as what they are, thus show themselves in their being)—into a sovereign figure, understood as an agent who holds the power over being (be it a human or a transcendent sovereign), a power over life and death, that the whole problem of the age, in which we still to a degree find ourselves—an age that revolves around the figure of the God Father and, jointly with it, around sacrifice—lies.

For sacrifice, we can say, is situated at the very heart of the question of the shadowy stain, thus of the disruptive appearance of the medium. We can understand the appearance of the medium as that which happens at the limit of the world, or, in phenomenal terms, at the edges of the frame (of appearance), thus that which is neither regular worldly content nor the medium that opens us to worldly content (and that we can call the world as such). In this sense we can say that sacrifice, whether as an object or the subject of sacrifice, as self-sacrifice, is that whose function is to allow the communication between the one and the other, thus between worldly content and the medium, the world as such.[5] The sacrificed is that which is withdrawn from the world in order to touch that which is beyond the world (a beyond that is nothing but the medium of the world). The sacrificed is annihilated (as an occupant of the world) to coincide with that nothing (i.e., no positive thing, but the potentiality for appearance of any positive thing) that is the medium. Additionally, we can say, the sacrificed (essentially tied to the being of the sovereign, or sovereign moment) is the appearance that of all appearances shines most powerfully (hence, for example, that element of fire often associated with it, as in the sacrificial ending, as well as the beginning, of *Apocalypse Now*), an appearance occurring at the dual moment of being consumed out of appearance (the white light famously shining at the moment of dying) as well as being born into appearance. This shining appearance of sacrifice is the appearance that appears the most, so to speak, since the very medium of appearance is inscribed in it. It is therefore an appearance that shines with the power of the medium itself, that which by definition illuminates all appearances (yet cannot itself exactly be seen and, as such, blinds), allowing them to appear to begin with. The shine is not exactly an appearance but is rather the becoming-present or operative of the power, the potentiality, for appearance that the medium is. The sacrificed, the utmost appearance, withdrawn from the world and shining powerfully at the world's limit, is something that has only, to use Walter Benjamin's term, an exhibition value, not a use value ("use" in this context understood as having a certain function in the world).

Needless to say, that which shines fierily at the edges of the world/frame has not only a positive connotation, and is no less demonic than divine, no less contaminated (since stained) than purifying (erasing the stain through its consummation): It is a damning, shadowy threat to the world (being positioned at the point of its possible annihilation) as well as that through which the world is blessed and comes into existence.[6]

Yet this sacrificial element has never been simply that which shines at the blinding limit, a pure appearance and activation (of the) "beyond" the world (the beyond understood here as nothing but the medium, which is beyond any content, in the terms of the previous chapters "more-than" any content, since it is what gives the content or allows it to appear), as the image, ideally, in its liberation from sacrifice, will come to be. Rather, sacrifice has also always been associated with rituals of actual destruction and annihilation controlled by agents seen as having, or devising strategies for having, power over death and life (or at least seen as being entitled to perform rituals whose task is to establish a communication with an agent, possibly transcendent, possessing such power), being and not being. Sacrifice thus also always implied, to a lesser or greater degree, the demand to construct an agent (human or supernatural—thus transforming, in the case of a supernatural agent, the beyond that is the medium—which is beyond any actual content—to a dominating, sovereign ground, an actuality beyond the world) to take possession of the limit, of that excess over anything and everything in the world (the excess that is nothing but the medium itself).

The aim of such taking possession is to eliminate the most threatening aspect of the medium itself, the fact that it is something to which we are fundamentally exposed, in relation to which we are absolutely passive, and in which is inscribed our coming to our limit, our going out of appearance, no less than our birth into appearance. To liberate the Image from sacrifice will be, as we will develop, to create moments of shining at the world's limit that function neither as a ritual aiming to take possession of this limit nor as that whose function is to erase the stain through purification (the exiling of the stained Oedipus meant to exorcise the plague); these moments are simply pure appearances, blinding appearances that inscribe the very medium of appearance, a medium that comes to shine in and through them. These appearances give us the world (in the sense that the world is our medium) beyond what we can will, even as they show us, simultaneously, the world, or our own place in it, coming to an end.

The aim of the Image will be to allow the medium to shine in (as) the world at its moments of creation and destruction, even as it liberates us from the sacrificial fantasies (fantasies being various scenarios circulating around the appearance of the stain, transforming it into narratives whereby a demonic or blessed agent appears as either taking hold of or being blamed for a situation[7]) that have always taken over, at least partially, the place of the Image, not allowing it to fully come into its own, and that irrupt, unconsciously, often in horror, at the heart of a humanity encountering the stain, bringing it to seek the apocalypse (touching—reaching even at the price of self-annihilation—the limit of the world), and to seek it now.

We will come back to these issues, but for the moment we can start to examine how some of these questions are at stake in the scene under consideration. As we saw, the father's exposure to the camera's movement simultaneously signified the emergence of America, his failure as a traditional father, and the appearance of the shadowy stain out of which the Godfather will emerge (the stain itself quickly transitioning from being the inscription in the field of perception of the very medium of perception that by definition cannot appear, into something acquiring moral value—failure, sin, uncontrollable destiny, etc.). We can therefore say that, at least from a certain point of view, we can understand the Godfather (whose reasons for emerging in relation to the question of America we will examine) as a fantasy construction whose aim is to compensate for the father's failure (thus for the abyssal emergence of the freedom of America, a fundamental expression of a new openness associated with godless modernity) and to take possession of the exposure of/to the camera by becoming an agent having power (or being in communication with a transcendence possessing such power) over death and life. In this sense, the figure of the Godfather, and the place he comes

to occupy in American life, will be, from one perspective at least, a fantasy construction created by trying to defend against the failure of the traditional father brought about by the coming to America/modernity.

We have seen in earlier chapters that we can understand the cinematic frame as premised on the division between what we see on-screen, worldly actualities, and the empty dimension of an off-screen that signifies, most fundamentally (when it does not simply mark the place of actualities not captured at the moment by the camera but that can be shown if the camera just changes its position), the potentiality for seeing, the nothing (actual) that is the medium, activated by the exposing camera (the messenger of potentiality) that itself does not appear (but can become marked in an anxiety-provoking stain). In this sense, we can say, that from the point of view of the question of the medium of film the character of the Godfather is a fantasy construction whose purpose is to allow one to take possession of the cinematic frame, as well as of the exposing camera, protecting the failed, exposed father (that dominating function in all of us) from them, restoring his control.

Yet in its remarkable complexity this opening scene is, of course, not satisfied in showing the fantasy mechanism responsible for creating the agent of sacrifice that is the Godfather, appearing out of the stain. Rather, the scene already stages the dismantling of the fantasy, exposing in turn its future failure as well as marking the place of another logic, that of the image. For, we soon find out, the failed father appealing to the Godfather is an undertaker, thus someone located at that mysterious intersection between death and life and therefore occupying—much as the fantasy agent of sacrifice who is the Godfather does, but differently—the limit of the world. To this limit figure the Godfather says, just after the undertaker has fully embraced designating him as the Godfather, that he himself might, in his turn, ask this man for a favor in the future, as if he would one day need to petition him the way the undertaker has petitioned the Godfather here.

Just before indicating the possibility of a future favor where it will be the Godfather who needs the undertaker, we are presented with the composition wherein Sonny Corleone (James Caan), the Godfather's eldest son, is shown as caught between the two fathers. It is Sonny's future death, marked as he is by the undertaker, that is thus already announced. This future death will in turn signify the Godfather's failure, and his passivity, an encounter with the limit between life and death that cannot be dominated or regulated by any sacrificial mechanism (the multiple slaughters at the film's end—juxtaposed with the baptism of Connie's baby—ordered by Michael, the new Godfather, will of course function as well as a sacrificial takeover of, an attempt to regain control over, the intolerable failure of the first Godfather expressed in Sonny's death[8]).

It is in relation to Sonny's death that the Godfather, in turn, will come to make a plea to the undertaker. What is this plea? To make Sonny's ravaged corpse look decent enough so that his mother can look at him. The undertaker will serve, then, in answering the helpless father whom the Godfather will become, in his capacity as an image maker, transforming the limit between death and life into appearance, the very appearance of the limit itself in a tolerable, thus not totally devastating way. Thus, in a sense, the undertaker with whom the film opens is an avatar for Coppola the director, the one who turns the failure of the Godfather qua sacrificial agent into the place of the emergence of images: pure appearances of the limit in which the stain comes to shine without fully consuming its beholders.

Thus, we can also say that in the exchange between the two pleas, the one to the Godfather and the other to the undertaker, we are witnessing the transition from the construction of a fantasy to the creation of an artistic image (the true artistic image being the crossing or overcoming of sacrificial fantasy), and it is Sonny's ravaged body, in a way—the dead son marking the failure of the father, as well as the failure of the attempt to turn the father's failure into a sacrificial mechanism restoring control and meaning to this failure, to turn Sonny's death into the origin of a redemption—that will be the site of connecting, and distinguishing between, sacrifice and image.[9] As we mentioned, this moment of tension and exchange between the sacrificial mechanism inscribed in the Godfather and the image-making one will be repeated and deepened in the movie's second major episode: the trip made by Tom Hagen, the Godfather's messenger, to Hollywood and his visit with the film producer.

Modernity and Tragedy

But all these questions are not simply posed within a general allegorical context. As we have started to see, they are situated in the specific context of the question of the cinematic medium, insofar as it relates to the question of America (and the belief or nonbelief in it) and, we can add, the historical moment when *The Godfather* takes place, roughly 1945–55, thus the first decade of postwar America, as well as the historical moment when the film was released, 1972, making it thus a product of the years leading to the end of the Vietnam War. In many ways the historical logic leading from the one moment to the other is here exposed.

We might thus make a few structural/logical as well as historical points. We can say, first, that the film's opening gives us a glimpse of a general mechanism of fantasy construction, a mechanism that can be said to have dominated much of human history, wherein the experience of a "stain"— the inscription in our existence of that dimension that cannot be possessed nor appear as such, which I have been calling throughout this book the dimension of the "medium" (a Medium writ large of our existence that the cinematic medium is a specific activation of)—is transformed into various sovereign figures, be they men or gods, who are understood to be agents of domination (as well as of responsibility and blame) who erase the stain within the context of a system of sacrifice. This general sacrificial mechanism, responsible for the creation of humanity's sovereign figures through much of its history, has been subject to a partial dismantling—the very investigation of its logic of construction in our scene, in the manner of a genealogical deconstruction (or a critique of ideology), being an essential moment of such dismantling—upon the emergence of what has been called the modern, thus post-theological, age, the age of the demise of the gods, thus of the sovereign figures guiding humanity (the *Gotterdämmerung* Coppola famously refers to in *Apocalypse Now*). This modern age, we can say,[10] as our deconstructive opening scene demonstrates, is also characterized by the appearance of excessive, horrifying stains, damned spots, inscribed as mysterious shadows in the holes left by the gods' absence,[11] an absence in relation to which, or on the site of which, the medium of film, and all modern arts, emerges. Nevertheless, these holes (full of erotic excess, anxiety, and paranoia, perhaps paradigmatically expressed in cinema in the black abysses around which David Lynch's films circulate) will now also be the site—in complicated tension with the emergence of art—of the emergence of modern types of sovereign fantasy figures such as the Godfather. These modern sovereign fantasy figures—such as Hitler (a would-be painter)—always come in complex tension with the question of the emergence of art, and it might be that the opposite is true as well, that modern art always comes accompanied by the possibility that such figures might emerge.

In this sense, the dismantling of sacred logic is far from having been completed in the modern, "godless" age (an age that might mistakenly think that it has left ancient sacrifice behind), and we can say that traces of sacrificial sovereigns now appear in the cracks of modernity, in the places where the holes/stains left open by the flight of the gods (to use a Hölderlinian term) remain inscribed as a negative and horrifying shining at the heart of a modernity that has been unable to emerge as an organization of life that has figured out how to live with the traditional gods' absence, that is, how to live without sacred sacrificial logic.

This resort to sacrificial logic at the heart of "godless" modernity seems to have been necessitated by the fact that the Medium, that in which humanity must ground itself in order to connect to its origin and resource, to that which makes it what it is, continues to call it, even as the connection to it has been blocked by the flight of the gods (those who still allowed the Medium to have some sort of presence), and a genuine new relation to the call of the Medium that will ground humanity in a new way has not yet fully emerged. Can there be a reconnection with the source and power of the Medium, thus a true way of presencing the Medium as an excessive, ungraspable, inappropriable "blinding light," outside of the logic of sacrifice? This might be the main question around which the project of modern art (an art that in this sense aims to be neither sacred—i.e., framing the Medium through a logic of domination—nor profane—i.e., trying to repress the very mystery of the Medium in its ungraspability) revolves.

Another way of asking this question would be: Can there be a way for humanity, by means of the dimension of the poetic, or art, to be appropriated to its essence (appropriated to the inappropriable), thus to its "own" medium, that which makes it what it is, and thus come to belong to itself, and to feel at home, and to overcome its tragedy? For tragedy is, I suggested, what characterizes the age of the twilight of the gods, that transitional moment (in many ways extending, though to very different degrees and in many different modalities, from the Greeks to our own day) from the age of sacrifice to that of (still to come?) the Image, where the sacred/sacrificial home is no longer available even as the emergence of a new home (home being that which is grounded in the blindly shining presencing of the medium) is blocked. Christianity, at the center of which is Christ—simultaneously a paradigmatic figure of sacrifice and a paradigmatic name for an Image (as emphasized by Saint Paul and Saint Augustine)—might be said to occupy the precise center of the tragic age to which we still partially belong, maintaining sacrifice and Image in a powerful equilibrium. A stronger connection to our medium seems to have characterized the various ages of the gods (thus Christianity included), or of sacrifice, even at the price of being partially grounded in a fantasy of domination, a fantasy that—by definition, since it is unreal—had to collapse, yet still seemed to inscribe in itself a more powerful connection to our truth, thus to our appropriation to our essence/medium.

America, as a place that repeats the Greek democratic and tragic moment, as well as the place that radicalizes the modern moment of the demise of Christian Europe and the opening of the call for another space, seems to be an essential site for working out this question of the possibility of a post-tragic humanity implicated with the question of the emergence of a new type of image, a new type of communication with the medium of our existence, one liberated from sacrifice. Both the tragic nature of America and the possibility of its overcoming in the direction of the discovery of a new kind of image at the heart of a new kind of place of human habitation are at the heart of Coppola's cinema.

The tragic side of America—its failure to develop a form of modernity (or of something beyond modernity, if we understand modernity as the age of the death of the gods that has not yet risen up to a new relation to the medium of our existence) that truly reaches beyond sacrifice, and is thus caught between the moment of a sacrifice (yet without the gods who give sacrifice meaning) and that of the image, comes into full view for Coppola in the historical stretch that provides the focus of his investigation in the first two *Godfather* movies and in *Apocalypse Now*: the span between the triumphal end of the Second World War (which seemed to signify the full emergence into historical dominance of the American solution with its irreversible modernity) and the disaster of the Vietnam War. Through this disaster, what came into sharper view was the presence of American modernity's heretofore unacknowledged shadowy side, the stain that indicated the nonachievement of a fully "modern" solution to the question we have called that of the medium, the stain from whose direction (precisely because the stain can no longer be sublimated/appropriated through a sacrificial mechanism) there erupts a tragically violent, bloody force. It is perhaps around the Vietnam War as bringing into full visibility the American tragedy—the unconscious attachment to a violent force in a tragic age caught between sacrifice and another world that has not yet arrived,[12] emerging at the spot of the failure of American democratic modernity's full emergence—that fundamental aspects of this tragedy, the various horrors associated with the history of slavery in America as well as America's treatment of indigenous Americans, came into sharper view as well.

For Coppola, I suggest, film is the American art par excellence through which the American tension between sacrifice and image is expressed—a tension, perhaps, that comes into particularly clear view in the American cinema of the 1970s—as well as the art, and here we can possibly distinguish it from Greek tragedy (a distinction made possible by the Christian highlighting of the question of the image—a highlighting containing the seeds to go beyond Christianity itself, which still partially belongs to a logic of sacrifice—that nonetheless has not fully seen its tension with the logic of sacrifice and tried to harmonize them), that strives to liberate the image from the shadow of sacrifice and as such to become the poetic ground (in the sense of that which connects to the origin, now understood as medium) of a modern democratic life beyond tragedy.

Image and Law

A crucial additional element in our opening scene needs to be mentioned before we can move on to the scene that follows, an element essential to any attempt to think the question of the inscription of the limit of the world (a limit we have called the medium, i.e., that which is "outside" the world precisely to the degree that the world opens through it), an inscription around which the modern question of art will come to revolve in a new way, I argue. This element is the Law. When the undertaker asks the Godfather to kill those who hurt his daughter, the Godfather answers that he cannot do that since they didn't kill her, and at the end of the scene he tells Tom Hagen (Robert Duvall), his lawyer,[13] "We are not murderers, in spite of what this undertaker says." The limit of the world (figured in the transformation from stain to Godfather) always comes as a Law, *the* Law, and the Law is always essentially, first, that which demands a correct recognition of the nature of the

Law, its true form (you shall have no other God), and second, deriving from this first requirement, that which demands a fundamental distinction, the distinguishing between a justified activation of the limit (understood as the limit between an actual human existence and its medium[14]) and unjustified activation, the latter forbidden, strictly speaking, as such. At the very heart of what the Law forbids, thus at the very heart of an unjustified activation of the limit, lies the forbidding of murder (the Godfather is in a way forbidden by the Law from killing the daughter's attackers, or he forbids this in the name of the Law: This would be an unjustified crossing of the limit that would count as murder).

What would count as a justified activation of the limit? One that serves as a site for the true presencing of the medium, thus as the site for allowing the medium to show itself as medium, to shine in its own light, thus as what is responsible for the world's opening and is thus the origin of human life, in the light of which (by the correct showing of which) human life thus needs to be guided. The Law as Law of the medium comes to shine in and through the justified activation of the limit.

But it is, of course, a question of the way the Law—which always makes its voice heard, even if in a distorted manner—is understood. We can say that in a sacrificial regime, for which the Godfather to a degree stands, the Law (of the limit) is understood, first, as that which separates life from death (terms very vaguely understood, according to a distinction between actual reality and its lack, both terms remaining themselves unclear), and then as that which can be represented by an agent, the agent of sacrifice (i.e., within the sacrificial regime, the one in charge of the limit's correct and just activation) who, as the agent through whose action the presencing of the Medium/ origin-of-the-world is effected, is seen as entitled to bring about, thus to control and possess (or to act in the name of an entity seen as controlling and possessing), the elimination or annihilation (the turning into nothing) of an actuality so that the power beyond actuality will come to show itself as that in the light of which life should be guided (this will be the Law of the paterfamilias in its ancient sacrificial form[15]). Any annihilation not in the service of this purpose is considered a murder. The moment or ritual of sacrifice itself, we can say, is that event where the presencing of the medium is understood as happening, or at least as being sought, a moment of a mysterious shining of the light that is supposed to orient all existence.

Within the context of our movie the Godfather behaves as the agent of a sacrificial Law, standing for an entire consistent regime he sees himself as responsible for (hence the dignity, and to a degree the awe associated with his figure), whereas his son Michael will not be the agent acting in the name of the Law, be it even a new Law or a new understanding of the Law but—since he no longer fully belongs to a sacrificial framework as his father does, nor does he belong to a new legal framework—will become a tragic figure and a murderer. The murderer (in Michael's case, literally, the murderer of the family, thus the one who lives the tragedy of the destruction of the paterfamilias logic, as we will elaborate) is either one who crosses the limit without being guided by a medium at all, or one caught in the tragedy of no longer having a consistent medium which she or he is to adhere to, or caught among several interpretations of the medium, several Laws.

If the image, as I have been arguing, is to be understood as a paradigmatic site for the inscription of the medium (most fundamentally as the arrival of a strange stain), it will also always be a site where the question of the Law (which is always the Law of the medium, that which answers a demand that seems to come from the direction of the medium, the demand—demand here standing for a power in excess of the will—to adhere to the medium's truth) and of the manner of understanding it is opened and reopened. It is of course no accident that the Second Commandment—preceding even the (Sixth) Commandment not to murder—thus the one following the First Commandment to recognize the true nature of God (i.e., the Medium writ large) immediately jumps to the question of the creation of images, in this context forbidding it. We will not here wade too far into this complex question, but we can say, first, that this iconoclastic commandment forbids the creation of images precisely to the degree that the image is the Medium's place of inscription, though, from the biblical point of view, in the wrong way, missing the true nature of God (i.e., of the Medium understood in a monotheistic context), and, second, that the attempt—initially of Christian iconophilia, and then, more radically, of modern art, art from the early Renaissance to our own day—to allow the creation of images to occupy a central or originary place in human life is grounded in the insight that in images the Medium (the origin) can come to show itself in an essential aspect of its truth. The image will no longer be forbidden as distorting the true showing of the Medium but, to the contrary, will be invested with the desire to find a site (a desire whose source is the question of desire itself) for a fundamental occurrence of such showing, which is to exceed the showing and understanding of images (but, as a consequence, also of the true nature of the Law, that is, of the demands of the Medium) held by previous regimes.

There cannot be a true Law—a Law grounded in the very demand of the Medium, a demand that needs to display itself in the realm opened by the Medium, namely, in the world—without leaving an essential place for the shining of an image as an immanent dimension to the Law: So goes the hidden assumption of modern iconophilia, yet such shining cannot be understood as being in the service of an agent of sacrifice. As site of the Law it will now be a question of distinguishing the true image (where the Medium is seen as inscribed in its truth) from the false one (thus distinguishing, for example, in the Bible, between the burning bush out of which the voice of God speaks and images that are false showings of the gods, such as the Golden Calf), and of forbidding false images, now counted among them the sacrificial fire (with which *Apocalypse Now* begins and ends, framing its tragedy with the becoming consumed by a sacrificial, even murderous, fire, from which it distances itself by transforming it into another kind of image).

The Law without the shine of the image—that is, without the appearance of that which is more-than appearance, the medium-of-appearance—is to a degree a not fully satisfying Law, that is, it is a Law not fully grounded in the "fire" of our Being or in the coming to be inscribed in, thus the revelation of, the medium in one of its essential aspects, that of the shine, the appearance of the "nothing" that is an empty power to appear. Such Law that seems partially unsatisfying and groundless is the Law culminating in post-Christian secular modernity, a Law that (starting perhaps with the Protestant Reformation and its attendant iconoclasm) desired to disconnect itself from the still sacrificial aspect of Christianity or at least Roman Catholicism (separation of church and state), but did so at the price of becoming detached from an essential dimension involved in the demand of the Medium and to which the fiery sacrificial regime, and to a degree Christian Catholicism as a partial continuation of this regime, still held a stronger connection, the dimension of the revelation of the Medium's shine as such, thus of an essential dimension of the source of Law. A Law without a connection to the revelation of the source of Law in its shine (or what we earlier called its passion, the passive receptivity of the gift of the Medium), thus to the Medium in its power as origin of appearance (rather than the Medium seen only in its aspect of forbidding, the aspect that is at the heart of formal Law), remains in a way empty, ungrounded, and thus disconnected from true Justice. Thus, as we may recall, when the question of Law was first mentioned in our scene, it was when the father (coming to beseech the Godfather to kill those who hurt his daughter) says that for Justice one must go to Don Corleone. The regular, formal Law, the Law of the modern legal state, failed to give him satisfaction, having meted out an inadequate punishment to the offenders, leaving the father, in his words, standing in the courtroom like a fool.

Thus it is as if the figure of the Godfather—who, we saw, appeared out of the stain, out of the inscription of the medium, as simultaneously a figure for the inscription as well as a phantasmic attempt to take it over and cover it up—is brought into the scene as the one through whom Justice, the grounding of the Law in the shining revelation of the Medium, can appear (in the historical context when such grounded Law is no longer available, and there is only the Law of the modern state that, by disconnecting itself from Christianity and its sacrifice, has also disconnected itself from the passionate shining of the Medium). Such appearance of Justice, though, is of course a regressive one, tied to the attempt to restore a pre-tragic, premodern sacrificial regime at the center of which is the figure of the paterfamilias. If the Godfather thus indeed stands as a sovereign figure within a sacrificial regime, this indicates, as we have started seeing, that at the heart of the sacrificial regime (a sacrificial regime making a return into groundless modernity) is to be found the question of Justice, the grounding of the Law in the true "appearance" of the Medium.

Cutting Beauty

As the opening scene comes to its end, this appearance is shown to essentially revolve around yet another dimension with which the sacrificial figure of the Godfather is intimately related, a dimension that—brought in at the very end of the scene and thus in a way shown to be the crux around which its whole logic revolves—is fundamental to his role as paterfamilias-guardian-of-the-Law and is, at the same time, at the source of his undoing and with him of the entire logic of the sacrificial regime, as well as being at the source of the promise of a new modality of the inscription of the Medium, beyond sacrifice: This is the dimension of beauty, and its accompanying questions, passion, desire, sensibility, and by extension, the dimension of the work of art.

Thus, immediately after the Godfather Vito Corleone articulates his position as agent of Law in the context of what we called a sacrificial regime, telling his lawyer that they are not murderers, he lifts his lapel to smell the red rose on it, a gesture indicating the relation of his figure as paterfamilias to the question of passion, desire, love, sensibility, and beauty. These are, to repeat, essential aspects of who he is and of his role as sacrificial paterfamilias, even as they mark his limits and the exposure at the source of his fall, the way the stain (as inscription of the medium) has not been fully converted into the sacred figure (not having been fully taken over by the sacrificial agent) and erupts as his undoing. This tension at the heart of the question of the sacrificial Godfather—a tension inscribed in the question of beauty, a tension around the question of art, which thus makes its initial, still very implicit, appearance in the movie at the very end of our scene—between the dimension of beauty as something essential and internal to his position as paterfamilias and of beauty as that which becomes the seed of his (and the whole sacrificial logic's) undoing, is expressed in what immediately follows the smelling of the rose: the cinematic cut, which will lead us to the next scene.

What is the cinematic cut? It is the most fundamental inscription of the cinematic medium as such in the diegetic world, or in the content, of the film, as its interruption. The cut is the purest "showing" and activation of the medium in its most essential aspect, which we have called exposure to the "off," that pure openness, beyond any given direction or aim, that which is nothing, beyond any content as such, since it is not content but is the medium through which any content can come to show. The cut is thus the interruption of content by the medium as pure openness without any direction or predetermination, and it activates the most essential aspect of this openness, which is the possibility of pure discontinuity. This is the case since, the cut being completely open and beyond any content, there is no specific content we are legitimated in expecting from what the medium will give us next. There is no continuity implied in the medium as medium of pure openness/exposure to the off (or what we also called the poetic medium as the messenger of the Medium writ large). Thus, any scene can follow any scene once the cut is introduced. The cut, in this sense, is the ultimate stain, the becoming-present of the medium (that nothing that is beyond any content) as interruption of content and continuity.

If the cut immediately follows the activation of the question of beauty by means of the rose (itself a flower that has been cut), it does so because beauty has to essentially be thought in relation to the question of the cut. Beauty is the shining emanating from the cut, understood as the coming to be inscribed of the medium in the world of appearance (of content) as its interruption. That which we call beautiful is that out of which (as in the cut rose) radiates the nothing of the medium that is always most fundamentally inscribed as a cut (or stain), making the appearance through which it radiates an appearance beyond any regular appearance (thus cut off in a way from the continuity of appearance, standing apart from it[16]), since it is an appearance out of which the origin of appearance, the medium (or more precisely specific poetic medium as well as the Medium writ large) of all appearances, itself strangely "appears." This appearance beyond and apart from appearance is the heart of what we call an image.

If, as we said, the Law is always first and foremost the Law of the medium, that through which the medium "utters" its demand (a demand indicating we must adhere to something beyond our will)—which is first of all to correctly recognize the medium and guide one's life through the correct relation to that in which life is grounded, the medium of life—then at the origin of Law there has to be a moment of beauty, the shining or radiation of the medium. The Law always has to shine at the moment of its reception (which is the moment of passivity to it, or the passion of the medium), as the shining face of Moses coming down from the mountain to bring the Law so paradigmatically indicates, a Mosaic shine that of course needs to be differentiated from the fetishistic shine of the Golden Calf (itself to be destroyed by fire, thus by another shine). This shining of the Law at its origin is that around which the true image comes to circulate.

This cut of the Law, appearing in its foundational moment as beauty or image, is what is gestured toward by the ending of the opening scene we have been following, concluding with the rose in its relation to the cut. This conclusion indicates that the Godfather as the spokesman for the Law is not only one in whom is inscribed the power over life and death, thus the possession of the limit between being (an actuality) and nothing (the medium), and the decision about the correct activation of the Law (to be distinguished from murder); he is also one who has to be a site essentially related to beauty, thus to the shining of the cut. Yet precisely this relation to beauty, the shining place of the cut that the Godfather as holder of the Law must inscribe in his figure, is where the seed lies that will lead to the undermining of his power and the demise of the logic for which he is the sovereign figure. Already inscribed in the cut marking the end of the movie's first scene are the failure of the Godfather's Law, his death, the death of his firstborn son (the most important figure of the continuity of power in the logic of a sacrificial regime), and the descent of the realm he stands for into the murderous domain it will become by the movie's end.

What is the reason for this failure? The fact that while the very essence of the Godfather as sacrificial sovereign with a power over life and death is to take over the stain/cut, thus possess the event of the medium's inscription, the medium is by definition that which cannot be possessed but can only be passively received. Our capacity to possess anything, thus any content, depends on our being open to content, thus on our living in the light of the medium that is at the source of our having content to begin with, of our having a world, but that cannot as such itself be content and thus cannot be possessed. The medium inscribed in the stain, the cut, as well as in the shining moment of beauty, is the inappropriable. To encounter the medium through the shining sites of its inscription is thus to suffer a dispossession.

This moment of dispossession, which is also a receptive moment, that is, a moment indicating the passive, unwilled, and unwillable reception of the medium, is also the moment when the two sides of the Law are heard:[17] On the one hand, the Law says, "You are forbidden from possessing the medium" (which in fact means you cannot possess it, since it is not possessable), "and if you try to possess it, this will cost you your life, since its force of inappropriability will mark the site of your dissolution."[18] On the other hand, the Law says, "You must receive, thus are passively subject to, the medium, to this 'nothing' that opens you to the world and allows you access to any worldly content. You must, in other words, receive the Law in passion." The Law is thus simultaneously a site of prohibition and the site of forced passionate reception, and passion, we can say, is first and foremost the expression of passivity to the medium. Passion is being forced to become open to, to receive as the reception of a gift (a paradoxical gift—that which by definition arrives beyond what one can will—which one *has* to receive), the medium as that which gives us the world and that as such is always more than anything in the world. Thus this more—the more of the "nothing" that is the medium in excess over anything in the world—is most fundamentally what is heard in the Law of passion, another word for which can be "desire," especially as developed in the discourse of psychoanalysis. Desire is first and foremost the desire of the more (the nothing) of the medium.[19]

The demise of the Godfather and of the logic of sacrifice of which he is a sovereign representative is thus inscribed in the cut—which is also a cut to the power of the Godfather—as the appearance of the Law as the inappropriable.[20] Yet this demise is also the result of a tension internal to the logic of the Law itself (thus, even beyond the incompatibility of the will, namely, the power to possess, and the Law) between what we can call the No of forbidding and the Yes of passionate reception. For the Law that forbids (forbidding, first of all, the possession of the inappropriable medium) is itself subject to an even higher Law (as we also saw in the transition between the two Laws that marked Lincoln's process of initiation), that of passionate receptivity, or the Law of desire, which starts to be inscribed in our scene with the smelling of the beautiful rose.[21] It is in the inability of the Law of forbidding to recognize a greater power than it, an even higher Law, the Law of desire, that also lie the seeds of the destruction of the paterfamilias.

Though traditionally desire has often been regarded as being in tension with the Law, and in fact as that which the Law must discipline, it has less often been seen that desire itself also expresses a higher aspect of the Law, inscribed in the cut of the medium, an aspect of the Law that is beyond the No of the Law, beyond forbidding. Deeper than, beyond the, No lies the Yes of passion.[22] It is in many ways this Yes that most powerfully shines in and as the moment of beauty, a moment that the Law of forbidding erroneously tries to dominate rather than expose itself to it.

It is the opening of this tension between the two Laws (of forbidding and desire) around the moment beauty and the suffering of the cut that announces the transition to, and becomes the very question animating, the scene following the cut, the subject of which is the most paradigmatic cultural ritual revolving around the relation of Law and Desire: the wedding.

Law and Desire, or the New Marriage

Let us move on, then, to the wedding scene, in many ways *The Godfather*'s central scene (and perhaps one of the most densely orchestrated and significant scenes in the history of American movies), in which all the forces leading to the tragedy (i.e., to that limit of the logic of sacrifice, a limit that has not yet been fully traversed in the direction of a new logic where the image will fully take on a new role) gather. We can say that the traditional bride (an essential site of the shining of beauty) is one of the paradigmatic figures of sacrifice, of that moment when the inscription of the limit (the medium) is allowed to shine—yet in such a way that the shining needs to come under the power of a sacrificial agent who possesses it, establishing himself as Law (in the sense of an original forbidding, forbidding all but one from possessing the moment of the beautiful shine). The traditional bride is supposed to serve as the site where desire is introduced at the moment of its shine into the domain of the husband as paterfamilias, who is seen as thus having the bride/shine in his possession and thus coming to dominate the limit and resolve the tension between the No of the Law and the Yes of desire.

In many ways, the liberation of the bride from sacrificial logic, making her a bride who comes to shine in a new light—a bride who is no longer part of a sacred marriage dominated by the paterfamilias but a member of a marriage that desires to be conceived in a new way, as the realm of a passionate sharing of a Yes beyond forbidding—is one of the most essential figures for the birth of the modern image in excess of the capturing of the limit within a sacrificial logic. This is true especially of film (at least from Jean Vigo's *L'Atalante* onward), haunted as it is by the figure of a bride who needs to exit a marriage in order to return to a new kind of marriage. This insight is most likely at the core of Stanley Cavell's celebrated concept of the Hollywood comedy of remarriage, which we can now understand as marriage moving from the realm of sacrifice to that of the image (a new image for which "Hollywood" stands), bringing with it the arrival of a new Law, a paradigmatic name for whose activation will be the arrival in "America." America, from this perspective, can be seen as the promise of a new configuration of Law and desire, now understood as the attempt to think in a new way the Law's two sides, its No and its Yes, that were hitherto deformed through making the shine that which needs to come under the possession, be it of the sacrificial dominating Will or even of the Law of forbidding.

It is in the cut, then—which opens the question of the becoming-inscribed of the Law both in and as the figure of the Godfather, yet also in excess of the figure of the Godfather, to the degree that the cut (both in its aspect of standing for the Law's absolute No of possession of the medium and in its aspect as the shining of the Yes in beauty) is a cut to or of his power—that plants the seeds of the opening of the question of marriage in the scene that follows the film's opening, as well as of the tragedy of the marriage (thus its exiting the realm of sacrifice but not yet finding a satisfactory new site[23]), and with it the transition into tragedy of the entire sacrificial realm whose ritualistic center the marriage is, and of the Godfather himself, the sovereign center of this realm.

This position of simultaneously being inside the sacrificial realm of the Godfather, thus belonging to his Law, and outside it, witness to his exposure to an excess over his Law that lies at the root of his undoing, is also expressed in the way we are positioned as viewers vis-à-vis the wedding in the opening of the scene. Thus, as we transition to the scene following the cut, we get a long shot of people passing through some sort of gate and, in the distant background, a group of people dancing in a garden. The screen is almost precisely cut in two, via a wall: On one side of the separating wall are the people inside the wedding party, occupying what we soon learn is the compound of the Godfather's family, and on the other side of the wall, outside the compound, from where the people enter the gate to pass through it, are mainly empty cars, though the area will soon be filled with FBI agents, representatives of the Law of the state.

Even before treating the two sides of the wall, we can say that the wall itself now functions as the inscription or embodiment of the cut, as it were, in the diegetic world. The wall thus repeats the place of the inscription of the medium occupied in the opening scene by the stain and the editing cut, even as the wall starts giving the cut, which is most fundamentally the inscription of the emptiness of the medium, substantial content that defends against it. In this sense the wall is a paradigmatic worldly mechanism established at the place of the empty cut, at the limit of the world (qua inscription of the medium that by definition is outside the world, as we saw, being that which opens the world), functioning simultaneously in a number of ways,

American Tragedy Between Sacred Sacrifice and Democratic Image 131

of which I will mention several: From one point of view, the wall marks the limit of the realm of the Godfather, signaling an excess beyond it indicating, in the manner of a cut to which sovereign power is exposed, the demise of the Godfather's power, and even the reaching of the limit of the whole sacrificial regime. It is because the wall signals the limit of the sacrificial regime, the exhaustion of a specific logic of responding to the demand uttered from the direction of the medium inscribed in the cut, that the other side of the wall will be one dominated by another logic (that is, another way of trying to respond to the cut and open to the Law of the medium), the logic organizing the Law of the modern state, most specifically of the United States of America. From the point of view of the realm of the Godfather and his family compound, what the wall signifies is that at the place of the cut and exposure a defensive mechanism is instituted that tries to eliminate the power of the cut, take control of it, and thus eliminate the threat of the outside. (In this sense, the wall marking the territory and the sacred marriage taking place within it have an interrelated function.)

From our own point of view, as spectators, positioned as we are neither fully inside nor fully outside the family compound, the wall functions as a cutting split between two realms, now to be divided between the sacrificial realm of the family—dominated by the sovereign figure of the paterfamilias at the moment of trying to assert himself through the family's central ritual, the wedding—and the realm beyond the limit, one that can no longer be appropriated to the paterfamilias, already marking the tragic demise of his realm, a beyond the limit soon to be associated with the Law of the state. By thus suffering the split, most fundamentally a split in the manner of the Law's becoming-present, the question awakened in us is "Where do we belong?," which is always the question "To what Law (i.e., demand uttered from the direction of the inscription of the medium) should we be appropriated?" Should we be appropriated to the sacrificial Law of the paterfamilias dominating the family compound or to that which is beyond it, soon to be occupied by the representatives of the Law of the state?

To a degree, we probably desire to be appropriated to the Law of the paterfamilias, to come to belong to the family, and for several reasons, just two of which I will mention: first, because we already began being appropriated to it in the first scene, through the way the paterfamilias appeared out of, and as a response to, the anxious stain, suturing it; second, because the sphere of the paterfamilias to which we open is a festive realm, its festivity revolving around the ritual of the wedding, the task of which is to find a place for desire, thus for the Yes side of the Law's inscription. This means that making a place for desire is at the heart of the sacrificial realm and of the family compound. As such, it is to the presence of this desire that we respond and would like to belong (and thus to find a place for our desire), while the realm beyond the compound's wall is, at first, empty, then populated by forbidding agents of the state's Law, lacking any element of desire. This outside realm, a realm without desire, is under the sway, as will be increasingly emphasized in the *Godfather* trilogy, of empty, thus ungrounded, Law (a Law that cannot really display, or even connect to, the medium that is nevertheless its hidden source), and capital, that is, the force of groundless exchange (i.e., exchange without the cutting Law of the medium to guide it).

Nevertheless, our place as cinematic spectators is that of viewers positioned at an indeterminate point neither inside nor outside the compound. Unable to be appropriated to the realm of the family, we remain in suspense between the two Laws. For though the barring wall forbids us from being appropriated to the sacrificial family,[24] this does not mean that it consigns us to being appropriated to the undesirable modern legal realm of the state. As we will soon see, though, our being positioned by the camera in this specific way will open for us a way to transcend this dilemma between the sacrificial inside and the desireless outside, through its making us what we will call witnesses of the modern image.

An important aspect of the question of desire here has to do with the fact that the modern realm of desireless state Law is something that feels its own lack and desires something beyond itself, desires desire we might say, from the sacrificial realm. This desire of desire from the point of view of one living in the realm that has been disconnected from it is embodied in the figure of the WASP Kay (Diane Keaton), who, in spite of the criminal aspect of the family (as well as, of course, because of it, crime itself inscribing in a distorted way the call of that which is beyond the modern Law of the state, a Law to which she cannot fully feel herself appropriated), is in love with Michael Corleone and will marry him in an obviously doomed attempt to be appropriated to the sacrificial family and the desire it allows for. Kay and Michael, neither inside nor outside (the wall), desiring each other, the outside wanting in, the inside wanting out (Michael himself wanting to leave the family and its compound, since at the heart of the sacrificial regime there is an uncontainable excess, inscribed in the stain and the cut), are also of course in this sense stand-ins for our own position vis-à-vis this scene, and the movie in general, as if, occupying as we do the legal state, we would like to be appropriated to the sacred realm of the Godfather and the family, to become one of its children, so to speak; yet, at the same time, as witnesses to the excess of the cinematic screen, we are looking for an outside beyond the compound, beyond the wall, that nevertheless does not coincide with the state and its empty Law.

Being able to fully belong neither to the sacrificial family as we might partially desire, nor to the modern legal realm, the very nature of a possible community (thus of a joint manner of appropriation to a Law) that we are offered seems to have been split into two, and in a perhaps irreconcilable way. This split is embodied most fundamentally, in the diegetic world of the film, in the tragic figure of Michael Corleone, the war hero who will neither belong nor not belong to the Corleone family and who will end up a murderous figure destroying the very logic of the sacred family—a destruction culminating in the killing of his own brother in *Godfather II*. The split also seems to echo (with a modern difference we need to inquire into) the Greek tragic split familiar to us from *Antigone*, which Hegel has famously articulated as involving an irreconcilable tension between the Law of the family (which Antigone, wanting to bury her brother, follows) and the Law of the polis or of the state (represented by King Creon, who forbids her from burying the treasonous brother).

The artistic image as place of the medium's inscription, thus as site for the demand of the Law—in its threshold moment in the tragic age (in many ways leading from the Greeks to our own era) when the logic of sacrifice has reached a limit and was thus exposed to the possibility of a new Law—is always structured around the drama of conflicting laws, thus of conflicting ways the demand of the medium/Law comes to be heard. This drama can be, for example, between the Law of sacrifice and another Law, or between two Laws that aim to be different solutions to the new Law beyond sacrifice; or it can dramatize what we have described as the most fundamental demand of the Law that comes in dual form, and is thus in a way involved a mysterious conflict internal to the Law itself, that between the forbidding No and the Yes of desire to which we must expose ourselves, an inappropriable gift that, paradoxically, we must welcome.

We have seen that sacred Law was an attempt at a solution to this double demand of the Law, a solution involving the appropriation of the inappropriable Law, even as one allowed desire in (because it became possessable). This solution centered in many ways on the relation between the sovereign paterfamilias and that most fundamental ritual where desire and Law, in dramatic tension with each other, reached a stable place: the marriage ceremony, in which desire was appropriated into the sacrificial Law. Thus, when the Law of sacrifice reaches its limit and is exposed to something beyond it, its solution of appropriating the inappropriable no longer deemed faithful to the true demand of the Law, it is the crisis of marriage—as in the case of Antigone, for whom, as she says, the tomb becomes the bridal chamber—that often becomes the focal point around which the entire possibility of a new Law revolves.

At the heart of the question of the image in the tragic age, that inscription of the medium that starts to shine at the limit of the logic of sacrifice from the Greeks to our own time, is the question of the crisis, or dissolution, of marriage (as sacred sacrificial ceremony) and indeed the search for a new sort of marriage, a new union of Law and Desire, or of the two sides of the Law, a One from the Heart, as Coppola will indicate in a later movie of that title, the subject of which is the dissolution of marriage and the attempt at its reconstitution. In many ways the ultimate image searched for by the post-sacred world is itself a "marriage," that which displays the unified-yet-still-in-tension double demand of the Law, its No and its Yes, its forbidding and its desire shining as beauty.[25] Until there is no new successful image, no new "marriage" as a shining of the medium fully exceeding the logic of sacrifice, and going beyond the tragic moment of the clash of Laws that remain irreconcilable, there is no post-sacred democratic life guided by the new Law/inscription of the medium.[26]

Being neither inside the walled area, occupying the family compound and appropriated to the sacrificial realm and its paterfamilias, nor outside it, appropriated to the desireless Law of the State, we become, we cinema watchers, what we can call witnesses to the problem of the image as it arises at the place of the tragic split between two Laws. The possibility implicitly splitting us as a result and on which our very fate depends is the following: Will we experience this birth of the image (in the sense of that which emerges out of the demise of sacrifice—its exposure to that which exceeds it—at the site of the inscription of the medium) as a birth of tragedy, doomed, like the protagonists of the diegetic world of the film, to be destroyed by the irreconcilability of the two Laws, of the two sides of the wall, or will we, through becoming initiated, qua film watchers, to the work of film itself in excess of its diegetic content, and to the possibilities film offers as a manner of inscribing the medium, as a manner of creating images, manage to become initiated into something beyond tragedy, and through it to a true democracy, in the sense of a way of life no longer grounded in the hierarchical logic of sacrality but by a new Law, a new "marriage" of the No and the Yes, forbidding and desire, and thus truly arrive in "America"? These, I suggest, are the central questions implicitly guiding Coppola's development of the question of film. In this sense, the arrival in "America" (a subject treated at length in *Godfather II*, most explicitly in the Ellis Island episode) is understood as a project that needs to be grounded in a true initiation into film, that is, a new initiation into images qua the inscription of the medium in which a new Law is implied, the Law of film, or the Law transmitted through film.

The Law of the Camera

But how exactly are we to be initiated into this new Law? From where will its command be uttered? In taking a look at our position vis-à-vis this scene, occupying an elevated and indeterminate perspective and split by the wall, we have momentarily omitted a crucial element, the relation to which is at the heart of Coppola's cinematic attempt to exceed the tragic split. This element is the camera. What is the camera within the context of the cinematic medium, and, more specifically, how does Coppola interpret and develop its function here?

We can start understanding these issues by examining the way the question of the camera is raised at the opening of the scene at hand, indeed opens out of the transition into this scene, a transition, we saw, that consisted of a cut. What is the relation between the cut with which the opening scene ends and the camera's strange, indeterminate, and elevated perspective through which our vision opens to the second scene? It indicates that the view given us by the camera is a view opening out of a cut; that is, it signifies a new understanding of appearance, of the appearance of the world, or of the world's content, as that which is grounded in (thus receives itself from) the cut.

We have seen that the cut is what we have called the inscription of the medium, medium understood as the nothing (actual) beyond, or more-than, any actual content.[27] To be grounded in the cut means that the camera inscribes in itself the quality of the medium/nothing/more-than-(actuality) to be a completely unpredictable, ungrounded openness. The camera is thus the agent of an openness, the appearance out of which (and to appear in this new understanding is to open in relation to this unpredictable openness of the medium) is itself always unpredictable, not grounded in any given order or readymade organization.

This pure unpredictable openness of which the camera is the agent, an openness that means there is no readymade, predictable perspective out of which, or in relation to which, that which appears appears, or opens, is expressed in the unpredictable, unrecognizable, indeed unmappable perspective that the camera as agent of the medium comes to occupy at the opening of our scene. We have seen that the medium, inscribed in the cut, is what can be understood as the inappropriable, an inappropriability that, on the one hand, we can never possess, never own, and in this sense never fully identify (with), remaining as it does essentially external to us, to our capacity for (self-)recognition; and, on the other hand, this inappropriability is what is completely intimate to us, indeed what is most intimate to us, to the degree that it is that which makes us who we are, that through the mediation of which we open to the world, or open to the appearance of the world's content. In this sense we can say that the medium, and its secret agent the camera, is simultaneously external and alien to us, at the same time as it is most intimate to us. The camera, to use Lacan's famous and crucial term, is thus extimate to us, something we can also understand as an intimate alien.

This extimacy of the camera, its bringing us to occupy a position of intimate alienation, is essentially tied to its being a technological, nonhuman, or inhuman, apparatus, an opening of vision that is not the vision of a human eye. The technological here is that which occupies the threshold between the medium/the dimension of more-than—which is, by definition, nonhuman to the degree that it is that which calls the human into being in the first place, makes the human the openness that it is—and the human eye. In this sense technology is always uncannily extimate to us, inscribing in itself the excessive more-than of the medium, which is always more than any particular capacity we can be the proprietors of, and thus also more than any specific human organ we can activate. The technological camera inscribes in itself an excess over the human eye, an excess out of which the world opens for the human and to which the human is passively exposed and can never appropriate. As such the camera occupies an inappropriable blind spot at the heart of the eye. The technological camera is a more-than the human eye that is intimate to the human eye, a nonhuman, or inhuman, technological extimacy.

The human eye can never coincide with the camera eye, for the latter emerges via technological means out of the blind spot or stain of the eyes, the eyes' inner cut we can say, the inscription of the medium qua nothing "in" the eye. This extimate inappropriability of the camera that can never coincide with the human eye is at the heart of an essential dimension of any exposure to a view given us by a camera (and especially like the one we are currently examining where the camera, due to its strange and unmappable position, becomes increasingly noticeable or hauntingly present as a camera), and this dimension is the simultaneity of watching the view given us by the camera at the same time as feeling that we are being watched by something, most concretely the camera itself, which is inaccessible to us. This inextricability of watching and being watched, activated by any camera view but becoming more noticeable in a view like the one under discussion, has to do with the view that we receive emerging out of that which we can never grasp and being an inhuman more-than us intimate to us, occupying a fundamental blind spot at the heart of the opening of our vision. To be watched is, in this context, to be exposed to this inhuman intimacy inhabiting our constitutive blindness, where that which we cannot appropriate is actually that which gives us the gift of watching, or of being open to a world (or open to things through the medium/world).

In this sense, we can see how the camera potentially inscribes in its very activity the two sides of the Law we have been discussing, the No and the Yes. For the camera, being the embodiment of the inappropriable with which we can never coincide, in a way forbids us from possessing it, forbids us from trying to coincide with its excessive view (in the sense of a view opened through the inscription of the excess that is the medium) and become the masters of that which appears, as if we were the agents upon that which appears depends.[28] At the same time it is the camera through which we receive, unwillingly (in the sense of receiving from that which is beyond our control and appropriation), the gift of the world, which paradoxically forces us to say Yes to the world to which we passively (i.e., unwillingly and beyond our control) and passionately open. To be initiated into the Law of film, or the Law of which the art of film is a singular messenger, would then be to learn to open up to the camera in a correct manner, that is, to learn to accept its No and to passionately welcome its Yes, and thus allow it to become the site or medium of a new "marriage" of Law and desire, or of the two sides of the Law.

From our description of the logic of sacrifice as having at its heart the idea of an all-appropriating agent, a God Father, it is easy to see that the principle of the sacrificial paterfamilias is in tension with the Law of the camera as extimate uncanny alien. In this sense the Godfather either would be one who cannot allow the camera at all or would be one who tries to appropriate it and become master of the camera, have his eye coincide with its eye, have the family (the general name for that realm over which he is the sovereign) and the camera's eye fuse in a union without remainder. And indeed this is precisely what happens as our scene progresses.

A world, the modern world (and it is a question how far back we want it to stretch, be it to the first age of tragedy with its bringing together of a constitutive blindness and a disastrous infection of the home; the birth of the unprecedented biblical God who announces for the first time the simultaneity of an uncanny foreign gaze that cannot be located anywhere specific together with a new experience of exile/alienation; the post-medieval age; or technological modernity), is a world where the sacrificial paterfamilias starts to be exposed to the uncanny gaze that the camera embodies, a gaze the experience of which had to start disturbing even before the actual invention of the camera, an experience that is undoubtedly at the source of the camera's coming into being in the first place. This modern exposure of the paterfamilias as a center of a whole sacred logic to the camera's eye, an exposure through which a technological, extimate, alien principle enters (yet is rejected as a destructive threat rather than becoming the vehicle for a new relation to the world), becomes the heart of a world whose inner blindness, the cut of the medium, irrupts into the open, and with it the experience of a horrifying (since it destroys the very structure of the world of sacrifice) alien gaze by which one is watched, to which one is helplessly exposed. Such exposed world announced by the demise of the paterfamilias without being yet replaced with a new relation to the alien principle is a paranoid world in the sense that the pure exposure to the inappropriable is phantasmically transformed into the feeling that an all-dominating agent inaccessible to us is controlling that to which we are exposed. This exposed paranoid world is also a world of surveillance, where the experience of being "watched" by the alien gaze is transformed into the doomed attempt to try to avoid the gaze to which one is exposed, avoid being cut, by becoming invisible and watching others from this invisibility, thus trying to "heal" the cut by both extricating oneself from the visible and putting the visible under one's power. This modern paranoid world of surveillance is a cold, disenchanted world where the passion and desire that the sacrificial regime enabled (even as it tried to possess them) have become, as a result of the demise of the sacred regime, the index of the horrifying exposure to the foreign, extimate gaze, and have as a result been subject to repression. This cold, loveless, desireless, disenchanted world of surveillance and paranoia, opening in relation to the question of the camera, is brilliantly explored by Coppola in the film he made in between the first two *Godfather* films, *The Conversation*, thus pointing more precisely to the question of the medium—and more specifically the way it is inscribed in the camera and modern technologies of recording in general—that stands at the background of the world he explores in the *Godfather* trilogy, with its tensions between sacred logic and the modern one.

We can see how the principle of the sacrificial realm, and of the Godfather who is at its center, enters into an intense, rivalrous relation with the modern principle of the extimate camera by following the trajectory of the question of the camera in the wedding scene under discussion. Thus, after giving us the unmappable and uncanny view of the screen divided by the wall, there is another cut, and the camera, as if actualizing the power of the cut (qua inscription of the medium as more-than, in excess of, anything actual), moves inside the compound, ignoring the separating wall (an actuality), as it were, and crossing it easily. The camera, we can say, thus functions in excess of the wall, overcoming its power of separation, and this overcoming is the first thing it does in the scene, as if declaring its independence from the wall and from the power of the paterfamilias it embodies. It reactivates the cut that the wall (in its attempt to dominate the helpless exposure to excess) tried to defend against, to block, and thus announces itself as a principle in excess of the principle of the wall, an extimate technology—a technology whose task is to bring the cut into the world in a new way, as a source of a new opening of appearance (an appearance opening, passionately, out of the inappropriable medium inscribed in the cut)—against another technology (that of the wall) whose function was to eliminate, and defend against, the cut.[29]

We have seen that the name for the unwilling reception (in the sense of the relation to an inappropriable one must receive—like a reluctant prophet addressed by God—and cannot intentionally decide upon) of the more-than, the excess that is the medium, activated by the camera here is passion, or desire, and in this sense what enters the family compound, symbolically announcing the compound's dissolution, is the principle of excessive desire, thus desire beyond the capacity to possess it that the paterfamilias stood for, and whose culmination is supposed to be the sacred marriage. The entrance of the camera qua activator of the passionate cut thus already announces the sacred marriage's dissolution or failure, and it is thus that the scene will end with the paterfamilias dancing with the bride, the beautiful shining of his supposed power to possess desire, only to experience the cut leading to the next scene, the nightmare of the cut horse's head, which we will come to. The entrance of the camera to the compound thus announces the intrusion of the passionate cut and the subsequent opening of the nightmare, nightmare being the moment when the excess of the image (a blind eye to which one is exposed and by which one is "watched") emerges beyond the power of the sacrificial rite.

These relations among the movement of the inhuman camera, the cut, unconscious desire (in the sense of desire—the inscription in us of the more-than that is the medium—beyond our capacity to possess it, taking us over unwillingly) and the opening of the nightmare (out of the dissolution of a sacred marriage) are perhaps most powerfully worked out by Coppola in his *Dracula*, both in its entirety but especially in the great scene (Dracula himself being interpreted in that movie as the embodiment of the desirous, nightmarish aspect of the camera movement that destroys any principle of the sovereign paterfamilias, and that in fact emerges out of the sovereign's self-destructive collapse following the death of his sacred bride at the beginning of the movie) where the traditional marriage between Mina (Winona Ryder) and Jonathan (Keanu Reeves) is intercut with (thus undercut by) Lucy's (Sadie Frost) uncontrollable erotic nightmare. It is in the nightmare that the camera most strikingly "shows itself," moving in a completely unpredictable, and indeed inhuman way, an extimate alien gaze (and Dracula, in his various inhuman—at times animalistic, at times monstrous, at times invisible—manifestations, is the camera's inhuman and passionate power) embodying the uncontrollable force of Eros beyond any limitations (actuality), even those of life and death.

But let us continue with our scene. Having entered the family compound as an unseen (since inscribing the non-actual more-than of the Medium) alien intruder, the camera now makes its first appearance in the diegetic world of the film, bringing into an explicit thematization the question of its activity. For, immediately upon our first view of the compound from inside, we see a photographer approaching, ostensibly to take the family photograph. What is the purpose of this photograph? To establish a harmony between the family as a whole, thus as a unit fully under the dominion of the Godfather, and the gaze of the camera, whose implicit threat to his very principle the Godfather seemingly wants to possess and dominate, to bring under his own power the alien gaze that challenges it, in the manner of the wedding where the excessive power of Eros is supposed to be brought under the power of the sacrificial father.[30] The successful marriage and the united-family photograph thus depend upon each other, as it were. It is as if there cannot fully be a successful marriage without the successful, unified photograph. And indeed this is the case, since this family photo ends up not being taken—on the explicit order of the Godfather, who cannot accept the photo being taken without the missing son Michael, who has not yet appeared. Michael is thus already announced as a principle foreign to the family, out of the unified picture, so to speak, inscribing in himself a disuniting, threatening excess that will prove to be at the source of the family's destruction, if not as a capitalistic enterprise, then as a unified sacred realm. Indeed, we can say, the out-of-the-picture Michael comes to be associated here with the uncontrollable excess of the invisible camera and with its cutting power, which the Godfather cannot control. It is no accident, then, that the ultimate moment when Michael assumes his power and acts in excess of all the family's precedents—a moment that is also the preparation for his most blatant act in the first *Godfather* as destroyer of his own family, that of killing Connie's husband, putting a final nail in the coffin of the sacred marriage with which the movie started—occurs via one of the most celebrated sequences of intercut editing in the history of film, that of the slaughter during the baptism of Connie's child, where the cut itself, as it were, is the principle allowing for the destruction of all the heads of the crime families, and with them the old world, at the center of which was the sacred Godfather.

This taking over of the world of the film via the intercutting power has, in a way, three main functions. First, it announces that the realm of the Godfather, the world of the family compound with which we started, a realm that has been infiltrated, at first discretely, by the alien, extimate power of the camera, has finally been completely undone by the principle of the camera as emissary of the cut. The protective walls have fallen.

Second, once the principle of the camera has taken over, when the wall between the two Laws (that of the compound and that of the state) has fallen, we find ourselves caught among three main options, as the movie will slowly develop them, culminating in the intercut scene of the final slaughter. One is the emergence of the abovementioned cold and paranoid world of surveillance (which seems to be the one characterizing the modern state, its agents in this wedding scene basically occupying the position of spying and surveillance), where the cutting power of the camera is phantasmically appropriated in a specific way we briefly discussed earlier. Second, let us call it the "Michael way," where the cutting power of the camera is phantasmically appropriated in yet another way, through the embrace of the cut as an unbridled power of destruction (this receives an even more striking actualization in the great intercutting scene at the end of *Apocalypse Now*, where the destructive activity becomes literally that of cutting). This means that one does not limit one's relation to the cut through attempting to suture its power, as in the paranoid-surveillance-defensive effort, but, in addition (and it is always in addition, the paranoid position, so well represented by Michael too, being the ground position vis-à-vis the cut, or vis-à-vis the cut when it is perceived from the perspective of the paternal regime, as a threat to its unifying logic), one tries to take possession of the cut, thus desiring to be the godlike master of the medium, of which the cut is the inscription, through the extraordinary unleashing of destructive violence, as if becoming oneself the cutting power. As a result it is as if one is not exposed to the cut oneself, or helpless vis-à-vis it. This is, of course, another fantasy, and as Michael's case (as well as, most famously, Norman Bates's case) proves, the more one tries to become the master of the cut/camera, the more helpless and exposed one becomes, until one finally is completely abandoned and destitute (or has one's head cut, as in Kurtz's case).

The third option vis-à-vis the cut is that of the movie director, which itself might actually straddle all three options. But starting with the third we haven't mentioned yet, we can call it the poetic way, or the way of the Image. In the way of the image it is a question neither of suturing the cut nor of trying to possess it through becoming an agent of a cutting destruction, but of becoming the one who is able to activate the cut as an inscription of the medium through which a new realm of appearance is now to open. The director/image maker does not want to own the cut, nor to suture it, but wants to welcome it and show it as the very heart of the medium, thus allowing the nothing that is the medium—in relation to which we are passive and that is the more-than we can only receive passionately or as unwilled desire—to become "present" in such a way that it becomes that through which our eyes are now made to open, welcoming the gift (in the sense of that which we receive but cannot will) of the world. It is by thus learning to welcome the cut in a new way that one finally comes to adhere to the Law of the camera, or the Law of film.

Needless to say, the director is not fully liberated from either the paranoia and feeling of surveillance/the need to occupy the position of an unseen spy activated by the camera, nor is she or he innocent of a certain destructive desire, the need to wound and introduce cuts into the body of the visible by way of trying to master one's helpless exposure to the camera. Nevertheless, the artist/image maker is the one who also manages, at least partially, to transcend these two tendencies and welcome the cut as the passion of the world, the passion through which the world is now given to us according to a new Law. The artist is the one who, paradoxically, can activate passion, or at least become the site of the welcoming (like the welcoming of the arriving immigrants to America at the beginning of *Godfather II*) of that which one cannot will, traditionally called being inspired by the Muse. Thus the famous intercutting slaughter scene at the end of *The Godfather*, the moment when Michael turns into a full-on destructive murderer by assuming the fantasy of being the master of the cut (already announcing the destruction in Vietnam that will start being unleashed in America a couple of decades after these scenes take place and that will occupy *Apocalypse Now*), is simultaneously the moment when the director achieves perhaps the most breathtaking activation of the medium, unconsciously instilling in us a new passion and a new Law, as well as making us members of a new community, a community gathered around the image understood as the inscription of the cut, rather than a community of the church, or at least of one aspect of the church that continues the sacrificial logic. For the church, we might recall, occupies the center of this famous intercutting scene, a center that is precisely decentralized (losing its power as the head of the world) and interrupted through the intercut, or comes to be dismantled, much like the sacrificial family compound, by the arrival of the extimate camera. But we will return to this intercut scene and consider it a bit more.

For now, let us examine the moment when the filmmaker is educated away, as it were, from being the master of the camera—in the manner of the Godfather trying to stage and control the cutting image—and becomes the recipient of a new Law, the Law of the camera that he doesn't (since he can't) will. For this education, we can say, is the subject of *The Godfather*'s second major scene—immediately following the wedding that was disrupted, in a way, by the intrusion of the extimate camera—the scene whose subject is the encounter of the world of the godfather/family compound with that of the filmmaker: the Hollywood producer suffering the nightmare of the cut horse's head.

As we first encounter the filmmaker in this celebrated section, we do so in the Hollywood studio where he is making a film. When the Godfather's messenger, the carrier of his Law, the lawyer Tom Hagen enters the studio, we see the filmmaker basking in the glow of the camera flashes surrounding him. The intrusion of the cameras here, at first, does not seem to serve the function of introducing the disruptive cut but rather in the way that this cut, as the lightning power of the medium, the medium/the shining more-than/the nothing as that which opens visibility, seems to be easily appropriated by the filmmaker, who is seemingly the exceptional figure capable of becoming the master of the source of the shine, the one capable of withstanding its disruptive power and coming to dominate it. In this sense, the filmmaker is still like the Godfather, a centralizing agent who can come to possess the power of the shine and through this possession become the source of illumination of the world around him. This parallelism to the Godfather is also emphasized by the way the young starlet next to him embraces the filmmaker, the paterfamilias of the movie world, in a way very similar to Connie's embrace of the Godfather during the dance that ends the first scene, just before they are cut (though of course, in the case of the filmmaker, with an erotic excess, indicating that the realm he occupies is no longer the paternal realm where desire is possessed by sacrificial Law but a realm opening in relation to the excess of the Image upon the demise of sacred Law[31]).

American Tragedy Between Sacred Sacrifice and Democratic Image 145

The education of the filmmaker into the Law of the camera, an education whose beginning is the subject of this second scene of *The Godfather*, thus has to pass through exposing him out of, away from, the fantasy of being the origin of the shine qua master of the illuminating power of the medium in his ability to withstand and dominate the flashing of the camera. This exposure away from the mastery of the shine is at the heart of the cut horse's head scene, undoubtedly one of the most celebrated moments of cutting in the history of film.

In general, the dominated horse is one of the great figures from mythical sacred history, and shining is an example of the exceptional power of a sacred leader. This shining of the leader of sacrifice is of course also famously displayed in the cutting up of animals. Our scene merges both resonances of the logic of sacrifice only to expose them to a cut that exceeds them, transforming sacrificial shine into a different kind of image, one where the camera asserts itself and announces itself as inscribing the birth of an image that exceeds the realm of sacrificial possession and domination, one that expresses an uncontrollable dispossession. Thus, as the Godfather sends his "message" in the form of putting the cut horse's head in the filmmaker's bed (a cutting that, from the point of view of the Godfather's sacrificial logic, announces that he has the power to possess the sacred object of the rival paterfamilias—the prized horse of the filmmaker—thus submitting the rival to his own sacrificial dominating force), it is the film cut that exposes the screaming director, waking into a nightmare, into something beyond the controlled and controlling logic of the sacrificial paterfamilias, into an uncontrollable opening. Each scream and cut—not unlike the camera movement we have dealt with, which exposes the beseeching father at the film's opening into an expanse in principle without measure, since it is grounded no longer in any order but in the pure indeterminate openness of the off-screen—exposes the "castrated" filmmaker (castration being in this case the deprivation of the paterfamilias from the sacred object of potency, thus of control over abyssal exposure) to the ungrounding power of the off, the indeterminate more-than any actuality. The modality of this indeterminate opening, in relation to which the filmmaker is helpless and which inscribes a dimension, that of the off, beyond that of the ordered world guiding sacrifice, is that of the nightmare. The nightmare, that strange infliction with a horror of an uncontrolled opening by which one is dispossessed, here striking the sleeping filmmaker in his royal bed, is perhaps the originary inscription by an image emerging out of the threshold between a world of sacrifice and a groundless world exposing beyond sacrifice, an image that often takes the form of a beheading, thus of the elimination of a controlling center of power. In this sense we can say tragedy—that "genre" that emerges between a world of sacrifice and a liberation into an image beyond sacrifice that is yet to come—always revolves first and foremost around a nightmare, a nightmare out of which, and this is tragic, it finds no way out, failing to fully open into the dimension we have been calling the image. The education of the filmmaker, as we have been calling it, an education into the image and the Law of the camera or film, into the power of the cut qua the inscription of the inappropriable medium, is, then, an education that has to initially undergo the suffering of a nightmare.

Arriving in America

The ultimate task of such an education will be to find a way out of the nightmare, and thus also beyond the paranoid attempt to suture the nightmare through surveillance or to take possession of the nightmare by trying to become the master of a cut in the manner of unleashing destructive violence through the infliction of cuts. Finding a way out of the nightmare will most essentially consist in coming to open, via the camera, to the Law of the Yes as that whose significance is the welcoming of that which arrives beyond one's will as an alien surprise, the welcoming of that which has no assigned place in an order, the medium, and of its messenger, the camera, that which can activate the medium, or the world, as pure, surprising, and indeterminate openness. Most essentially, perhaps, a way out of the nightmare will be found by the welcoming of those who inscribe in themselves that unpredictable excess of the world, its indeterminate openness, thus those who, as inscriptions of the pure openness of the world-as-such, have no determined place: the immigrants. It is the ultimate task of the camera qua activator of the passion of the medium to be that which opens a cutting through the power of which the immigrants can be welcomed, a cutting welcoming whose aspirational name is "America."

Needless to say, perhaps, such an education beyond the nightmare will not be achieved within the diegetic content of *The Godfather*,[32] which ends with the unleashing of the ultimate attempt to become the master of the cut in a scene of pure bloodshed and slaughter. However, such an education is nevertheless glimpsed in the relations that open between this violent intercutting scene occurring toward the end of *The Godfather*—simultaneously announcing the unleashing of Michael as a murderous power of willful cutting in excess of the sacred law of the Godfather as well as announcing a dizzying and liberated filmmaking that fully embraces the power of the cut as that around which a community of film watchers assembles in excess of the sacred community of the church—and the opening of *The Godfather II*, tracing as it does the transition from a Sicily dominated by religious and sacrificial Law to the arrival in America of the absolutely displaced, thus placeless and powerless, alien immigrants, at the center of which is the mute and poetic child Vito, before his transformation into the sacrificial Godfather.

Thus, in the early part of *The Godfather II*, after Vito manages to escape Sicily, we get a view from an indeterminate place of New York Harbor and the Statue of Liberty, an indeterminate view that, like the unmappable camera view overlooking the compound at *The Godfather*'s opening that we have analyzed, marks the fact that also here at stake is the question of the camera, whose view from nowhere determinate is to be the source of a new understanding of the question of appearance, one grounded in the cut and in the indeterminate-in-advance openness it inscribes. It is this new understanding of appearance into which the immigrants, following the cutting that opens the view of the Statue of Liberty, are now welcomed. It is as if the Statue of Liberty, an image for the image, comes to be inscribed by the power of unprecedented openness announced by the camera in its relation to the cut (and in this sense, the Statue of Liberty functions as a rival inscription of the stain of the medium to that of the Godfather, an inscription that does not aim to take possession of the stain as a power over it), a power that the immigrants on the ship are now welcomed into and out of which they will start watching. To watch like the immigrants do, and as we are called to do, is to watch out of the position or, more accurately, exposition to that groundless openness announced by the camera whose view is marked by the pure openness of the cut.

Thus, as we first receive the immigrants after having been exposed to the placeless view of the camera as it opens to (inscribes itself in, and as) the Statue of Liberty, we see the child Vito among numerous immigrants. Suddenly it is as if the child is responding to a mysterious call, the call by the camera and its cut, a cut inscribing the medium as openness (to suffer or receive a call is to be exposed to the dimension of the medium as what one cannot will). As he receives the call, the child stands up and starts to walk, and his walk is accompanied by the movement of the camera itself, indicating the association between the camera and its openness—an openness that is a new principle of movement in excess of any specific and determined direction, an open, free movement—and the immigrant child, who as if can start to walk freely because he has been called by, exposed to, the movie camera.

As the moving immigrant child—having become the one paradigmatically inscribed by the camera and its indeterminate freedom—starts to walk, looking in the direction of the off-screen (an off whose figure/image here is the Statue of Liberty), thus of the indeterminate openness of the medium/the more-than-actuality, all the other immigrants start to rise, themselves looking toward the off, as if called by the moving child who is himself (standing as the avatar for the director) the inscriber of the call of the camera, transmitting its freedom to the immigrants. One by one we see them standing up and mysteriously looking toward the off as the camera passes them by, as if the camera's principle of openness inscribes itself in the very activity of their watching. They have been seen by the blindness of the camera transmitted to them by the child, a freeing blindness, a principle of haunting extimacy, out of which they now start to watch, not in paranoia or in a desire to cut into the body of the visible, but in a mysterious hope. It is the blind eye of the camera, that is, an openness of visibility grounded in the nothing that is the medium (an openness that in this sense cannot be the expression of any willful transcendent gaze) that welcomes them into America, an America that from this perspective is the name for a new openness of the visible, one not grounded in any transcendent gaze and as such one that does not see them as this or that determinate person with this or that function or place in a hierarchy but as free immigrants, those who inhabit the new openness that America aims to name and that the camera as America's messenger aims to activate.

Yet this look of freedom activated at first by the child Vito qua inscriber of the camera's blind freedom and its indeterminate open movement is soon to be extinguished, as they are all heralded into the imprisoning enclosure of Ellis Island and its cold, paranoid state bureaucracy. It is this movement of freedom upon the sight of the Statue of Liberty, and the subsequent move to the enclosing Ellis Island facility, that already determines the fate of Vito as one who, though inscribed by America and its messenger the movie camera as a new principle of openness, will be haunted by a traumatic imprisoning imposed by the cold and paranoid state, a hostile principle that he will unfortunately counter not by becoming a poetic liberator of the principle of America by inscribing it, for example, in the potentiality of the camera (a poetic potentiality clearly inscribed in him—a fact emphasized by his moving singing as he finally breaks his muteness upon seeing the Statue of Liberty from the open window of his Ellis Island prison cell—a singing to which Coppola as poetic activator of the camera is seemingly the heir[33]) but through the founding of a family compound reinstating a logic of sacrality from which America had been the potentiality of liberation, as if trying to return to a sacred Sicily and eliminate his father's death, thus regressing to a regime of which America was supposed to free one.

Being tempted by the lure of the sacred family compound governed by the paterfamilias, but desiring to open oneself to the freedom of the camera grounded in the cut—this is the trajectory that the cinema of Coppola (as the inscriber of the call of America and as the attempt to welcome the immigrants, to establish an immigrant eye or an immigrant mode of watching beyond the prison of state paranoia) and perhaps the life of Coppola (who has established a California winery—a domain clearly reminiscent of the Godfather's compound, a winery operated by him as a paterfamilias businessman—which he finally sold in order to make what he surely aims to be his last major movie event, *Megalopolis*, transforming capital—by insisting on spending his own money, through an almost sacrificial expenditure—into poetic excess) call on us to open to.

FOUR

An American Revolution

SOFIA COPPOLA'S *LOST IN TRANSLATION*
AND *MARIE ANTOINETTE*

"The Americans are asking for help with their revolution," declares the French minister of finance to the young King Louis XVI, hoping he will approve sending them assistance, in a subtly essential scene in Sofia Coppola's *Marie Antoinette*. While this demand for help is presented as part of the film's narration of scenes from the Versailles of Marie and Louis, it should also be read, as this chapter aims to show, as a meta-poetic statement about *Marie Antoinette*, as well as about Coppola's cinematic project in general. It is the medium of film, I claim, and Coppola's singular way of inflecting it and activating its potentials, that is called upon to help with a historical project, the American Revolution, which has not yet been completed, is still happening, as it were, and is still in need of help.

To understand Coppola's mediumistic-historical procedure, we need to grasp both her singular approach to the medium of film and the unique way she envisions the relations between this medium and the question of history. I will try to at least begin developing these issues by looking at two of her early paradigmatic films: *Lost in Translation*, her second feature and the film in which she hit upon a new method of creating images, and thus a new systematic way of understanding and activating potentialities inherent in the cinematic medium;[1] and *Marie Antoinette*, her following film, through which she forged a connection between this new method and an approach to history, resulting in a new kind of historical film.

Cinema Between Sleep and Waking

The screen is dark. Then we open our eyes to the first image: a scantily dressed woman lying on a bed, her back turned to us, the space she faces (is it a window, or perhaps the limit of a stage?) fully covered with curtains. The upper part of her body, shoulders and head, as well as her feet are cut off from our view, off-screen. Who is this woman? Is she sleeping; is she possibly in the middle of a dream? Is she awake, perhaps engaged in deep contemplation? Is she an actress, preparing for the curtain to rise and face her audience? Is someone already watching her, perhaps even someone whom she is in the middle of seducing? And if she is seducing someone, is she aware that she is doing so, or is the power of her seduction increased precisely because of her unawareness and even ignorance of the watcher(s) because of her *withdrawal* (possibly a withdrawal called sleep, or perhaps a withdrawal into her own solitary realm) into a somewhere that is inaccessible, to them and possibly to her as well? Needless to say, we cannot know.

Here highlighted, through the cutting of the woman on her bed, is the decontextualizing cut—a cut characterizing any screen image, as we kept seeing in all our discussions, insofar as the limits of the screen interrupt the continuity of a world that we would otherwise have expected to be privy to due to the passive nature of the camera, which simply records what is in front if it rather than create its image, the way a painting, for example, does. I have been steadily trying to show that in many ways the mystery of the cinematic cut—a cut that opens a decontextualized zone of a new kind, one that is (because it is the site of a recorded projection) *part* of a world assumed to continue beyond it, yet at the same time *apart* from a world from which it has been separated by the abyss of the cut[2]—lies at the center of investigation of many, perhaps all, of the major cinematic auteurs.

This is the case since, in the terms of several of our previous chapters, the cut, as interruption of any positive content, is the activation of what we have referred to as the medium, which is not any content itself but rather the potentiality for any content whatsoever, and as such is no-thing. The cut introduces and brings to the fore the no-thing of the medium. As we have also seen, our most primordial relation to the medium is passivity, insofar as the medium is always in excess of our will. While we *can* will positive or actual things, we cannot will that which is *withdrawn* from all actual things, the no-thing that enables our opening to all things to begin with. Thus, when the cut is activated in key moments of essential cinematic works, what is at stake in the cut is the way these works understand the nature of the medium itself, as well as the manner in which we encounter our passivity toward the medium, the precise way in which we are cut by it. I would thus even argue that the singular way a specific cinematic auteur interprets the cut—and thus interprets what precisely is at stake in the decontextualizing cutting out of the surface of the screen from the continuity of a world—is what defines what we might understand as their poetic *signature*, the singular way that, for them, the essence of cinema lies.

We might thus say, for example, that Alfred Hitchcock is the director who fully developed the cut as that at the heart of which lies suspense, that is, the suspension of any determination through cutting a surface out of a world, a cutting that leaves the world hanging over a vertiginous abyss. This cinematic abyss is nothing but the emptiness, the no-thingness, of the medium into which one falls, that is, in relation to which one experiences a fundamental passivity. The guiding question regarding such an abyss, which will define the existential choice regarding the space of the screen, would be whether one should try, futilely, to dominate it, paradoxically being swallowed by it completely, as in *Vertigo*, or whether one should transform one's relation to it (most importantly, through love) and be rescued from the fall, as in *North by Northwest*. Or, as in the case of Robert Bresson, the cut becomes a crack through which a spiritual realm enters the (actual, determined) world, a world whose mode of determination is conceived as a prison. It is the crack opened by the cut that allows for escape from such a suffocating world through courage, love, or death.

If Coppola is indeed an auteur—someone activating in a new and essential way the potentialities of the medium of film—what would be her singular discovery (what Deleuze would have perhaps called her cinematic Idea) regarding the relations between the decontextualized screen and the cut, a discovery that informs every aspect of her films, from the way they are edited, to their camera movements, to their being saturated by affects in excess of action, to her directing of the actors and her use of music? I suggest that her discovery lies in her understanding of the realm of the screen and its relation to the cut via the relations between sleep and waking. Sleep would thus be understood as a cut that occurs at the heart of waking life (inasmuch as the major cinematic cuts in her films introduce the dimension of sleep—and that of Eros in its association with sleep), and as such is interpreted as that in which the experience of our relation to what we have called the medium, understood in an existential way, is at stake.[3]

To withdraw into sleep is thus to suffer (i.e., experience a passivity to) a cut(ting out of the actual world), to become exposed to that which is withdrawn from any content, which is at the same time what makes the opening to any content possible, the medium. An Image, as a consequence, would be understood as that which brings into appearance the way waking life is haunted by the medium as the suffering of falling asleep. At the heart of visibility is a fatigue, our exposure to an invisibility (the medium in excess of any content) that overwhelms us to the degree that we cannot will or determine it but are passively exposed to it. The Image is that wherein the dimension of a primordial fatigue makes its claim heard and comes into visibility, paradoxically since it is the "visibility" of the fatiguing medium's invisible dimension.

Hence one of the primordial sites, perhaps the most primordial for her cinema (though there are a few others), which Coppola associates with the space of the screen in its exposure to the cut, as the opening image already indicates, is the bed. I can think of no other director for whom the bed is so essential cinematically. The bed—rectangular in shape very much like the screen, and into which one resorts as one withdraws from the world of daily life—is a paradigmatic site of the image, insofar as it is where waking life and sleeping, opening to worldly content and the cutting withdrawal into the enigmatic medium, come into contact most essentially. In many ways the essence of Coppola's cinema can be summed up thus: The bed's place at the heart of our life has never been correctly understood, and thus we have never correctly understood the relation of our waking life to the sleepy withdrawal from it (and as such have also never correctly understood Eros either, nor, very significantly, the feminine). It will be the task of the cinematic screen (and of the being of America) to serve as a site through which the bed's existential significance comes into view and informs our life.

In the opening image, we saw, it is a cut *woman* who lies in bed, withdrawn from us and possibly from her waking self. This brings us to the question of the relations between the issues we have started exploring and the question of the "feminine." By no means confined to women in Coppola's films, the "feminine," as she explores it, is an essential moment of the human's relation to that excess we have called the fatiguing medium (which through, or by the means of which, we open to the world). This cutting moment is nevertheless more central perhaps to the being of women, a moment with which their lives seem to be more engaged. This seems to be the case for historical reasons but also for more fundamental causes related to the way the medium's excessive dimension is inscribed in the two sexes differently (a difference Coppola hardly ever thematizes—except perhaps in *The Virgin Suicides*[4]—but subtly points to in many ways), an inscription at the heart of what we call Eros.

Eros, that excess in us we cannot will and that we suffer as the cut of an arrow, names, I suggest, the way the human body is inscribed by the emptiness (from any content) of the medium (an emptiness it cannot will, thus in relation to which it is passive) through which it is taken outside itself and is exposed to the world. In this sense the erotic, as inscription of the medium in the human body (what psychoanalysis would come to name, with Jacques Lacan, jouissance) is one of the fundamental dimensions in our life through which we experience the suffering of the medium (i.e., our relation to what we have also referred to as existence[5]) as, first of all, that toward which we are passive or, in the terms of our Spielberg discussion, are passionate. The cutting Eros is a fundamental dimension through which we experience the passion of existence (our medium).

However, the male body's inscription by Eros comes to revolve around a privileged organ as its center, a center of mediumistic inscription called the phallus by psychoanalysis (that discourse privileged to be the first to delineate a dimension in our existence that we can understand as being neither that of meaning, i.e., of the medium insofar as it functions as giving us a world, nor simply that of a body or a content in the world, but the way the first is inscribed in the second as a mysterious excess). This center, because attached to a specific organ and thus being a determined content, seems to imaginatively come to play in our unconscious lives (differently for each of the sexes but nevertheless in both, a point Freud insisted on) the role of a unique, exceptional content (potentially sacred),[6] whose possession (since, unlike the contentless medium that cannot be possessed, an object is precisely what *can* be possessed) will enable the possession of, and thus the power over, the medium. The possession of such a magical object, as a consequence, is seen as that which can also become the means to have power and control over any erotic manifestation (and, perhaps most of all, of women), eliminating as a result the threat of existential passivity, a threat always expressed by Eros. In this sense the phallus can come to serve as a defensive mechanism against (and a phantasmic power over) the passion of existence. It is thus a defense against "femininity," if we understand this term as the name that stands for our passivity to, our passion for, existence, at least insofar as it is experienced via bodily Eros.[7] Though man's relation to the erotic cannot be reduced to the phallus (and is thus characterized as well by a fundamental "femininity," the passivity to the medium inscribed in/as Eros), as Coppola frequently emphasizes (mainly through artistic characters such as the actor in *Lost in Translation*, or Elvis, or even Louis XVI, whose resort to objects serving as avatars for the phallic object—such as swords, or a gun, or even a glass of whiskey[8]—is shown to be very unstable, a defense against another power that overwhelms him), the phallus (qua the inscription of a privileged bodily object by the empty, excessive medium) nevertheless always seems to powerfully haunt men, in the manner of an originary divinity forever uttering its claims.

"Femininity," then, as displayed by the withdrawn, cut woman of our opening image—withdrawn from being a content we can grasp—expresses the passive and passionate relation to the medium at the moment of the cut. As evinced by the image's ambivalence, which our previous analysis started to point to, such passivity and passion involve three fundamental and interrelated aspects. There is sleep (the withdrawal from waking life into the enigma of the empty medium, from which one is to draw one's resources to open to waking life). There is also seduction, which we can define as the communication of, as well as the being addressed by, that withdrawn dimension of excess. This excessive dimension is one that we cannot, strictly speaking, willfully communicate—since only a content or a specific meaning can thus be communicated—nor intentionally be addressed by, for the same reasons. In this sense we can say that seduction is the paradoxical communication of, as well as the being addressed by, the incommunicable withdrawn. Finally, there is artistic performance, or more generally the creation of artistic images. We can define these—a dimension going beyond the communication of the incommunicable associated with seduction, which we can understand to a degree as unconscious—as the paradoxical showing, thus the bringing into visibility, of the dimension of the withdrawn (the medium) *as* withdrawn, a withdrawal at the heart of waking life. If a major dimension of the passivity to the withdrawn medium is, as the opening image shows, the mysterious experience of being watched by no one specific (being "watched" indicating, in this context, the passive exposure to that which opens the world, yet which we can neither control nor see, since a contentless invisibility opens our vision to begin with), then the artistic image can also be understood as the paradoxical ability to bring into appearance this dimension of being watched by no one specific, by the medium as such. The artist, then, is the one who can open to the excessive dimension of sleep, extract its erotic, seductive (qua the communication of the incommunicable withdrawn) resources, and bring about a new type of display, that of the paradoxical showing of the withdrawn, a showing who no one specific watches.

After the "feminine" opening image of *Lost in Translation* brings these aspects together, the opening scene immediately following develops them further, adds new dimensions, and now connects them to the question of the relations between art and the "masculine," examined from the point of view of their *non*alignment (a question doubtless fascinating for the cinema of Coppola, the daughter of a male cinematic artist), through the figure of the actor Bob Harris, one of the film's two protagonists.

As the screen goes blank again after the opening image, thus after suffering a cut introducing the dimension of sleep into the heart of our watching, we hear a plane, followed by a female announcer saying in Japanese and then in English, "Welcome to Tokyo International Airport." Let us read this allegorically, if we understand allegory (derived from *allos*, other to) as the investigation of how the dimension of the medium, that which is other to any content since it is that which any possible content emerges out of, interacts with the dimension of content. From this point of view the blank space and the cut are to be understood as the intrusion into the film's world of the empty dimension we have called the medium, an intrusion, we will soon see, involving the introduction of an excess that brings with it the dimension of sleep, as well as the suffering of a displacement and the arrival at a strange, foreign zone, where one is *lost*. The space of the decontextualized screen will now be allegorically conceived as a foreign land, a place where the coordinates—linguistic, cultural, and so on—that have guided the world and allowed it to be understood as a *coherent continuity* and interconnectedness, have been lost.[9]

Language and Eros

But what exactly *is* this foreignness introduced through the decontextualizing cut, a foreignness most essentially inscribed in the encounter with a foreign language? Or, to ask slightly differently, what is this foreign language the screen as a decontextualized zone confronts us with? Obviously, the film's content, realistically understood, would make the answer seem simple: We are in Tokyo, where Japanese is the predominant language. Yet, if we read the film allegorically, thus in relation to the intrusion of the empty medium through the cut screen, foreignness and the foreign language as it functions herewithin the context of a cinematic work need to be understood differently. Foreignness is first and foremost the intrusion of the dimension of the medium qua that which is *absolutely foreign* to, Other than (*allos*), any content. In fact, we can say that as we are exposed to a foreign language, we first of all experience a *passage through the cut* (which in fact happens to us here, in the blanking of the screen as we arrive in Tokyo), that is, the intrusion of the dimension of the empty medium (which we have also associated with the term "existence") as such, a dimension whose emptiness means precisely that it can never be exhausted by this or that specific content or a specific language that would seemingly fully coincide with it.

The dream of a pre-Babel language, perhaps a *natural* (and sacred) language of humanity,[10] is of course the dream of a congruence between an actual language and the medium as such. However, at the heart of the question of existence as an empty medium is the necessity that there always be a plurality of languages, since no actual configuration can exhaust the purely indeterminate opening that is the medium. From this perspective, to be lost in translation is the fact of having to suffer the passage through the emptiness of the medium as one moves between specific languages, an emptiness or a pure openness that is disorienting and is thus the source of being lost, precisely because, by definition, it determines in advance neither any given meaning or direction nor any set of rules through which meaning is to be brought about. Any meaning or direction as well as any system, such as a specific language, that codifies certain options of making meaning and giving directions always emerges in relation to the empty excess (an excess that of course keeps haunting and is inscribed in each actual language,[11] in different ways) that is withdrawn from all of them, an excess by the direct encounter with which one feels an originary disorientation or lostness.

From this perspective, the cut screen will be that through which one connects to the empty excess of the medium, an excess at the heart of all particular languages and that we can perhaps associate with what Walter Benjamin called a pure language. Such pure language, existence understood as a medium-as-such, exceeds every actual language, allowing us to stay open in excess of the historical and grammatical determinations of these languages. The work of art is what introduces, in our case via the cinematic screen, a cut, overwhelming us, through our exposure to it, by the foreignness of pure language/existence.[12]

Yet, in addition to being exposed upon the cut to the dimension of pure language, we are exposed to a second dimension of foreignness in our scene, and in the movie in general, which has to do not simply with the suffering of the passage through the absolutely foreign (i.e., the cut or the medium) as we transition between specific languages, but also with coming to occupy the foreign land of the screen qua a detached zone upon whose surface the invisible dimension of the pure medium/language (invisible since empty of any content) nevertheless seems to leave enigmatic traces, or paradoxically to show itself through the appearance of strange, enigmatic marks. Such marks or traces (we have previously analyzed one such mark, the shadowy stain in *The Godfather*'s opening scene) count as enigmatic to the degree that, on the one hand, they are withdrawn from clear meaning and comprehensible language yet somehow, on the other hand, still belong to the dimension of meaning, or more precisely to that dimension *through which* various meanings emerge, the dimension of the pure medium (existence).

Being neither meaningful, thus belonging to what we might metaphorically (echoing, in a way, Maurice Blanchot) call the light of day, nor non-meaningful, thus totally devoid of light, belonging to what we might call a total night (or death), these marks instead flicker (like the flickering lights surrounding the enigmatic Japanese signs and writing, welcoming Bob Harris as he arrives in Tokyo) in between full light and total night, withdrawn from clear meaning even as they communicate something to the degree that they display the paradoxical presence of the excessive medium in its withdrawal. Such marks also always come to belong to, or resonate within, a mysterious zone, a twilight zone of Eros and dreams, a zone of sleep, or a zone between total sleep and waking life. Every site, such as the cinematic screen (or the bed), that is cut off from the continuity of the meaningful world unfailingly comes to be inhabited by such enigmatic marks communicating the dimension of the withdrawn medium, and thus also begins to function as a site of Eros and dreams, a site circulating energetically around flickering enigmas.

We have seen that Eros is the enigmatic inscription in the body of the excessive and empty medium-as-such at the moment of the cut, that is, the moment of the passive and passionate exposure to the medium. Thus, every strange enigmatic mark or trace qua "material" or bodily inscription of the cut (enigmatic marks, such as the Japanese characters—at least for those who cannot read them—of *Lost in Translation* or the stain Marie Antoinette's signature leaves on her marriage document) begins to be filled with Eros. Yet the opposite is no less true, for every bodily erotic site, which is every bodily site that is somehow disconnected, cut, from a continuity (for example, the continuity of the body in its organic functions) and begins to be haunted by the excessive and empty withdrawn medium (for example, as with, beyond the bodily sites we most often consider erotic, the many decontextualized body parts, such as feet, nails as they are being painted, eyelashes, etc., that Coppola is so fond of, as was Melanie Klein in her thinking of partial objects), also emits enigmatic marks.

The realm designated the unconscious by psychoanalysis is the twilight realm of Eros and dreams circulating around these enigmatic marks, those emitted from the erotic body, from the site of its cuts, as well as from any body, such as the screen, that begins to function as a cut site inhabited by enigmatic traces, that is, by the paradoxical presences of the absent medium.

To be lost in translation from the perspective of the question of these traces would be to wander in a space between this detached, enigmatic zone of dreams and Eros and the meaningful world of waking life, not knowing how one can be translated into the other or the place of the one with regard to the other. To sum up the question of foreignness, we can say that pure language (or existence-as-such, understood as our medium) and the enigmatic inscriptions it casts as its traces—and around which the unconscious realm of dreams and Eros circulates, or from which this zone receives its communicative energy[13]—are two fundamental dimensions of foreignness to which we are exposed via the work of art. We can also understand the expression "lost in translation" historically. In such case we can say that these dimensions of foreignness (always in the background, of course, of our waking lives) erupted in a particularly powerful manner at the moment when we experienced the loss, the being *cut out*, of a world order, a loss that we have been associating since this book's introduction with the emergence of modernity, following the demise of the order called Christian Europe, a demise we have also been associating with the Nietzschean phrase "the death of God." This modern death of God has spread, through the Europe that has suffered the trauma of this loss, across the entire globe, which in its wake is now modern.

We have also been associating "America" with this modern moment of the death of God, understanding America to be the expression of a call (a call initially heard in a particularly powerful way by displaced Europeans, cut out of the old world and thrown into a strange, decontextualized—for them—new foreign land) to organize human life in a new way, one that takes into account the consequences of the modern crisis, thus of the death of god. We can now understand this crisis to involve, through the cut that is modernity, the introduction of the two dimensions of foreignness mentioned earlier, two dimensions to which we have been powerfully exposed, that of pure language/existence-as-such and that of the enigmatic, unconscious realm of Eros and dreams. It is modern humanity who is lost in translation, exposed to a pure language we cannot understand and that disorients us, and suffering enigmatic inscriptions (the traces of this pure language) that afflict it with excessive Eros (an Eros we can also understand as exceeding the phallic way of determining it, which has to a degree dominated the traditional world) and that haunt it with new dreams. It is "America" that simultaneously names the fullest discovery of this modern lostness in translation experienced by the displaced, those who have been cut out of the older ordered world, and that serves as a call to organize human life so that this lostness, meaning the exposure to the dimensions of foreignness, is not to be erased but is to be grasped as a fundamental dimension of human life, a dimension that has been to a degree covered over by tradition.[14]

As we discussed in this book's Introduction, it is "America"—understood as the call initially heard from the land of decontextualized Europeans, cut out, displaced from their traditions and world order and carrying the death of god with them to the new land where it most fully came into view—that perhaps stands most importantly for the call for such a reorganization of life, a life in which these two dimensions of foreignness and loss are now immanent. However, it may be that the modern discovery of a new double foreignness comes into view most fully, both conceptually and artistically, in the early twentieth century, especially around the moment of the final blow to the old European world order, the First World War. We thus simultaneously have the conceptual emergence, with Walter Benjamin (the most influential theorist of translation), of the term "pure language" (as well as the distinction between language-as-such and the language of men); with Heidegger, of the term "existence" and/as being-in-the-world (both to be understood as what we have been calling the absolutely foreign empty medium); and with Freud, of the unconscious, the realm of Eros and dreams and the enigmatic traces around which they circulate. This moment, of course, is also when cinema emerges as the most important art form of the century, and perhaps most strikingly in the case of American cinema, which has become the site where this major new art comes to haunt the most fundamental modern land of the displaced (fundamental to the degree that its entire being, its constitution, emerges at, and out of, the modern moment of the cut, expressing the death of god that in Europe could still be covered over through traditional ways of life and customs).

Eros and Existence

Let us continue to follow our film and see how all these questions come into focus through the adventure of its two protagonists, displaced Americans (and Americans, as I indicated, are by definition the displaced, cut out from the old world and lost in translation, i.e., exposed to a new foreignness) making their way through the foreign land of the screen. Thus, after the cut marking our landing in Tokyo, we see a man. It is night, his eyes are closed, his head is leaning on the window of a car, a window through which we see, in a blur (thus with nothing determinate and meaningfully visible), against the background of the night's darkness, some lights. He intermittently opens and closes his eyes, clearly (like us movie watchers) in a state of neither full sleep nor complete wakefulness. As he looks out the car window, he sees buildings with numerous illuminated signs, which for most of us (in that most of us are not able to read Japanese) and clearly for him are nothing but a series of enigmatic marks, seemingly wanting to tell us and him something though we have no idea what (since there is no translation provided). As he thus (and we with him) continues his night drive and is exposed to more enigmatic illuminated marks, his eyes constantly closing and opening as he gazes out the window, he lacks any clear sense of the topographical arrangement of his whereabouts (since we mostly get close shots of very restricted areas) and thus has nothing with which to orient himself and hence to be able to understand the world as meaningful. Suddenly he sees something familiar yet strange: It is none other than himself, but he is illuminated and enlarged, occupying a billboard. Shown in profile, he holds a glass filled with some drink, his hand lifted in the direction of his face. On the corner of the billboard is a nice-looking glass bottle containing that same liquid, with more enigmatic inscriptions to be found next to both the bottle and his face. Seeing this strange image, he rubs his eyes in disbelief, as if thinking, "Am I dreaming, or am I awake?," "Who is this? Me?," only to see a large, flashing, enigmatic sign that obviously provides no answers to his questions. Finally, he reaches his destination, a hotel (a transitional space essential to Coppola's cinema, most importantly in her *Somewhere*), where a group of people he obviously does not know greet him in rapid succession, not really making him feel himself to be in a more recognizable setting, a place where he can start to orient himself. His sense of alienated isolation and loss is only increased.

What is happening in this remarkable opening scene? It is a particularly successful cinematic dream sequence precisely because, among several fascinating touches, it does not frame itself as such, as in Hitchcock, for example—nor does it appear as pure surreal strangeness, as in Luis Buñuel or David Lynch—and remains uncannily and indeterminately hovering, lost in translation, between the feeling of a dream and the feeling of reality, dream and wakefulness.[15] There is also a further essential question: What precisely is the relation of this scene to the opening image of the woman on the bed with which we began?

Let us try to start unpacking these questions using what I've called the allegorical method of understanding the way the medium (of film) interacts with (through, among other means, cuts, enigmatic marks, etc.) the content of what we see. As a displaced surface, thus a surface cut off from the world's continuity and exposed to the medium's indeterminate openness, the screen, we can say, is a car, or is itself a moving vehicle through which (via the window) we start opening to the world, a world characterized by its strangeness or foreignness, that is, as displaying itself to us beyond any familiar coordinates and conceptions we might have had in relation to it. Movement itself, though, now needs to be understood differently, as implying the dimension of the pure medium. To truly move, in the way the work of art activates movement, is not to transition between different actual locations in space and time but to undergo a *passage* through the empty medium, becoming exposed (via the displacing cut) to the medium's indeterminate openness, such that anything that appears now seems to do so out of the unpredictability of this openness. Not only have we become strange to ourselves through this displacement; because our eyes are made to undergo a passage through the pure medium, rather than this or that determined frame such as a specific language, that *to which* we now open is itself strange, that is, it is not determined by any readymade coordinates. Thus, a third dimension of foreignness opens here, we might say, a dimension not only of pure language or the empty medium or of enigmatic traces, but the strangeness of anything *to which* we open in the world *with the means* (the mediation) of the empty medium.

In addition to the surface of the screen as a bed into which we withdraw, Coppola returns again and again to an understanding of the screen as a moving vehicle, a vehicle of displacement through which the world reveals itself to us in its strangeness and foreignness.[16] Movement and foreignness are shown to be essentially interrelated. Though films have been interested in the relations between the cinematic screen and the moving vehicle almost from the first film, the Lumière brothers' *Arrival of a Train in La Ciotat* (1896) (or, nearly as early, George Méliès's 1902 *A Voyage to the Moon*), Coppola introduces a dimension that is unique as far as I know, and that indeed connects the screen as vehicle with the screen as bed. The characters looking out of their respective vehicles in her films (the carriages and boat of *Marie Antoinette*, the cars or trains of *Lost in Translation*, etc.) almost never simply observe intently the world outside the vehicle but are constantly in transition between looking outside and withdrawing inside, often due to their falling asleep but sometimes through simple *distraction*,[17] that is, through being pulled by an excess that forces no specific direction or orientation on the part of the gaze. It is as if she understands the specific type of watching that opens with the means of the screen-as-moving-vehicle to be such that it is grounded in an excess, that of the empty withdrawn medium, which starts to weigh on us and impose itself, drawing us away from the world or forcing us to withdraw from it. This excess is nevertheless the condition for opening to the world, the world in its strangeness. A withdrawal from watching (which signals the becoming present of the medium of watching as such), of the sort that happens in sleep or even in distraction (itself always on the border of sleep), is at the heart of a kind of watching: cinematic watching, as one's opening to the strangeness or foreignness of the world, which is a world not determined by any preexisting coordinates.

This strangeness of the world to which one opens in movement, a movement enabled by the passage via the excess of sleep, is one dimension of that foreignness Bob Harris is exposed to when he drives through this new, unrecognizable landscape. Three other aspects, characteristic as well of much of Coppola's cinema, are related to this strangeness: call them the blurry, the atmospheric, and the affective. All three facets have to do with the dislocated screen having become a moving vehicle, via which one undergoes a passage through the empty medium, thus through an open indeterminacy. Hence the blurry, characterizing our first view out of Bob Harris's moving car (and many views taken in by the movie's heroine when she gazes out her hotel window, as well as taken in by Coppola's many heroines when looking out their windows, from Marie Antoinette to Priscilla), marks the fact of the world appearing in relation to distracted looking, that is, looking pulled by an excess that prevents it from having any determinate orientation and thus any capacity to fix things in a precise place, allowing them to come into focus and be bestowed with a recognizable, determined identity.

The atmospheric (and the various additional terms that can be attached to it, such as the enigmatic, the foggy, the moody, etc., all present in one way or another in all of Coppola's films) has to do with the loss of clear, determined meaning and orientation, once the foreign and excessive, empty, and indeterminate dimension of the medium makes its entrance. The "atmosphere," a word originally referring to the vapors and gases surrounding a planet, names the effect of blurring and covering over any determination, thus any clearly grasped contextual configuration in a world experienced as meaningful continuity. A scene becomes atmospheric once a feeling of indeterminacy pervades it, when everything specific in it seems to become covered over by a *displacing namelessness*, an unplaceable excess (the excess of the medium over any determinate content, an excess that cannot be named since only what takes place in the context of the medium can be named, not the medium itself). In this sense we can understand the atmospheric as the paradoxical becoming-present, to sensibility, of the medium.

The dimension of affect names the mode or modality of presence of the empty excessive medium that we also sense through blurry appearance accompanied by atmospheric indeterminacy. Affect, or the being affected, most *noticeably* happens (though it is always in the background, not always noticeably so) at those passive moments, such as the car ride in our scene (or the entire existence of the film's heroine, finding herself at a moment of *suspension* in her life when she doesn't, in her own words, know what she wants to be), when, being deprived of determined and clear action and plannings or projects, one can be said to experience the passivity to, the exposure to, the excessive medium one can never control, will, or grasp, since it is that via or through which any grasping or willing can happen. If Coppola's cinema is a blurry, atmospheric cinema of affect in excess of action, this is because all her protagonists (the entrapped women and paralyzed man of *The Beguiled*, the blocked writer and her retired father of *On the Rocks*, the abandoned adolescents bereft of an orienting familial framework in *The Bling Ring*, etc.) are at the (cinematic) moment of being suspended from, cut out of, their capacity to determine their actions, and thus experience, in anxiety, wonder, boredom, and so on, their passive, nameless exposure to the excessive medium.

The moment of the (cinematic) ride, then, is the moment (which we can also understand as the moment of the Image) when one opens to the strangeness of the appearing world in its blurriness and atmospheric indeterminacy, accompanied by the intrusion of affect in excess of action. This event of movement that is the cinematic ride, the moment of the Image, also or even primarily revolves around the exposure, through the cut, to that strangeness we have called pure language, as well as around the irruption of that twilight realm of Eros and dreams.

All these forms of displacement characterizing the (cinematic) ride, the event of the Image, thus of being lost in translation (understood both as transition between actual systems of meaning and as being in movement) at the threshold between sleep and waking, seem to strike the lost protagonist with two fundamental interrelated questions. The first of these questions, perhaps the two most fundamental questions at the heart of any human individual, we might call existential; it often takes the form, "Who am I?" (a question with its parallel utterance in the words of the woman protagonist, Charlotte, as we soon come to know her: "I don't know what I'm supposed *to be*"[18]). The second question is what we might call the erotic question: "What is my relation to Eros (or desire), that is, to that cutting excess that is inscribed in my body and overwhelms me as a moment of passivity or passion?"

We might understand the relation between these two questions as follows. The "Who?" question articulates our manner of being exposed to what we have called the empty medium. Before we are anything that can be determined, before we can *be* this or that, we are the passive exposure to the medium's indeterminate openness that occupies the heart of our openness to the world. The "Who am I?" question expresses the indeterminate openness characterizing a self before any of its determined actualizations. It is not a question one actively or willingly asks but a question that imposes itself (indicating the overwhelming force of the medium), unwilled, in a moment of lostness and estrangement. One is always surprised and overwhelmed by this question.

And what about the erotic question? We have seen that the existential passivity to the medium also expresses itself in bodily inscriptions we designate as erotic, corporeal sites of mediumistic excess. At such sites the body suffers the cut (the incision by an emptiness) of the medium and becomes filled with Eros and desire, thus with the paradoxical presence of an empty excess over any order and any directionality, an excess by which we are carried outside, beyond, ourselves, at the same time as that through which we feel what is most intimate to us, what lies at the heart of ourselves, that is, the medium/existence.

We have also seen that these erotic sites (which in principle, and not only in the most obvious erotic loci, or erogenous zones, can come to inhabit the organic body, as an alien invasion, anywhere) can be regarded as coming to function within a system of communication of enigmatic marks or traces, a system we have come to call, since Freud, the unconscious. These enigmatic traces, the communicative inscriptions of the empty medium as such, can emerge from the incision of any body (the organic body, the body of a word, a cut-off screen) when it comes to function mediumistically, that is, as belonging to the question of meaning but simultaneously withdrawing from any determinate meaning's grasp. The unconscious is that "system" through which all these meaningless (yet belonging to the communicative medium, or even incorporating it) traces begin to circulate and communicate among themselves. They are sites that become full of Eros rather than of meaning.[19]

Being full of Eros, which passively and passionately dispossesses us yet is empty (since it is mediumistic) of determination, the unconscious can be said to haunt our lives as a question. This question is itself unconscious and structural, in the sense that it is not necessarily an actual, conscious articulation that we have chosen or can will how to respond to but is, rather, the very manner of being of the unconscious, the realm of Eros. This realm, by definition, *is* a question since it haunts us as that which *puts us in question* to the degree that Eros is the cut we cannot control or will. The erotic unconscious forces an open nondetermination upon us: "How am I to live in relation to that erotic excess in me, that bodily inscription of the indeterminate and open medium?" We might even say that being the cutting passion that puts us in question, the erotic question that is the unconscious's very manner of being is always the question of what we have called the "feminine," or the question of the originary "femininity" in us,[20] a question faced differently, to a degree, by the two sexes: Women, and we will soon return to this, may remain (again, not consciously or willingly) more faithful to its originary structure.

Jacques Lacan famously described the unconscious as being structured *like* a language, and we can now understand this "like" as having to do with the being of the unconscious as a system of communication; yet it is an erotic communication of the excessive medium as such, circulating around enigmatic marks, rather than a linguistic system governing meaningful language.[21]

Unpossessable Existence/pure language, striking us with the "Who?" or "Who am I?" question, is thus inextricably interrelated with the ungraspable unconscious, haunting us as an erotic question. Whereas the "Who am I?" question can be said to be the very manner of being of our consciousness qua our indeterminate mediumistic openness to the world, striking us with a passivity, the erotic, "feminine" question, the being incised by a bodily excess (or excess neither body nor meaning but between the two), exposing us to the world while putting in circulation communicative enigmatic marks, is the very manner of being of our unconscious.

It is out of these implicit questions that the uncanny billboard (thus decontextualized screen) image mentioned previously of Bob Harris in profile, elegant and at ease yet also melancholy and contemplative, holding a glass of alcohol as he is surrounded by enigmatic letters, seems to emerge.[22]

Melancholically holding the glass as he does—and we soon learn Harris is an actor visiting Japan to shoot a whiskey commercial—immediately sends us in a certain sense to the heart of the matter, in that the gesture recalls that other melancholy actor (or would-be actor) who articulated most paradigmatically for modern theater (in a play that famously opens with the "Who?" question) both the existential question and the unconscious dream question and articulated them in their interrelation, revolving around the question of sleep and awakening: "to be or not to be . . . to sleep: perchance to dream." Particularly perhaps—and we can think, for example, of the Laurence Olivier version—the relevant moment echoed most immediately by the hand holding the glass is not that of the famous soliloquy but of the address to Yorick's skull.

The moment of the actor, the moment of acting, which is also the moment of the Image irrupting for the actor Bob Harris out of the questioning movement between sleep and waking as he reaches the foreign land (of the screen, as well as of Japan, if not Denmark), is, when read allegorically as we do here, initially that moment of passivity and withdrawal from/suspension of action in the world (a suspension expressed in the reposing moment with the drink, for example, in our case, and Hamlet, to recall, is the one whose capacity for action is suspended) when existence as a medium is revealed. This revelation of existence articulates itself in the form of a question, first "Who's there?" and "Who am I?," then whether to be (at all, as well as someone determined) or not to be, thus to withdraw into the no-thingness of the medium.

The actor, we can say, is someone suffering from the suspension of identity, the suspension of a determined place in an ordered continuity of existence within which one can will oneself to act, or not to act. Out of this suspension, a moment of withdrawal from any determination, the actor draws the resources to become various possible identities (the Japanese commercial director repeatedly instructs the passively sitting Harris to take on different personas, and the latter always obliges), various ways of being, usually identities that are themselves experiencing a moment of crisis, thus a moment in which their lives are critically suspended, subjected to being put into question by the medium.

What is the function of the prop or specific object (the glass of whiskey on the billboard, the skull in *Hamlet* or, earlier in the famous soliloquy, a dagger, and later a poisoned cup) that the actor relates to in his/her *melancholy* (the being possessed by something ungraspable that withdraws and that the self cannot access, most fundamentally the medium, as well as everything in which the medium inscribes itself in a cutting way), contemplative, suspended moment? It is, at least in the cases mentioned, double, inscribing in itself the two types of questions (the existential and the unconscious/erotic). First, the object inscribes in itself a threshold moment, situated between being and not being, between the possession of a specific determination and the dissolution of determination, the exposure to the nothingness. This is clear, of course, for the skull and the knife, but no less so for the glass of whiskey, through which, out of the cutting experience of a suspended action, one experiments (like any actor taking on various identities) with letting go of one's self-possession and its accompanying ecstatic pleasure.

Second, that object that emerges out of the existential suffering of primary passivity, the passion of existence/the medium, thus inscribing in itself this passivity, resonates with that other exceptional object, the erotic object we referred to as the phallus, which, even as it inscribes the moment of the erotic cut, of the decontextualizing (from the integrity of an organic body) force through which one becomes filled with desire one can never will or control qua excessive exposure outside oneself, also comes to serve, because of its objective determination, as the site of an imagined scenario of being able to possess and master the dispossessive ("feminine") power of desire (qua bodily inscription of the passivity to the medium). In this sense the prop comes to serve as that object through which, at the moment of suspension and exposure to dissolution, one plays with the mastery of the "feminine."

In such capacity the glass of whiskey becomes that magical object through which, at the moment suspended from action, which is the moment of the actor/image, one experiences the mastery over a femininity to which one has been exposed due to the suspension. Drinking from the magical glass, even as it enacts the erotic liquidation of self-possession, comes to serve as the masterful possession of, as well as a defensive mechanism against, this very liquidation, thus against Eros (hence the satisfied self-possession and ease in a world one feels is one's oyster also associated with the cool characters Murray plays for Coppola both here and to an even greater extent in *On the*

Rocks). This scenario, in which the object emerges in relation to the question of the phallus, is an unconscious one, having to do with the exposure to the "feminine" moment of passivity through which one is put into question by the very being of Eros, and as such it also revolves around the emergence of enigmatic marks, non-meaningful inscriptions of the medium (the source of meaning) that dreams are made of, hence the strange resonance in this scene of the Japanese written characters surrounding the whiskey-drinking actor.

Who am I? To be or not to be? To be swept by cutting, "feminine" Eros, or to *have* the phallus serving as a defense against, and mastery over, the "feminine"? These are the questions that open at this moment when the image is between sleep and waking. Yet of course this image is (also) a commercial, meant to supply answers to these questions, answers centered, precisely, around the supplying of a phallus (and the phallus is that which has come under threat at the "feminine"/erotic moment of the image) in the form of the magical glass of whiskey. It is as if coming to possess the magic glass allows one to find one's place in a world from which one has been cut off, suspended and exposed, lost in a foreignness, looking into an existential abyss and erotic horror (Eros is a horror from the point of view of the phallus, but it is of course, irrespective of the phallus a cutting exposure at the limit of death). The bottled liquid, poured into the magical cup, will enable the nightmare to be escaped through the simultaneous experiences of (self-)liquidation and its containment or control.

A few years before *Mad Men* and Don Draper (and Murray in the commercials, here and later in the film, is Don Draper-y *avant la lettre*), Coppola subtly points to the way the commercial, perhaps fundamentally an American type of commercial, has emerged as what serves as a defensive answer to an experience of displacement and loss, an experience that the artistic image also emerges from, yet with the aim of inflecting it differently. Her film itself, as exemplified by its opening scene, will present itself as a counterimage to the one offered by the commercial, a poetic American image offered as an alternative to the commercial one.

Dreaming of Escape

But of course, the questions to ask are where does the poetic image, as opposed to the commercial one, aim? How will it respond to the existential abyss and unconscious horror from which both sorts of image equally emerge? Is there another response besides that of the phallic fantasy?[23] To glimpse what that response might be, we need to think of the relations between this opening scene, culminating in the image/commercial of the melancholy man holding a glass,[24] and the opening image of the cut woman.[25] For this opening scene cannot be understood without bearing an essential relation to the opening image that precedes it, out of which, in a sort of reversal of Eve emerging out of the cut in Adam's rib cage, it emerges. Before we elaborate this, it is important to emphasize that the two images, relating to each other through the cut without any causal and explanatory order, immediately raise the question whether, in case there is any relation at all between the two (which is not necessary, though of course the entire movie will deal with the relation between the two protagonists presented in these first images), the second should be understood in relation to the first, or vice versa. Thus, for example, because we have established the cut here as indicating the dimension of the withdrawal into sleep, should we perhaps understand the opening scene with the man as being that which the cut woman we have first encountered is dreaming of? Or, to the contrary, since we have seen that the man just arrived in Japan emerges through the cut/sleep, can it be that the cut woman is what he had been dreaming of while on his passage to Japan, or perhaps such dreaming has even led him to come to Japan? Who is the dream of whom? ("You stepped out of a dream," the lounge singer at the hotel performing the Nat King Cole song will later sing.)

The answer of course, which is the heart of the movie, is that it is both. No less than the arriving man being the sleeping/seducing woman's dream, the sleeping/seducing woman is the dream of the man arriving in Japan in pursuit of something: officially, to make a commercial, but he is really driven by an unnamable desire he cannot conceive of, which will be at the heart of the question of the image (in excess of the commercial, thus of the fantasy phallic response—which is why the two will not have a consummated sexual episode but will rather end their encounter by sharing a kiss, and a secret, a point to which we will return).

Let us start with the question from the point of view of the man, since we have been accompanying him. If the sleeping/seducing woman is his dream, a dream in pursuit of which he goes all the way to Japan (thus, making a passage through the foreign),[26] then we might understand the cut through which he arrived to be an unnamable *call* inscribing itself in him as a cut he cannot master (the call being that pure excess of language/the medium over any of its specific actualizations, an excess one can only passively receive, without willing it). Such a call, in our case, emerging as it does from the unconscious realm of sleep, is also filled with desire or Eros.[27] Yet what is the Eros of the actor/artist (an Eros that will be inscribed in an artistic image) after; what does its call demand? Coppola's implicit answer: to experience itself (namely, Eros, desire) in excess of being captivated by the phallus (in excess of being trapped by that which the commercial revolves around); namely, to experience itself in its cutting "femininity." This is true in Coppola both for male artists (who nevertheless seem to always waver between this desire for excess over the phallus and the demand of the phallus—Elvis being the most elaborate figure in Coppola's work for this hesitation,[28] wavering as he does between singing and the gun) as well as for women in general, though regarding women it is mostly female artists, or at least artistically inclined figures such as Marie Antoinette, who hold Coppola's interest.

From the point of view of the actor/artist, then, we can say that a tension emerges between the cutting "feminine" call—the being subjected to the excess of the cut—expressed already in the half-sleeping, half-awake cinematic ride we have been following, and the (unconscious) "commercial" attempt to defend against this call through the selection of an exceptional object through which one will be able to contain and control passionate excess. This tension is expressed in the resulting image situated between the melancholy suspension from action and direction, surrounded by enigmatic marks, and the emergence of magical containers that aim to anchor one in a world one can control, a world that is one's oyster and pleasurable habitat. Yet the artist is not only subjected to this tension, meaning exposed (through being overcome by a fatigue withdrawing one from the world) to an excess over the phallus and to the "commercial" temptation to restore the phallic (which can stand for modern capitalism's whole temptation, having felt the threat of the death of God involving, to a degree, a phallic loss) but is, more profoundly, someone looking for an *escape*,[29] that is, among other dimensions, looking to liberate erotic passion from phallic captivation. How can this be done? Only when one comes to establish a relation to the world—a relation the artistic image, in distinction from the commercial, circulates around—that is not characterized as a possession, where the world (i.e., that which we are passively and passionately exposed to) does not end up being owned and mastered. Such a nonpossessive relation will come about through the encounter (prepared for by following the call of the realm of Eros and dreams) with the cut woman. One cannot escape without being rescued,[30] without, that is, accepting a certain passivity. Only once this happens can the artist leave "Japan," that foreign land he entered that was the stage for the tension between the erotic and the "commercial."

Yet before we get to this, we first must understand the relations between the opening image and the opening scene from the perspective of the cut woman. For, we said, this might not be the man's dream; it might equally be the case that the man arrives in Japan out of the woman's dream. This can be understood in at least two ways. First, the cut woman may have created a dream image of a specific man that will be a response to a desire in her, a desire (as we defined it) to escape, or it might be that the cutting of the woman—thus the suffering of "feminine" passion overtaking her in sleep/seduction—involves the issuing of a mysterious call to which the arriving man responds as if he were telepathic. In this case the aim of his arrival, as in many a fairy tale (which *Lost In Translation* also is) is to rescue the woman, to allow her to escape her imprisonment in the tower (the Park Hyatt Tokyo hotel).

Yet what does the woman need to escape? No less than the man, a certain unconscious captivation by the phallus. It might be that in the woman's case two forms of relation to the captivating phallus are most prominent, both of which need to be escaped from (yet ultimately all forms of relations to the phallus, as captivator of "femininity" from which the poetic aims to escape, can exist in women and men alike, precisely because the phallic fantasy inhabits the unconsciousness of both sexes, even if the phallic "object" exists only in men). First, there is the question of the woman's own unconscious phantasmic desire, or partial desire, to *have* a phallus, thus to come to possess "femininity" (a question apparently not of great interest to Coppola[31]). Second, there is her unconscious desire to be *possessed by* the phallus, possessed, it is assumed, by another (a desire that seems to particularly mark the young bride Marie Antoinette, or the young bride Priscilla, or the young protagonist bride of *Lost in Translation*). Yet such a fantasy of being possessed inevitably fails, since the men Coppola's women are waiting for to fulfill this fantasy are usually artists (or are interested in locks more than the sword, in the case of Louis, or have been paralyzed by a leg wound, as in *The Beguiled*) and have thus been more acutely exposed to the fact that one *cannot have the phallus*, one cannot possess primordial "feminine" exposure. Thus, these men either leave the women frustrated, as in the case of Marie Antoinette, or, more frequently, as in *Lost in Translation* and *Priscilla*, act out (more explicitly in the case of Elvis, less so Charlotte's husband, another artist, in *Lost in Translation*) their frustration with being exposed to a "feminine" excess they cannot control by trying to violently possess the women, indeed to unconsciously desire to kill them and thus to erase the reminder of the originary wound.

This male fantasy of killing the woman, both for Elvis and in *Lost in Translation*, comes in the form of the attempt to put them permanently to sleep. Thus, Elvis, as if by mistake, gives Priscilla a too-powerful dose of a sleeping pill (on top of many other pills supposed to undermine her self-possession). This fantasy expresses itself even more subtly in *Lost in Translation*, where on one occasion the photographer husband urges the wife to go to sleep as he puts his hands on her neck in a "loving" way (he has grabbed her by the neck on several other occasions) as if unconsciously aiming to suffocate her into permanent sleep.

It is as if the threat of the woman resided in her waking relation to sleep, that is, in her bringing into the light that "feminine" passion and withdrawal from the light (a cutting withdrawal we called the medium), a withdrawal and passion that are the condition of the light, or of being open to the world, yet this is a condition that undermines the desire to be in the world as possessing it. The woman (insofar as being a privileged inscriber of, or witness to, a "feminine" cut) is neither the "night" (withdrawal from the meaningful world) nor the "day" (the world of continuity and meaning) but is the *night in the day* (i.e., cinema, or *La nuit américaine*, as François Truffaut would have it). The phallus, in this sense, is a refusal to sleep or, perhaps more accurately, a desire to dominate the night. Only once the night (in the sense not of the natural falling of darkness but of the cutting dimension of the medium as the absence of determination to which we are forcibly subjected) is dominated can one actually sleep (at least according to what we might call a metaphysical conception of sleep), resting secure that even the enigmatic dreams haunting one and putting one in question do not pose a threat.

We can also think of this question historically. The event we have referred to as the death of God, emerging upon the cut we associated with modernity, can be said to have exposed humanity to that cutting, "feminine" passivity to the medium, a passivity that the figure of God as an all-powerful dominator—a power that, from the unconscious point of view we can call phallic and, from the point of view of the question of existence, we can associate with the grounding figure that metaphysics (the name given by modern thinkers to that conceptual tendency to dominate the passion of existence) has termed the Subject[32]—had still protected it from, even as God (being a withdrawn figure rather than a fully present dominating agent) had still partially exposed it to. Upon the demise of such protection, all that the cut is inscribed in, "femininity," the night of sleep, death, and so on, erupted with unprecedented threatening power. Two directions seem to open for the modern world in relation to this demise of the divine, which had been a controlling figure yet nevertheless a withdrawn one and thus had still allowed a certain exposure to what we have called the medium: either a compensation for the horror of exposure via the bringing forth of fully present dominating/suffocating figures, in the shape of ersatz divinities, fascistic figures of sovereignty whose aim is to fully coincide with, and be in possession of, the medium; or an attempt to open up to a way of life that exposes itself to the passivity to, and passion of, existence (existence naming the dimension of the medium without its theological/metaphysical grounding) in a new way.

In relation to the dimension of sleep and waking, we can say that without the protective powers that have defended it for millennia, a world that has lost its theological bearing has come to suffer terrible fatigue, endured without the possibility of sleep. Neither a true night, the welcoming of which has become too horrifying, nor a true day, which is what can be opened to only in relation to the welcoming of the night (the withdrawn medium) that is its condition, a sort of permanent insomnia seems to have started troubling humanity.[33] It might be that we have never had a true night and day, since the theological age has itself been, we have seen, a defense against the night, yet nevertheless the protective figure of the divine allowed for a certain openness to the medium/night, even if in a partial way, and thus allowed for a certain sleep through which both a partial night and a partial day could at least be glimpsed. But for the moderns, it seems, "Not poppy, nor mandragora, / Nor all the drowsy syrups of the world, / Shall ever medicine thee to that sweet sleep / Which thou owed at yesterday."[34]

Since the (metaphorical) night—the withdrawal from any determination we called the pure medium—has no actual time and place, serving as it does as the opening of any determined time and place, one is displaced when exposed to it, we can say, in the sense of being taken out of one's actual time and place. Being subject to the passionate calling of the night in an age when this passivity has become all too threatening, resulting in insomnia, also means that one comes to reside in permanent jet lag, that is, one cannot coincide with one's (actual) time, being constantly haunted by that non-actual time (perhaps pure time) that is the medium.

Such insomnia and jet lag characterize our two poetic protagonists occupying the foreign land of the screen/Japan for much of the movie, wandering the hotel and the city during their nights that are not nights. The murderous desire to inflict sleep via suffocation—characterizing the attempt of phallic domination at its extreme limit, a limit that can also be said to characterize one major tendency of an entire historical age in which the seeming security of such domination has come under increased threat—is the attempt, then, to eliminate insomnia, so as to allow one to "go to sleep," as Charlotte's husband tells her.

Yet the threat of the "feminine" is the source of insomnia only from within what we might call the phallic and to a degree theological logic, that is, the logic circulating around the relation to the passionate cut as that which needs to be dominated and possessed. Thus, in their insomnia Charlotte and Bob, though exposed to the "feminine" cut and experiencing the dimension beyond the phallic, are still trapped in its logic. To escape, for them—that is, to escape the phallic fantasy of domination—also requires that they escape their very insomnia, which is still an aspect of this logic of domination. To escape would mean to learn how to fall asleep in a new way: to have a different relation to the night and to the "feminine" cut.

How will this escape be possible? By using the very resources, we might call them the poetic resources, found in insomnia itself. That which is glimpsed from the heart of insomnia, an excess over the phallic, will need to be opened to in such a way that it liberates the protagonists both from phallic captivation and from insomnia, insomnia remaining, to repeat, an expression of an anxiety in the face of excess, an anxiety that is part of the phallic logic, grounded as this logic is in the need to dominate erotic excess. One needs to experience insomnia, which indicates a phallic crisis, the exposure to a cutting excess over phallic domination, in order to escape the phallus, but one needs to escape insomnia as well by liberating the excess glimpsed through it from the phallic anxiety that is the very source of insomnia. One needs to fall asleep according to a new logic and to cure/escape both one's insomnia and one's jet lag.

And this is indeed the poetic trajectory taken by Charlotte and Bob in *Lost in Translation:* Having called each other through their dreams, and both of them having reached the foreign, cut, realm of the screen, embarking on its ride, that is, the passage through the medium between sleep and waking, suffering as a result from jetlag and insomnia, they will learn over the course of the film both to escape phallic captivation (Bob going perhaps beyond the dimension of the "commercial," Charlotte seeming at least to have begun liberating herself from the unconsciously murderous suffocation by her husband) and to cure their insomnia. This will be achieved through what we might understand as a mutual giving, or gifting, of the night to each other, learning to sleep in a new way.

"Can you keep a secret?" Bob asks Charlotte in one of their fundamental exchanges, "I'm trying to organize a prison break; I'm looking for an accomplice." "Are you in or are you out?" he asks. "I'm in," she responds. We have already seen that there can be no escape without an accomplice, or that one cannot escape without being rescued, that is, without welcoming a passivity that one cannot dominate. This welcoming of the need for an accomplice in escape (which Bresson has also profoundly pointed to in his escape movie) lies at the heart of a new relation to the world or to existence, a relation not of possession but, Coppola indicates, of *sharing*, sharing being the relating to another through the welcoming of what withdraws and exceeds one precisely because it is that which no one can possess.

Bob and Charlotte will thus, increasingly over the course of the movie, come to share the withdrawn, in the form both of sharing their nights, going out together on various nocturnal adventures, and of sharing a bed, the withdrawn zone of sleep and Eros (in a couple of beautiful scenes of conversation), though this latter sharing, crucially, is not explicitly sexual. An affair, Coppola seems to indicate, would still be too tied to the phallic logic they are trying to escape.[35] And indeed, after some scenes of sharing their nights and bed without sexual consummation, they will both be able, at first very briefly and increasingly more successfully, to fall asleep, into a sleep that is not achieved as a result of a phallic conquest (over erotic excess). This new sleep, the new relation to the night, indeed the new relation to Eros and the new overcoming of anxiety will thus involve the sharing of the cut, thus of the passion, of existence, initially glimpsed through their insomnia but now going beyond it.

This sharing of the cut is also at the heart of the experience of the cinematic image as Coppola understands it. The cut screen—because no one can own it, exposing as it does everyone to the excessive medium, in passion—is what we all come to share as the sharing of the withdrawn, of the call of the night and the source of dreams, and of the day.

Perhaps the secret is the ultimate figure in *Lost in Translation* that stands for this sharing of what one cannot possess. We have seen Bob ask Charlotte if she can keep a secret, and at the very end of the movie, when Bob and Charlotte separate and bid each other good-bye, at the culminating moment of their existential and erotic adventure, Bob holds Charlotte tight and whispers something in her ear, something that remains a secret from us. Then they kiss.

To share the withdrawn, which is what connects the two, even as it is that which is at the heart of their separation, their being cut from each other, is to share a secret, that is, to share that which does not communicate any open meaning but only communicates the withdrawal from meaning (and ownership) that is at the heart of all meaning, the medium itself. And it is the kiss that becomes the erotic manifestation of this sharing of the secret par excellence, both in that it is an activity of the mouth, the site of speech, at the moment of its secretive withdrawal from saying anything specific and when it is engaged only in communication as such, and in that this place of pure communication of what exceeds all specific meanings, the place that is thus a site of a fundamental sharing of what cannot be owned, the secret, is also the site of a fundamental erotic connection, that is, of that bodily inscription of the excess of the medium in relation to which we are passive and passionate, expressing itself at the moment of welcoming existence as a fundamental sharing.

After this erotic/existential sharing of the cut in the secretive kiss, the two can separate—and welcome the morning. For this scene of separation (and/as the culmination of their connection) happens in the morning, the first time they share something other than the night. They can do so because they have connected to the night in a new way, welcomed it through a sharing of withdrawal, and thus welcomed it as the secret resource allowing for the coming of a new day. To enable the new day in this way is also to allow film to begin, and to end, as the welcoming of the withdrawn medium/the cut of sleep as the source of a new appearance.

Watching the Sunrise—Marie Antoinette

"The problem of leisure, what to do for pleasure"—so blasts the post-punk band *Gang of Four* singing "Natural's Not in It" on the screen's dark background before the film's first image appears. Then, after a few more sung lines, the inaugural image: Marie Antoinette, lying on a chaise longue, her head leaning backward, her eyes closed, seemingly bored and lacking much of a desire to do anything. Surrounded by sumptuous pink and white cakes, her head adorned by an enormous set of feathers, she can hardly bring herself to lift a finger and taste one of the cakes (her eyes still closed, though her head is turning a bit in our direction, even as she seems to be unaware of us) as a maid at her feet puts on her pink slippers. Suddenly she lifts her head, opens her eyes, and looks directly at us, as if deigning to acknowledge our presence; she smiles a bit, seemingly quite ironically, then turns away from us again, closing her eyes and again leaning her head back. She's done with us. Cut, then the movie's title: *Marie Antoinette*.

Very much like the opening image of *Lost in Translation*, the image here brings to the fore the following dimensions, which I will mention briefly so as not to be too repetitive: a bed or bed-like surface, upon which a woman who is mostly withdrawn from us passively lies. She might be in the state between sleep and waking, but it also might be that of seduction, between being aware and unaware of being watched. Also, perhaps we are dealing with an actress, and with a performance in the context of a theatrical or cinematic setting, especially since her image emerges immediately following the appearance of the name "Kirsten Dunst" on-screen.

But a few further elements are added. First, an aspect that might also have been present in the earlier image but is greatly intensified here: The indeterminate suspension between an actual woman, say, Marie Antoinette, and an actress, say, Kirsten Dunst, brings with it, among other elements, the question of time, especially since Marie is a historical figure. When exactly is what we see supposed to be happening? Are we seeing an eighteenth-century person or a twenty-first-century actress? It is the cut nature of this opening image—its being a totally decontextualized image that is not even part of the movie's main narrative but takes place in the suspended zone of the opening titles—that is, of course, at the heart of this temporal suspension. The decontextualizing cut, we already saw, inscribes the dimension of the withdrawn medium as such, thus the dimension of a pure opening that is also, we can add, that of a pure opening of time, temporality-as-such, before any actual time and place. As a result, any cut image belongs to an actual time but also inscribes in itself a pure temporality in excess of any actual time. Thus, any cut image is in a sort of jet lag as we defined it earlier, being both in (actual) time and withdrawn from actual time, relating to a supra-temporal, or a-temporal (in the sense of temporality-as-such), or, most appropriately for this image and the film in general, an anachronic dimension.

It is this anachronic dimension belonging to any (artistic, or poetic) image that here takes the form of the hesitation between Marie Antoinette as an actual, historical person belonging to a specific time and place and the actor/performer Kirsten Dunst, who, we can say, is someone activating the role or image of the actual person. When an actual person has been transformed into a role or an image that an actor then takes on, this role/image, by definition, no longer belongs to any specific actual time but can be activated, or *repeated*, in *any* time and historical age. This also means, as the duality Marie Antoinette/Kirsten Dunst shows us here, that the actual historical person who has been transformed into an image/role that the artist/performer/director chooses to repeat has already inscribed in herself an anachronic dimension, something not simply belonging to her specific time and place. Artistic or theatrical/cinematic performance/image involves the activation of this dimension that exceeds actual historical time as if calling to be cut from its time, decontextualized and repeated in very different historical moments. What repeats is that which expresses or inscribes an excess that does not belong to, or is exhausted by, their (actual, historical) time.

We can thus say that Marie was someone who did not belong (to her time and place), "containing" or inscribing in herself a dimension of excess beyond any specific historical time. This dimension of excess calls to be constantly repeated and returned to. We can designate this excessive dimension, which specific actual people seem to inscribe in an exceptionally powerful way, the dimension of *fascination*. The fascinating person is someone expressing an excess beyond, or withdrawn from, their actual time, which is the source for their becoming an image/role that can be infinitely repeated across many different historical contexts. What is this fascinating dimension inscribed by Marie or by any fascinating, memorable (memory in this context being the activation of the repeatable) figure that human culture feels compelled to keep returning to? It is, precisely, the dimension we referred to as enigmatic withdrawal, the dimension of a cut inscribing the pure medium, understood both as existence/temporality/pure language as such and as ungraspable erotic excess around which the unconscious circulates.

Yet not only is Marie a fascinating, withdrawn, anachronic figure expressing the pure temporality/existence that is the medium as such, and that always needs a decontextualizing cut, as in our opening image, in order to come into "visibility" or be activated as the pure interruption (of any actual content) that it is. She is also the inscriber, in Coppola's interpretation, of the medium/cut in two very specific ways, both of which are at the heart of her significance for modernity and for Coppola's understanding of what is at stake in modernity (and in America).

First, as this first image already shows, Marie's inscription of the medium/ cut is through a withdrawn "femininity," the inscription of the passive exposure to the medium as both sleep and Eros. Second, Marie is not just the inscriber of a passive "femininity"—this would not have been enough for her to become as fascinating as she is—but is a poetic creator, an artist. As a poetic creator Marie will be someone who entertains a *reflexive* relation to her passivity, thus be someone who grasps such passive "femininity," and this is at the heart of her revolutionary significance, as the site of the call of the excessive medium, against a tradition that saw such passivity (a passivity implying the threat of exposure to excess), as something that needs to be dominated (which also always means something that requires to be captured through the logic of the phallus).

If this first image already hints that Marie, in her relation to Kirsten Dunst, is an actress, thus a poetic figure activating the anachronic power of repetition (which is always the repetition of the medium in excess of any actual content, and thus a repetition as the always renewed possibility of activating the pure cut), this is because she implicitly relates to the excess (of the medium) in her, inscribed in her passive withdrawal into sleep and her erotic pleasures (already grasped as opening to seduction and, beyond it, to performance) as a revolutionary, thus cutting, resource, for escaping her time and historical context, defined by phallic domination and by a metaphysical subjectivity (that is, by the king as a figure who serves as determining ground for everything that arrives).

The excess in Marie is thus not only something she is passively exposed to but—and this is the general paradox of the artist (understood as an activator of the excessive medium in relation to which the artist is passive)— something she *learns how to creatively activate*, seeing in it the essential dimension of a new opening and transformation of existence. Creativity (as the outcome of the passage, in this context, from passivity to seduction, from seduction to performance/power of repetition) is learning to activate the power of the cut, the power of withdrawal from any actual context and order, and to reopen the world as that which is not grounded in any given order.

Thus not (only) will Kirsten Dunst and Coppola be artists portraying/ repeating, through activating the power of decontextualization, a fascinating figure from the past. Marie herself is already the performer relating to a supra-temporal (temporality-as-such) excess inscribed in her as the source of a cutting power she can learn to activate (which is not the same as having power over it) in such a way that she can escape her context, the poetic power of repetition. Thus, later in the movie Marie, after a long process of what we might call becoming an artist—and the film is very much a bildungsroman, a portrait of the artist as a young woman—will indeed be transformed into a performer singing onstage. Marie will thus be an actor (and director) activating a *revolutionary* power of repetition—in the sense that repetition is the power to cut or interrupt any order—that Dunst and Coppola will be heir to.

I have mentioned that there are two additional dimensions activated by this first image beyond the opening image of *Lost in Translation*. The second dimension, in addition to anachrony and acting/performance as activation of the power of repetition, is what we might call a genealogical critique or deconstruction of an image through the highlighting of the logic of its artificiality and constructedness ("natural's not in it," we recall, the band sings). What this means in this context is that rather than simply present us with a realistic image of the decadent Marie, which we expect the film to later show us in greater historical detail, this opening image works as a trap from which we, not unlike Marie, will need to escape. What is this trap? Like any trap or

An American Revolution 183

imprisonment in Coppola's films (most importantly in this film, the trap of Versailles itself), it is a metaphysical/phallic trap.

How does the trap work here? By giving us an image of Marie that corresponds to the clichéd idea of her that history has bequeathed us, the decadent, privileged, and detached "let them eat cake" Marie, an image we will need to slowly learn to see (or unsee)—and this is the trajectory the film will take us through—as having been an attempt at a captivation of the withdrawing, passive, seductive, performative Marie by a specific historical logic. Such logic, call it phallic/metaphysical, informed much of Marie's historical reception. Such reception has emerged, and this is Coppola's implicit argument, as a response to the threat that is Marie's exposure to the passion of existence and erotic excess. This metaphysical/phallic reception desires to dominate Marie's excess, and to do so through what we might understand as a sacrificial destruction.

The Marie we receive through this opening image is thus the Marie sacrificed by a history (at a specific moment when the metaphysical/phallic power dominating it has increasingly started to show itself in demise) threatened by her revolutionary passion (which parallels the French Revolution but also exceeds it), a Marie that history attempted to dominate. It is a Marie—which the image shows us as well nevertheless, in spite of its constructedness through phallic/metaphysical captivation—of passivity, passion, seduction, and cutting performative repetition, who has been transformed by those who felt threatened by it into a symbol of that which needs to be eliminated/suffocated and put to "sleep." It is because the passion of existence activated by Marie, by definition, escapes any grasp and domination that it poses a threat to the viewers, who seem to feel rejected (by the ungraspability of the withdrawn and erotic Marie) and wounded. As a result, these wounded and rejected viewers (understood both as those participating in Marie's historical reception and us, the cinematic viewers) implicitly come to paint Marie's excess through an unconscious phallic projection (a projection that can belong to women no less than it can to men), interpreting it as meriting destruction so as to purify the community and deliver it from the threat of such excess.

This projection on Marie, the film shows, comes no less from her own social context of Versailles—where she is seen as a foreign intrusion and a disturbing threat, someone basically responsible for the phallic failure of the king—than from the broader people of France, for whom she stands as the paradigmatic symbol for all that is wrong with the monarchy. It is implied, though, that the grounds for the people to sacrifice Marie are not so much her belonging to Versailles and its decadence; rather, in their view she is to blame for the failure of the king/phallus to procreate (which is to say that the people see the problem with Versailles as not so much decadence as impotence, for which Marie is the ultimate symbol). In this sense there is the hint seemingly offered by the movie that the French Revolution was not a revolution *against* the phallus, but rather the unrest erupted because the phallus was failing. This unrest actually desires the phallus, is a revolution *for* the phallus.[36]

In this sense, Marie's revolutionary significance will stand out in her own revolutionary historical context precisely to the extent that Coppola sees her as exceeding it. For even as the French Revolution, as Coppola will hint, activated a certain novel/modern cutting exposure to a dimension beyond the control of the king (that sovereign entity combining the being of the metaphysical Subject with that of the unconscious phallus), and thus inevitably involved the eruption of a passive and passionate exposure to the medium/existence, it felt threatened by its own exposure to the passion of existence to the degree that it simultaneously needed to dominate and destroy any such exposure, expressed significantly in its destruction and demonization of Marie (and the reign of terror that followed the revolution, the rise of Napoleon, the restoration of the monarchy, etc.). The revolutionary cutting off of the head will have been, in this sense, also (beyond the cut of the king, thus the inscription of the medium of existence in excess of the king) the attempt to cut the more profound cut (the cutting of Marie), so to speak (and thus paradoxically to preserve the head/phallic domination in a way), or to destroy the threatening passion of existence that erupted with the revolution. Marie will have been, for Coppola, a revolutionary figure who goes beyond and escapes the metaphysical and phallic captivation of passion that the French Revolution partially resulted in: a figure of escape whose true place will be America (where she longs to go to at a certain moment) and film.

Our own passage through the film will in principle involve the call to escape this phallic/metaphysical history and free ourselves from its clutches and thus to go beyond the position of Versailles and of the phallic desiring revolutionaries, both positions ultimately aimed at the sacrifice of Marie. Going beyond both these positions we are to expose ourselves—both through, or with the means of, the image, but also against it, in a sort of genealogical critique or deconstruction—to Marie's poetic excess and receive her withdrawal (from our grasp and will) as the activation of the passion of existence and unconscious desire. Such opening to excess announces a revolution of a different kind, not the revolution of unrest that in many ways is indeed channeled into a desire to destroy power, but to do so not because its failure has become a crack through which a dimension beyond power (understood as phallic potency in that context, or as will to power) is glimpsed and aimed at but because power has, precisely, been failing, has shown itself as weak, having become, like Louis (at least in the first years of the marriage) impotent, manifesting a threatening impotence that one aims not to surpass but to eliminate through a phallic restoration.

The revolution that Marie will inscribe, which we might call an American revolution (Marie sets on such a path when she falls in love with a soldier participating in the American Revolution, but his absence allows her to go beyond the logic of phallic captivation that he also represents), as well as a cinematic revolution of the image, is precisely one that, experiencing the demise of the domination of phallic power (and what it works in tandem with, the metaphysical Subject/the theological divine), aims to exceed and surpass rather than restore it. This demise of phallic power, a demise at the heart of the irruption of the revolutionary cut, characterizes a whole historical age, modernity, an age of crisis expressed paradigmatically by Louis's impotence. But in the case of Marie's ("American") revolution, the revolution will aim not in the direction of actually bringing back phallic power but at the exposure, through the experience of the cut, to a new passion beyond power, a passion against which such dominating power was, to begin with, a defense.

It is such a revolution we are called to through our undergoing the experience of liberation from our entrapment by the clichéd image of history (the aim of which is to protect metaphysical/phallic power), represented by the film's opening image. Such liberation from the image is not to be understood as operating in a Brechtian manner, for example, as it is not learning to open to some thinking or judgment supposedly higher than captivating images, but rather is brought about by opening to the image's passionate potentiality in excess of its phallic/metaphysical captivation. It is the excessive image that we are called to open to, the true image beyond the dominated/sacrificial one, and, through this opening (which is the opening to film), we escape. A true revolution has to pass through the true image, the site of the cut, the exposure to Existence, and the passion that is Eros.

The Logic of the Palace and the Logic of the Bed

Let us accompany Marie, albeit briefly, along her cinematic trajectory, a trajectory of liberation from captivation, as it opens after this first image.

The screen is dark. Then, after the sound of a door opening, a tiny bit of light starts to infiltrate the screen. A maid opens a window to let the light flood in. At the front of the screen, very close to us, an adolescent girl is lying in bed, having obviously been awoken in this unwelcome way, her eyes starting to blink, opening a bit then closing. A cut. We are outside, in the morning light, with a stately palace in front of us in a perfectly symmetrical image. The voice-off of a woman, Maria Theresa, empress of Austria, declaring, "Friendship between Austria and France must be cemented by marriage."

The main opposition guiding the movie is already on display, with, on the one hand, what we can call the order of the palace, with the attendant full daylight it imposes and the marriage it desires (a phallic, sacrificial marriage offering up the girl), the aim of which is to cement and thus stabilize and ground that order, set against, on the other hand, the withdrawn girl in bed, somewhere between sleeping and waking, between eyes closed and opened, a girl on which the palace tries immediately to impose its light and order. The entirety of the movie will consist of the way the demise of the order and logic of the world of the palace (inscribing itself most symbolically in Louis's impotence and the non-consummation of the marriage at the heart of this order and logic) will be the occasion for the girl (a parallel to the French people, whose revolution also irrupts out of this crisis, but differently) to begin connecting to the revolutionary power inscribed in her withdrawal and in her attachment to this stage between sleep and waking—the power of the cut and performative anachronic repetition, the power of Eros, the power of existence as implying the presence of the night/medium-in-excess-of-any-content as the condition of the day—to start making its claim, a claim also to inscribe itself, perhaps essentially and necessarily so, in the achievement of a new image, most fully coming into expression in the cinematic image at the emergence of which Marie's revolutionary desire seemingly aims, beyond her time. The opposition staged in this opening scene can thus also be understood as the opposition between two types of images, between what we can call the metaphysical/phallic image, whose ideal is full visibility, chasing away any trace of the night, and the other image, emerging out of the flickering of the eyes at the moment between sleep and waking, darkness and light—an image we can call cinema.

It is Marie, then, who will come to stand for the cinematic image. In Marie a revolutionary call will be inscribed, desiring the emergence of cinema. Hence the film's anachronic nature—famously using rock 'n' roll and post-punk music, and so on, on its soundtrack—depicting a history that at its heart has a figure who does not belong to it, who exceeds it by bringing the anachronic, cutting power of repetition into it. Marie is thus a rock 'n' roll excess inscribed as an anachronic revolutionary uprising at the heart of the palace. Marie, as Coppola interprets her, should be understood as a proto-cinematic revolutionary, calling from her entrapment in the palace for the emergence of cinema as a new type of image. From another point of view, we can say that the film itself, in its activation of cinema as revolving around the adventure of Marie's desire, trapped as it is in the historical palace, will have the task of finally enabling the redemption of this desire. While it is through Marie's revolutionary desire that cinema can seemingly arrive, it is through the arrival of cinema that Marie's desire can find its place, and the movie house can replace the palace. Thus, at a beautiful key moment in the film, after her lover Count Fersen has left, Marie, gazing out the palace window, as she closes and opens her eyes, sees, as if upon a hallucinatory cinematic screen, his image fighting in the American Revolution. Cinema and America are the revolutions inscribed in Marie's desire for escape while captured in the palace.[37]

The first stage that will set Marie on her path, as if inscribing in her a first connection to her revolutionary powers, which is also the first connection to a new type of image, the cinematic one, occurs just following the opening scene we have briefly discussed. Forced to leave her home and move to France, Marie travels in a carriage. As with Bob Harris's car ride upon his arrival in Tokyo, Marie's carriage functions as a vehicle of displacement, the being cut out of one's place, that starts to take on the qualities of the decontextualized screen between sleep and waking, the withdrawn medium and the opening to the world. Thus, as she is on her way from Austria to France, Marie gazes outside the windows, then withdraws back inside her compartment, to sleep, or to play, in her semi-distracted, semi-sleepy way, which activates, we saw in our discussion of *Lost in Translation*, that new understanding of vision as emerging out of a withdrawn excess, that of the pull of the empty pure medium in excess of any content.

This, then, is the originary touch of cinema in her adventure, as she is displaced from her palatial home and exposed to the screen-like cutting out of the carriage and the view it opens. We cannot follow all the steps in her revolutionary trajectory, thus in the bildungsroman that this movie is, but let me just indicate a few. As she reaches the estranged foreign land of Versailles, much like Charlotte in Tokyo, Marie becomes a *watcher*, gazing, out of her withdrawn displacement, at everything surrounding her. It is as if the first stage of activating the power of the withdrawn is that of becoming an alienated watcher.

It will be the marriage to Louis that will seemingly have the task of eliminating the excess expressed in her alienated watching, and transforming it, or channeling it into the metaphysical/phallic logic of the palace. The marriage bed, one of the main foci of the film, will be the main site with the task of integrating Marie into the logic of the palace, thus capturing the excess that the displaced Marie brings with her. But because the marriage will fail to be consummated, the attempt to dominate the excess brought by the withdrawn Marie will fail as well, and this failure will allow her to slowly activate the potential revolution inscribed in her withdrawal in an unprecedented way. In many ways the opposition I referred to, which opens the film—between the logic of the palace and the logic of Marie in her bed between sleeping and waking—will have as one of its main sites, if not *the* main site, the opposition between two beds: the bed of the withdrawn Marie and the royal bed of pure visibility, the task of which is to transform the withdrawn bed into a site dominated by the metaphysical/phallic logic of the palace (hence also the wedding night scene with the entire court in the bedroom with the new couple, watching them, as if their withdrawal were not allowed). It is as if Marie's revolutionary escape from the logic of the palace will require her to draw on the resources of the initial bed (that of the girl between sleep and waking) so as to slowly transform this bed, the site of the withdrawn, into the poetic site of the screen as inscription of the medium, a site of the passion of existence and of Eros. This poetic trajectory of the bed of withdrawal, the bed between sleep and waking (which also needs to be transformed into an erotic bed before it can become a poetic screen understood as place of withdrawal, through which existence is grasped in its power of repetition), will have to come at the price of the destruction of the palatial bedroom, with its phallic bed of full visibility, lack of sleep (Marie is often shown as not being able to sleep; she is always already up when the chamber ladies arrive in the morning), and lack of Eros. And this will indeed be the final image of the movie, showing us the destroyed bedroom.

Yet before we get there, Marie, who has begun to be liberated through the phallic failure of Louis and thus be connected to her poetic withdrawal, her revolutionary excess, will have to go through some further transitions. We cannot go through all of them here, but I would like to mention a few. One important initial stage in the transition from the palace to art as activation of the withdrawn is that of excessive consumption, often referred to in Coppola's vocabulary as "shopping," whereby Marie, as if out of frustration of the phallic bed's failure, compensates by purchasing more and more stuff, more shoes, more clothes, ever more elaborate hairdos, and so on. Such scenes in Coppola are often interpreted as a critique of capitalistic consumption, decadent excess, and so forth, but their role and logic are in fact different and more complex. For, we might say, though we are dealing with a certain excess that is wrongly directed—in the sense that it is substantialized, expressing itself in the accumulation of things—this decadence is nevertheless the expression of her beginning to relate to her desire and excess beyond the logic of the phallus, even as she is still looking for substantial things to satisfy it.

This means that there is a *positive* dimension to the excess as it is expressed here, which is an excess that manifests itself as unregulated and thus out-of-control consumption. For such excess, coming as it does out of phallic failure (i.e., as supposedly a compensation for the failure of the marriage bed), is already the inscription of a connection to the dimension in excess over phallic domination. In this sense (and this is an essential aspect of Coppola's logic from *Lost in Translation* to *Priscilla*), it is not that Marie's excessive consumption is to be seen as a poor substitute and an inadequate compensation (in the manner of the early understanding of Freudian sublimation) for phallic satisfaction but rather that the failure of the phallus sets her on a liberatory trajectory of escape beyond it, toward the discovery of a more profound relation to the passion of existence and erotic excess, a trajectory with "shopping" as an early station.[38] In this sense, such shopping is seen as corruption only from the point of view of phallic desire for regulation; but from another point of view, that of the excessive logic of escape, it is an important, if still misguided, step toward the overcoming of the phallus.

If this sort of "shopping" is an index for an emerging eighteenth-century capitalistic excess, Coppola seems to indicate that an escape from capitalism will be in the direction not back to a more regulated, supposedly lost order but to a more radical relation to excess. This direction we have referred to as the decontextualizing cut (thus the cut out of any reliance on a given order/metaphysical/phallic domination) inscribing the excessive openness of the medium and a "feminine" erotic jouissance beyond economy (if we understand economy as having to do with the calculation through which excess is transformed into profit, and thus metaphysically/phallically captivated).[39]

Following this stage of excessive consumption comes a first escape from the palace, the first time Marie will have managed to exit it, going to a *masked* ball in Paris, thus also connecting for the first time to her performative dimension (she had already connected to the performative, but not yet actively, in her earlier role as an enthusiastic opera watcher). This exit from the palace will also, literally, announce the death of the king and his regime, thus functioning as a first revolutionary cut, for upon Marie's return to the palace from the ball comes word that Louis XV has fallen ill, and soon thereafter he dies. Louis and Marie's coronation follows, in a night of festivities that ends on a crucial note, the birth of a relation Marie establishes between a realm *outside the palace* (thus the realm of escape), which is connected to the idea of nature and the landscape (dimensions to which she has already been exposed in her carriage ride from Austria to France), and a new understanding of the poetic (she has already started, as I mentioned, connecting to her poetic nature, through opera performances *in* the palace and the masked ball outside it), paradigmatically taking the form of watching the sunrise.

For, having spent the night not in her royal bed but partying, Marie aims to end the night by going out of the palace to watch the sunrise. It is as if the outside of the palace, which takes on the character of the *landscape* (that to which one opens in movement, through a ride, thus via the passage through the cut, as the first carriage ride indicates, and as we saw in our discussion of

Bob Harris's ride),[40] connects her to a new type of gaze, in which the withdrawn and the opening to the world start to be understood as essentially interconnected. This transitional moment between the dark and the light, the withdrawn and the open, is the moment of the new image (culminating in film) Marie stages (she's the one initiating the excursion to watch the sunrise and is thus the director of the event, as if unconsciously desiring a new kind of image, one that corresponds to the logic of her withdrawn being) upon the death of the king and the (still momentary) escape from the palace.

Finally, the marriage is consummated and Marie gives birth, but luckily (as in the case of Priscilla) a girl is born, which means that the child is not a son whose duty will be to perpetuate the phallic order of the father but rather a new possibility beyond that order, a new opening of a crack. As Marie says to her daughter, whereas "a boy will be the son of France, you shall be mine": She will be the inscriber of an excessive passion, a revolutionary passion beyond the metaphysical/phallic palatial France, an excessive passion that will be transmitted to the future, as if announcing all of us as its heirs and heiresses, and a land populated by these heirs and heiresses beyond France (and even beyond the French Revolution, which, as we saw, still stood under an implicit desire for the phallic order): "America."

A Land of Her Own

Such a new "land" of the future, which Marie's passion opens, finds its first outpost outside the palace, in a place that is fully Marie's own,[41] the Petit Trianon, which she receives as a gift from Louis following the birth of her daughter and which she will establish as a new kind of realm: poetic, erotic, playful, and democratic. In the Petit Trianon, a proto-"America," Marie will fully become a performer, acting onstage and singing a song she (at least according to myth—"C'est Mon Ami") composed, and there, in the Petit Trianon, she will have her great love affair, a free erotic encounter whose form is not that of the dominating and instrumental palatial marriage.

The newness of the Petit Trianon as a realm outside the logic of the palace will also express itself in the double discovery of the relation between the landscape and the new image, now fully expressed as cinema in Coppola's direction. Thus, at a key moment, as she walks freely in the Petit Trianon, alone in her room with a seamstress, she tells the woman, "I want something more simple. Natural. To wear in the garden." After she says "natural," there's a major cut, after which we see her running freely outside, as we hear her disembodied voice speak "to wear in the garden." She runs toward the off-screen, exiting the screen, after which there is another cut. A series of cuts follow, giving us seemingly disconnected views of nature, after which we see a view of her daughter playing in the garden.

It is as if a *new cinematic language* has emerged in, or with, this realm of the outside, a realm of an unregulated openness achieved via a series of cuts (the first of which, between the room and outside, signifying the cut as that *through which* one exits into a new open realm), where the views emerging out of these cuts are neither ordered in any way (the disconnection between the voice, now disembodied, and the view, also being part of this general disconnection of ordering) nor seen from any large perspective through which we can grasp the way they are interconnected: a series of fragments with no governing whole. The question of a new language, which is perhaps no language at all or perhaps some kind of natural language, a language humanity is at home in, soon follows, when Marie reads to her friends, as they are sitting in an unorganized way outside, from Rousseau. "Rousseau says, 'If we assume man has been corrupted, by an artificial civilization, what is the natural state? The state of nature from which he has been removed? Imagine wandering up and down the forest, without industry, without speech, and without home,'" after which we get a scene of Marie's daughter looking at a bee, saying, in French, the only time French is spoken in the movie, "*regardez* la petite Abeille," as if calling to look, via a new, natural language, the language of her home.

While Rousseau's speculations—which echo (in) Marie's desire to escape, as she sits freely outside, from the order of the palace, taken to be a corruption of nature—seem to point to a primordial natural state, a state without speech, a lost state, Coppola's way of filmmaking and the insistence on speech (and on a new way of looking) seem to point in the direction of cinema not as a natural *state* (thus actuality) but as a natural language (thus mediality, an open potentiality). This language is the language one feels at home in—a new home in excess of the corrupt palace language in which one is trapped—and it is not something lost (or not exactly, since one can talk of it as having always already been repressed) but something *to be achieved*. It is as if the film provides an answer to Rousseau's question "What is the natural state?" by showing that it involves the achievement, the development, of a cinematic "language of unregulated cuts (i.e., inscriptions of the withdrawal that is the pure medium in excess of any content), which gives us an openness to a world that cannot be conceived as a given whole but is conceived as the relation between fragments exposed to each another because *there is no* given whole."[42]

"Nature," within this context of looking for the originary state of the human before corruption, is not a lost actuality that has been corrupted. It should be thought of through the Benjaminian concept we have mentioned of pure language, understood as that empty excess of the medium (existence-as-such) beyond any content and beyond any actual linguistic system, an undetermined openness that has been repressed ("corrupted") by metaphysical/phallic captivation. The home of the human is not a "nature" understood as lost actuality before the fall into speech (and society) but that enigmatic withdrawal of the empty medium, the "night," at the heart of a new "day" (a relation that cinema, the medium of watching the sunrise, is dedicated to in a particularly essential way). The new day (to which cinema as the watching of the sunrise aims to give access) is that to which one opens if one can activate the primordial exposure to the night that inaugurated Marie's adventure, thus of which she is shown to be an important, poetic witness, trying to remain faithful to it so as to escape the "corrupt" palace.

There is an intriguing indication in the movie that this new land, this new world (of which Marie's Petit Trianon is a herald) with its new nights and days, opened through the activation of the "natural" language of film (understood as the inscription of pure language with the means of the activation of unregulated cuts) is that which the name "America" aims to be or inscribe, and that toward which the American Revolution, haunting the film as a distant project to which Marie/Coppola can be of help, aims. And this indication has to do with how the cinematic language Coppola activates in this segment of the Petit Trianon clearly echoes that of Terrence Malick, especially the one he used in a film released a year before *Marie Antoinette*, *The New World*, dealing with the birth of America. Though Coppola has mentioned in interviews that she "references" Malick in this section of the movie, she has not explicitly said, as far as I could find, that she was thinking of *The New World*, yet it seems to me quite clear that she did, or perhaps that she intuitively sensed in Malick's cinematic language a dimension that both of them activated in a very similar way at almost the exact same historical moment.

Saying Good-Bye

Yet there will be one more essential step, beyond this poetic and erotic stage of the proto-American land of the Petit Trianon, that will announce Marie's final grasping of the implications of that revolutionary excess/cut revealed to her in her withdrawal on the bed with which the movie opens (the moment between sleep and waking, upon whose resources it is as if she is increasingly trying to draw in order to escape). It is this step that will finally enable her to take permanent leave of the palace: death. The coming to be inscribed by a relation to death—imprinting itself in her through the death of her son—is understood to be the extreme limit of that withdrawal into the night that is the condition of the new day. It is as if only upon this death will Marie understand the full nature of the cut of withdrawal that she has been witness to, and upon whose resources she constantly, unconsciously, drew, so as to escape. Only upon this death will she have grasped what is at the heart of existence, of the erotic and the poetic, and only by connecting to this most extreme limit will she have achieved her final escape, leaving the palace in the early morning, the beginning of the day, after the revolutionaries (who both parallel her adventure but also betray it, in that, as we saw, their desire finally aims, precisely, at not so much escaping the palace as taking it over, coming to dominate it[43]) come to occupy it.

Coppola very pointedly cuts the movie with this final carriage ride, when Marie, as she wavers between looking out the carriage and withdrawing into it, is finally leaving the palace. As she looks outside, Louis asks her, "Are you admiring your lime avenue?" (thus indicating her attempt to bring the language of "nature" into the palace so as to escape it). "I'm saying good-bye," she answers, followed by a cut to the destroyed palatial bedroom. It is in thus saying good-bye (not unlike the two protagonists of *Lost in Translation* at their final parting[44]) that Marie has finally embraced the extreme limit of the cut, "appropriated" that inappropriable excess, which is the withdrawn death, and has managed to depart to a new day. Though historically we know where Marie is going, Coppola insisted that this ride outside, her final escape, has no sequel depicted in the film. Marie herself might be going to her death, but the cinematic repetition of her cutting revolutionary excess, a repetition that reaches here its culminating moment, might point elsewhere. Where she is going, when her excess and power of repetition have been embraced by/as cinema, is open, an openness, a new relation between the night and the day, that might be called "America."

CONCLUSION

The Law and Passion of the Medium

Let us gather some of the most essential steps we have taken throughout this book. It is the question of the *conceptual* significance of the term "America" that set us on our way. It is a term, I argued, to be understood as a *modern* name for the question of the meaning of Being that emanates from the event that Nietzsche called the death of God, an event that Heidegger, in his turn, came to elaborate as the putting into question of what he called the onto-theological, or metaphysical, interpretation of Being. "America," I claimed, should be heard as the name in which an obscure call, here meaning the inscription of Being in us, before and in excess of any actual statement, increasingly started to resonate. This is the call of Being in excess of its onto-theological capture. It is a call the meaning of which we do not yet understand, but in the open indeterminacy of which is heard a demand, indeed a Law, to organize human life in a new way. At the heart of the *openness* of the call is the fact that the pure "to be" is not seen as determined in advance in any way, not grounded in any God or transcendent Subject, however conceived, that guides the Whole in advance and is under the power of no aim that prescribes it.

The United States, I suggested, as a modern *political* entity trying to organize the life in common of human beings, was perhaps the first such entity to have fully felt the pressure inscribed in the demand, or Law, of this modern call. The newly formed country of the United States associated this modern call, if obscurely and with all the problems and complexities we mentioned in the Introduction, with the term "America," and saw itself as trying to respond to it, indeed saw itself as being its privileged witness, guardian, and messenger.

The call of Being, or the call "to be" (understood as the exposure to an undetermined openness) is a Law, we showed, precisely to the degree that it is that to which we are subjected unwillingly. The call is beyond, or in excess of our will, for it is (as an empty openness by which we are inflicted and which exposes us to any possible thing) that through which we come to be (who we are) to begin with, those who are addressees of an empty call. The Law of the empty call of Being that exposes us to any thing—but which itself, in its emptiness, is withdrawn from any actual thing, being, strictly speaking, a no-thing—is characterized by two aspects, which we called the No of forbidding and the Yes of passive, indeed passionate, receptivity. In its aspect as No, the Law says: "You cannot possess, indeed you are forbidden from possessing, the call, or the Whole,[1] for it is that which marks the limit of your capacity to possess." In its aspect of Yes, the Law marks our passivity, thus our passion, to that indeterminate and open emptiness that exposes us to anything whatsoever and thus opens us (in spite of our will, beyond our control) to the world. "You *Must* receive the world," the Law says, and indeed, "receive it as a gift," that is, as something one could not foresee nor control nor ask for, for it is at the origin of our capacity to ask and control, and as such not subject to them.

In its capacity of being that withdrawal (from any actuality), a withdrawal that we have also called a cut out of actuality that exposes us to the world, we termed the call of the "to be" (the excess over any and every actuality, over any specific being) our Medium (writ large). By this we mean the post-theological and atheological Medium of existence, for which one of the preeminent modern names has been "America." How can this call of the withdrawn, thus invisible, modern Medium, how can the Law that is the call "America," manifest itself, be connected to, and activated? Here opens up the question of the modern work of art (Renaissance and post-Renaissance), and, more specifically, the question of modern artistic or poetic media as *forms* of making possible the emergence of specific contents, which are themselves not a content. These modern artistic media are in charge of creating zones that are detached and cut off from the continuity of the actual world. It is through this detachment from actuality that they expose us to a dimension beyond actuality and communicate the Law of the Medium. The modern poetic medium, we explained throughout, is to be understood as the medium of the Medium, or of the ungraspable Law of the "to be."

We have defined the manner of the Law's inscription in us, in its powerful mystery in a modernity in which the Law can no longer be appropriated by a transcendent agency, by borrowing, with slightly different aims, the essential Lacanian term of the extimate, or extimacy, denoting an outside that is the most intimate to us. Being beyond and before our capacity to will, and in excess of any actuality, it can neither be appropriated nor located and is thus absolutely "outside," but being at the origin of who we are, as those who receive through it the gift of the world, it is the most intimate to us, our very heart, absolutely "inside." Our heart, that which is most intimate to us, is the exposure to a world we receive as a gift we (or anyone, neither earthly nor transcendent agency) can never own or appropriate and is thus absolutely external to us.

If the poetic medium as messenger of the Medium is to be truly effective, it needs to be a site through which we connect essentially to our extimacy, through which we receive the Law most fully. This is where the remarkable nature of the cinematic medium makes an outstanding claim, which turns it into a particularly powerful messenger of the modern call/Law as it came to inscribe itself in the term "America."

This outstanding claim of the medium of film has to do most importantly with three characteristics: (1) the *cut-off nature of the screen* that exposes it to that which is beyond actuality; (2) the *passivity of the camera* as a photographic recording apparatus that registers what is out there rather than creates, as in painting, for example, what it gives us to see; and (3) the *extimacy of the camera*, which seems to function as simultaneously internal and external to us.

The three elements are interrelated in the following way. When we see something on-screen, the camera's passivity combined with the screen's cut-off nature results in our sense (unlike in painting, theater, music, literature, etc.) that what we perceive is always partial, that there is more-to-see beyond what we see, beyond the screen, a "more" that comes to haunt the screen (in the sense of a presence that is not actual and that cannot be identified or located).

Though we might say that this more-to-see could always be brought into actuality simply by turning the camera in its direction, the fact that what we see will forever remain partial—and by definition, since the "more" the cut-off nature of the screen implies can never be eliminated, there will always be something beyond the screen implied in the image—connects us to a more fundamental "more," that of the non-actual, withdrawn, Medium (which is a non-quantitative "more," in excess of any actuality), that thus as if comes into paradoxical presence, the "presence" of the withdrawn, with the means of the cut-off screen.

This coming to presence of the Medium *through* the limits of the screen—or *through, or with the means of, the cut*, or cutting off, of the screen—in its relation to the passive camera has the effect that everything we see is not a direct view but feels mediated by that which we cannot see. While the direct view of everyday perception can have the effect that what we see is experienced as our property or our possession, in the sense that its appearance depends on something we believe to possess, our capacity to see, our vision, the indirect view has the effect that what it lets appear seems independent of the source of appearance, thus disconnecting the possessive fusion that might occur, for example, in painting, where the appearance itself seems to be the direct possession of the source of its appearance. In this way we become dispossessed, as it were, of our "own" perception. It is as if it is not us who see, and who possess seeing, vis-à-vis the screen image. Rather, we become those who *receive our vision* from an emptiness, the Medium, which is simultaneously internal and external to us. We can thus be said to *experience, as it were, the very reception of our seeing as a gift from elsewhere*, that is, from something that we cannot locate or appropriate, possess, anticipate, something that thus dispossesses us (as well as coming to possess us, as a power to which we must submit), and comes in this sense to serve as our Law, that to which we are subjected, the Medium.

This Law has two sides. On the one hand, everything that we receive through it, every view, is a gift, to which we must submit, passively and indeed passionately (since it awakens in us a *desire*, that is, inspires us with an empty "more" over every actuality, a "more" we are forced to receive and do not possess) with a Yes. We must say Yes to that which we receive as a gift we cannot help but passionately accept. We must say Yes to the Law of desire we simultaneously suffer (forced to receive through a painful dispossession) and enjoy, by luxuriating in the desire it gives us. At the same time, that to which we must say Yes is accompanied by a forbidding No. Since the gift of appearance and of desire is always haunted by an inaccessible more (beyond the screen image, off-screen, the effect of the cut), the Law of the gift is simultaneously the Law that says "you cannot see, you are forbidden from seeing and possessing, the 'Whole.'"

This double side of the Law is a complex co-implication that our entire tradition has never fully opened up to, instead finding numerous strategies of defense against that which dispossesses us, whether by trying to possess the Law of forbidding in a phallic manner, or by subjecting desire to the Law of forbidding, and so on. It is that whose full acceptance would mean the acceptance of the modern call of "America," now understood as the name for the demand to open up to the complexity of the Law in a new way, adhering in a new way to the demand implied in the "to be." Our acceptance of this call depends on fundamentally changing our relation to the Law.

The double-sidedness that we have called the Law of Forbidding and Law of Desire, the No and the Yes, simultaneously and immediately inhabits *every* view of a cinematic image that thus becomes a privileged transmitter of its complexity and mystery. This duality of the Law that we receive through the cinematic image that serves as its messenger—a Law that announces itself first and foremost through an extimacy of the empty "more" that is the Medium, simultaneously coming from the outside as that which dispossesses us and intimately inhabiting us as that which opens our eyes, that *through which* we see—expresses itself particularly powerfully (as we saw most importantly in our discussion of *The Godfather*) in our relation to the camera that extimately haunts us. The technological, inhuman, and thus also the inscriber of a "more" than human, eye of the camera becomes the focal point of the Medium's extimacy, the prime messenger of its Law, as a foreignness that disappropriates us. It instills itself as an origin of our vision we do not possess, nor can coincide with, and at the same time serves as the gifter of our vision and becomes what is most intimate to us, haunting the very core of our being.

As an uncanny foreignness that is intimate to us, the camera is not only that through which we watch and see but that by which we feel watched, exposed to a gaze we cannot control. To be watched, in this sense, means to experience our exposure to a Law we cannot control but which is our very essence. This condition of watching/being watched immediately characterizes any and every screen image we receive through the camera's mediation. This character of the image is at the heart of the attempt to either try to disappear and avoid the camera's gaze that spies on us and exposes us or to dominate the camera, becoming the master of its gaze and thus eliminate our exposure to it.

These basic tenets of the medium of film qua messenger of the Medium/Law, the duality of which resonates as or in the call/Law "America" of which film becomes a privileged messenger, have allowed us to deduce all other aspects of the relations between film and "America." Thus, we saw in our engagement with Spielberg how the cinematic screen qua inscription of the "more"/the cut of Being or of the modern Law of the "to be" opens up the question of community as a multiplicity wherein each of the members is equally the sufferer of a cut (a cut of which the screen serves as a messenger). This means that even as each individual is the passionate, desiring, receiver of/sayer of Yes to the openness to a world determined by no transcendent agency in advance, an openness activated by the image, each is also forbidden from seeing themselves as possessors of the world, of others, and of themselves, in an interdiction delivered by the limitation of the screen.

The logic of the togetherness of this multiplicity that we can call "the people" (which is also the togetherness of us cinema watchers, each simultaneously opened to the world through the extimate camera and forbidden from possessing it by the limit of the screen) is that of a communication with the means of the cut. Communication here does not mean the exchange of opinions, knowledge, or ideas but of individuals having to expose themselves to each other and express the fact that they are together *since and qua* separate. It is a communication wherein all come to *share* a world precisely because none can possess it. This sharing is never a static state but is always a *sharing in movement*, a democratic sharing we can say, that is, a passage through the "more" that is the cut of the "to be," the call of which they are the passionate and desiring recipients. This call demands that they each take leave of themselves, exit their self-possession, so to speak, and expose themselves to the disappropriating indeterminate openness that is the world. Through this common movement outside they all come to share, they participate in the incessant *creation* (that is, a communication across an indeterminacy where nothing is given in advance) of the world. This creative communication inscribing in itself the cut of the outside or the Law-of-the-

Medium takes the form, in *West Side Story* (other forms are also possible), of song and of the movement of dance, a common-exposure-in-movement-across-the-cut-of-all-the-people-who-share-a-world, the most appropriate name for which is *democracy*.

Although the Law of passion and forbidding is inscribed in the cinematic image and in what the medium of film seems to *immediately* transmit through its basic tenets, making the demand of the Law visible, which also means making the demand of the cinematic medium visible, and thus allowing us to live up to this demand is not as immediate and is the task of the *poetic* image, and, more generally, of the *art* of film. The *poetic* image is not just the visible content that characterizes any image brought about by the technological medium of film. It is what we have defined as an allegorical image (the showing of the Other, the *allos*), now understood as the elucidation, illumination, and bringing into visibility of the medium (itself other to any actual content) as messenger of the Medium (other to all contents as well as all specific media), thus the medium as the messenger of the very (modern) Law that is at the background of the emergence of the poetic image.

This poetic task is not easily achieved and, even after the call is heard and the dimension of the poetic is born, is met as frequently by various defensive mechanisms against the demand of the Law that is the background of the poetic's coming into being as by attempts to open up to and adhere to it. The task of each poetic film, each in its own way, is to try to fully live up to and overcome as many resistances as possible to the demand uttered from the direction of the medium as messenger of the (modern, atheological) Medium emerging out of the ashes of the death of God, and thus to live up to film as messenger of "America."

This tension between the demand to live up to the call of film (or to the call/Medium "America," of which the medium of film is the messenger) and the various defensive blockages preventing it, is expressed particularly powerfully in a specific figuration of that moment of suspension (the moment marking that full adherence to the new Law has not yet been achieved, and "America" not yet been reached) by which the American screen (as well as the Bible, that ancient medium of the call of the Law) is haunted: the figure of the desert. The desert as a place outside any existing civil order, we saw with John Ford, is the place where the modern Law of "America" is heard in *ex*citing freedom (the being forced to open to the undetermined in advance). But the desert also indicates that we have not yet managed to overcome the various hindrances to fully opening up to and fully achieving a (modern, "American") world. Something seems to be missing, something we lost that haunts our memory, at the heart of this failure. This desert call accompanied by a blockage is at the heart of the melancholy and exciting genre of the Western, a genre that illuminates in an essential way what generally haunts, in all genres and all films, the poetic screen as that which comes under the demand of "America": How do we turn the desert screen, the moment of the call, into the successful democratic sharing of the world in common movement?

This desire for the transition from desert blocking to a democratic sharing of the world inscribed in the call of film is always accompanied by a reflection on genre. Genre means a specific way of inscribing the Law, in which a particular aspect of the Law comes into visibility and is activated, often through a defensive lens. Thus, for example, in the form of a Western whose desert simultaneously expresses the call of (the new) Law (which emerges out of the death of God) and the Law's blockage, or in a melodrama or film noir in which the excess of feminine passion—itself the expression, we saw, of the general passivity to the Medium in excess of its theological captivation—makes an appearance that is, from the point of view of desire for control, a destructive threat or the announcement of an inevitable demise. It can also occur in the form of the musical in whose singing and dancing the sharing of a world in open movement is expressed in a way that often goes beyond the defensive gestures of other genres.[2] From this perspective , the transition from the desert to full democracy can either be conceived of as the ending of and exiting from a specific genre (such as the end of the Western, which Ford constantly tries to achieve even as he is blocked from reaching it, an ending that would mean the final exit from the desert to democratic society) or as the transition between genres, say, from the Western to the musical, which is one of the paradigmatic genres (romantic comedy probably being the other[3]) where the possibility of happiness, thus of the achievement of the truth of the sharing of the world in democratic movement, is glimpsed. In fact, Spielberg's *West Side Story*, among its many generic mixings, is the attempt to show the fundamental relations between the Western, with whose desert the film in a way opens, and the musical (and of course of tragedy and melodrama as well).[4]

Perhaps most fundamentally from the point of view of the question of genre we saw in our discussion of Francis Ford Coppola, it is the possibility of the end of, and exit from, tragedy that is at stake, tragedy being that most general generic name for roaming in the desert suspension without being able to reach the promised land of democratic common creation, or co-creation of the world in movement. In our explorations we have looked panoramically at the history of modernity, following the not yet fully successful transition from an age of sacrifice to an age of democracy that can be read on the body of the Image-as-messenger-of-the-Medium as it struggles to transform itself from a sacrificial event to the shining of democratic opening to the atheological world. At its profoundest, the task of film as a uniquely powerful modern medium, serving as the "American" messenger for the modern atheological Medium and of its Law, is to allow us to transition from the tragic world—at the heart of which is Christianity, powerfully occupying the suspended position between the age of sacrifice and the new age of the Image—to the democratic age beyond tragedy. The modern work of art, or something beyond the work of art for which we do not yet have a name, is the messenger of the Law of the new Medium (of the world, of an existence in excess of its onto-theological capture) at the heart of whose command is the bringing about of a democratic world. This would be a world guided by a new relation between forbidding and passion, the No and the Yes. It would require a passionate transformation at the heart of which, we saw with Sofia Coppola, is a revolutionary opening up to feminine Eros.

It is finally here, then, that we glimpse the essential—philosophical and existential—stakes at the heart of the modern work of art (which we have also called the modern Image) that emerge during the Renaissance when Christianity—increasingly subjected to an excess of the question of Being over its theological captivation, thus the theological captivation of what we have called our Medium—starts to weaken. It is out of this weakening that a new, modern Medium, coming out of the ashes of the death of God, starts to emerge, and with it a new poetic medium whose task is to serve as the emissary of this Medium, the modern Image. It is this modern Medium, we have argued, for which "America" has become one of the most powerful names, and it is in the art of film understood as the messenger of "America"—thus an art whose definition exceeds its sacrificial, its Christian, and its aesthetic, frames—that the task of the modern Image has arrived perhaps at its most radical and promising manifestation.

Notes

Introduction

1. To speak here only of two faces, rather than five, as in Mattei Călinescu's celebrated study. See *Five Faces of Modernity: Modernism, Avant-Garde, Decadence, Kitsch, Postmodernism* (Duke University Press, 1987).

2. Peter Brooks has importantly drawn attention to the rise of melodrama in the age of the death of God; see *The Melodramatic Imagination* (Yale University Press, 1995).

3. I have discussed many of these issues in the first chapter of my book on the cinematic off-screen, *The Off-Screen: An Investigation of the Cinematic Frame* (Stanford University Press, 2017).

4. See *The World Viewed* (Harvard University Press, 1979); *Pursuits of Happiness: The Hollywood Comedy of Remarriage* (Harvard University Press, 1984); and *Contesting Tears: The Hollywood Melodrama of the Unknown Woman* (University of Chicago Press, 1997).

5. See my chapter on intolerance, "On the Origin of Film and the Resurrection of the People: D. W. Griffith's *Intolerance*," in *The Off-Screen*.

6. "Before finishing with these additions and multiplications, I would like to modify, if not quite to retract, what I said in my book about the delayed encroachment of modernism upon the art of film. Reacting against what I regarded as empty and prejudicial announcements appointing film as the major modern art, hence against certain definitions of that art, I insisted that the historical interest of film lies rather in its condition as the last traditional art, which means in part the last to find itself pushing itself to its modernist self-questioning. I was amply tentative about this, but it may well be too soon to be so much as tentative about such a ques-

tion, too soon conceptually as well as too soon artistically. It may be that the art itself and, more directly, the concepts in which one attempts to grasp its behavior, are too chaotic to allow of any such perspective now—except one taken upon the platform of a manifesto, which is not my business" (Cavell, *The World Viewed*, 215, 216).

7. It might be that some great American artists about which Deleuze is insightful, such as Melville or Welles, essentially waver between these two modern options. There are undoubtedly other projects beyond the European modernist and the "American" options of developing an art out of the ashes of the death of God. One can think, for example, of the cinemas of Satyajit Ray, Abbas Kiarostami, or Yasujurō Ozu, each trying, in their own quite diverse ways, to develop cinematic projects out of the ashes of the demise of their respective traditions.

8. Though Deleuze himself, unlike Cavell, would have probably not happily, or at least not fully, accept being thus put under the umbrella of the Heideggerian problematic, it does not seem to me to be too far-fetched.

9. A logic that guides, of course, such conjunctions in any of the arts, as in literature-philosophy, painting-philosophy, music-philosophy, etc.

Chapter 1

1. This chapter first appeared in essay form in *Discourse* 46, no. 1 (Winter 2024): 139–75.

2. In relation to this initial more-than-oneself there emerges another crucial aspect in human life: the unconscious.

3. Spielberg most famously connects aliens and ghosts at the ending of *Close Encounters of the Third Kind*, when the spaceship brings back missing pilots from the Second World War who were dead or had been presumed dead.

4. A Law "forbidding" from being the whole, forbidding the possession of speech, which psychoanalysis (especially in its Lacanian interpretation) has famously called castration. There is, of course, nothing that really forbids; the logic of the world simply dictates that we cannot be its ground. "The Law" refers to how this fact receives presence, so to speak.

5. To call art a human activity is of course not exactly accurate since, as tradition has always known, art in a way comes from beyond the human, or from the limit of the human, and cannot be willed; it is first of all received.

6. In this sense, the moment of art is the other side of the moment of Law. While the Law forbids our possession of the world, it does not deal with our involuntary reception of its infinite, and indeterminate, gift. Art is dedicated to this reception of the gift of infinity (infinity not designating an infinite quantity but the dimension that is Other than quantity, the indeterminate openness of the medium). Beyond the Law (which is not before the Law, nor against the Law, nor the Law's cancellation) as forbidding of the possession of world and speech is art as exposing

us to the gift of their reception, the reception of what we cannot will. The Law can be said to inscribe the place of the gift negatively by circumscribing a "limit" (it is crucial we do not hear limit as part of a logic of quantity but as marking the transition between the logic of quantity and the mediumistic no-thing, the more-than-one) we are not allowed to cross as possessor—but, like Moses, who cannot enter the Promised Land itself, there is a dimension beyond the Law whose task is to open us to the gift or to the promise (a major "concept" in *West Side Story* that we will explore as we continue), the dimension of art (and remember Stendhal's definition of art as the promise of happiness). We can also say that if classically the father is the figure associated with the Law, the mother will be the figure at the heart of art beyond the Law. The mother is "forbidden" (as in the psychoanalytic Oedipal interdiction) only insofar as she cannot be possessed, but she is the inscriber of an inspiring infinity-beyond-the-Law, the gift of which it is the task of art to enable us to receive.

7. It is interesting to notice that both Tony and Maria appear from above, in relation to each other, she toward him in the balcony scene, he toward her in their first encounter at the dance when she comments on his great height.

8. The case of the miracle is equally the case of dreams, which come from the world's limit and cannot be willingly summoned; one can only wait for them. As the Blue Fairy describes it to *A.I.*'s David, "At the end of the world where lions weep, that's where dreams are born."

9. In a way similar to Diderot's famous fourth wall, which forbids the actors from seeming to interact with the audience. The gaze that opens to the perceptible cannot itself be seen or, in eighteenth-century language, the illusion is dispelled.

10. See, in this regard, my discussion of Riefenstahl/Hitler's *Triumph of the Will* in *The Off-Screen*; Hitler, invisible in the film's opening, is implicitly posited as the power controlling the camera, the only one who is not exposed to it but possesses it.

11. It is interesting to note that the biblical logic of the marking of the borders of ancient Israel, a topic often on Spielberg's mind I think, at least from *Schindler's List* onward, tries precisely to delimit a land, a land standing under divine Law, which cannot be subject, logically, to ambitions of territorial expansion (although it was in fact subject to such ambitions during ancient Judea's brief imperial expansion). The limits of the sacred land thus mark the interdiction of a will over these limits. The sacred land is limited in such a way that it is strictly forbidden to transform the passivity regarding the Law into a willful activity and thus into territorial ambition beyond the borders.

12. For a brilliant attempt to think the Law in relation to a poetic dimension that exceeds it yet does not cancel or overcome it, see Shoshana Felman's "A Ghost in the House of Justice: Death and the Language of the Law," *Yale Journal of Law & the Humanities* 13, no. 241 (2001): 241–82.

13. Think of the great moment of the child's song as he sees the planes flying in

Empire of the Sun, Shug's exuberant final song in *The Color Purple* (as well as its opening song by the two sisters, "Makidada"), or the Israeli song "Jerusalem of Gold," heard as the Schindler Jews assemble at his grave at the end of the movie.

14. It's a messianic land of musical passion not in the sense that one comes to exist in a Rousseauian natural state and speak the primordial, pre-rational language of passions mentioned earlier, but in the sense that one comes to inhabit it in such a way that the Law in it is lived neither as pure limitation nor as what is transformed into the desire to possess the Law via territorial expansion, but as the gateway to something in excess of the Law, a gateway through which the medium comes to be received passionately, as origin and resource of our lives to which we have access in an unwillful, thus miraculous, manner. The social contract correctly understood, as common reception of primordial Law, is the gateway to the jazz musical, or the jazz musical is that through which the promise, the state of waiting for the miracle beyond the Law, and perhaps the miracle itself, is transmitted to us, in excess of the Law, but perhaps also in such a way that allows us a correct understanding of the Law and of the social contract implied in it.

15. Spielberg has called *Porgy and Bess* the greatest American opera and *West Side Story* the greatest American musical, for reasons that undoubtedly have to do with their relations to jazz but also with the singular relations that Jewish artists established with the black heritage of jazz music, connecting several kinds of American alienation within a new messianic genre.

16. Or Howard Hawks, or John Ford. In fact, many of the great American directors, in distinction from their European or Asian counterparts (with the possible exception of the great Russian directors), who seem to inhabit an already given society (even if they are investigating the ruins of that society), are always engaged in tellings and retellings of the mythical origins of community, as if emphasizing that the very question of America is nothing but this biblical question.

17. Which is also a glimpse of an Israel, the two questions being essentially connected for Spielberg, as two somewheres in touch with the question of a new origination of humanity, with the view directed toward a new possibility of community.

18. Among the major classical Hollywood genres, it is the Western that most often was dedicated to mythical narrations, understood as stories of the origination of common life and of the gods in relation to which this life emerges; the setting of events on the margins of the civilized world, the threshold of its origin, make it a "natural" candidate for such questions. In a way Spielberg uses the defining aspect of the musical, the intrusion of music and song, to raise the question of the limits and origins of language, thus making it equally open to being a "mythical" engagement with the question of the origin of the world and of community. Spielberg evokes the question of the Western in *West Side Story* by beginning with the whistle in a manner reminiscent of Ennio Morricone's famous theme for Sergio Leone's *The Good, the*

Bad, and the Ugly; this famous Morriconian whistle, I suspect, was itself probably inspired by the whistle at the opening of the original *West Side Story*, a film that in interviews Morricone has said was the only musical he liked as a younger man.

19. Later on during the song "Stay Cool," a scene we will not examine closely, Spielberg will stage the group as formed around the chain of transmission of a gun, a communicative transmission that the protagonist Tony will, unsuccessfully, try to arrest, in order to open a different kind of communication.

20. Thou shall not kill, one of the founding commandments of the Law, thus basically commands "Thou shall accept the Law," which is the Law of limitation as exposure to others in common life, characterized by an irreducible passivity to the medium.

21. Jacques Lacan has famously declared that the woman does not exist; in our context, this means that only actualities, the ones, exist, but that in which the exposing, cutting, medium is inscribed in such a way as to keep it manifest beyond the attempt at a possessive takeover is beyond existence (actuality). The woman, or perhaps the feminine more-than-one in everyone, is the infinite passion "to be," beyond and in excess of any existing actuality (which is of course the reason that it is Anita who bursts into the "to be" song—"I like to be in America"—and that it is Valentina who sings of America as a "somewhere," i.e., not an actuality).

22. Consider, in this context, the transition between the logic of revenge and the logic of the Law in Aeschylus's *Eumenides*.

23. And later on, in mockery of the Law, in singing about judges and cops (thus in excess over them), in "Gee, Officer Krupke."

24. It would be highly interesting to figure out the strategy through which Spielberg appropriates others' materials, absorbing them into his own system without violently altering them—almost leaving them in their original form with very little intervention. I would suggest that Spielberg metaphorically performs a mysterious alien takeover in the manner of *Invasion of the Body Snatchers*, where the recognizable form of those taken over by the aliens seems to remain the same, as if nothing has happened, yet their essential being has been completely emptied and transformed. There is undoubtedly something of this in Spielberg's various films where he takes over materials from others, perhaps most remarkably his completion of a Kubrick project in *A.I.*, resulting in a film seemingly very faithful to Kubrick, yet at the same time completely Spielbergian. In interviews Spielberg, in his slightly disingenuous self-effacement, sometimes likes to compare himself to Michael Curtiz, in that unlike great auteurs like Welles and Hitchcock who have a signature style, instantly recognizable, he has none, always fitting the occasion but supposedly not imprinting a clear signature. But of course this is the unique characteristic of the alien Spielberg's strange capacity for mimetism (remember E.T.'s learning about humans through mimesis) through which he can completely hide and cover himself—like the dream-spreading giant *The BFG*—only to better be himself.

25. It is also the moment when she becomes unrecognizable to herself. "Who could that attractive girl be?" she sings to her reflection.

26. For an important discussion of these issues, see Mladen Dolar's *A Voice and Nothing More* (MIT Press, 2006).

27. Spielberg examined this persistence of a love connection after the cut of death in *Always*, one of his least satisfying films.

28. On the other hand, when they first meet in the dance later in the evening, it is Tony whom she first sees against a background of a starry blue sky (the decor of the dance floor), and it is he who is like the tall alien coming from the sky, in the manner of the elongated aliens of *Close Encounters*. When they later meet, she is on the balcony appearing above him, and he climbs up to her. This seems to indicate they are both miraculous aliens to each other, but at the same time, I think, there is nevertheless an excess in her, having to do with occupying the place of the cut itself and of Tony's being in the Spielbergian position of the praying one who waits. This suggests that she is the alien miracle itself, even beyond Tony/Christ. It is also important to note though that Tony, not unlike Christ, has an excessive dimension that marks him as being inscribed to a great degree by the feminine cut; thus, as he arrives at the dance he is greeted in equal enthusiasm, which he equally welcomes, by Riff, Riff's girlfriend, and Anybodys, whose sexuality is undetermined, and played by a trans actor (Iris Menas).

29. An aspect we can call logical, in that the "feminine" here, more than designating a specific gender, designates a certain moment in the general logic of Being, that of the passion of existence, beyond and in excess of the Law of existence that announces: You are forbidden from possessing the whole. The precise relations among the gendered differences marking the human, the erotic inscriptions in gendered bodies (the way that the excess that is Being, the "more-than," expresses itself in different erogenous zones, zones that are "more" than their functional place in the body), and the logic of Being with its two fundamental aspects, Law and Passion, present too large and complicated a question for the present context, as is the question of whether the "feminine" and "masculine" are still the appropriate categories here. For the sake of convenience I continue to use them, but with the acknowledgment that the question regarding them has no clear answer.

30. "I'll get a terrace apartment," Anita later sings. "Better get rid of your accent," Bernardo retorts.

31. The welcoming of the alien in music, in relation to the problem of the irreducible multiplicity of languages, was a question that already occupied Spielberg in *Close Encounters of the Third Kind*, where the question of the translation between languages occupied the heart of the film.

32. Hence the less-than-hidden ambivalence toward Lincoln Center, erected according to a European model of a temple of the arts, replacing and displacing a multicultural neighborhood, thus a democratic place of habitation of the people in

their multiplicity. In the manner of a Jurassic Park, Spielberg, through the magic of the most popular of the arts, film, will re-create the neighborhood, as if resurrecting it from the grave to which history, dominated by the antidemocratic haves, assigned it. Is there also an implicit dig—with the flavor of the Marx Brothers' parodic *Night at the Opera*—aimed at Spielberg's former Dreamworks partner and erstwhile producer of popular music and song, David Geffen, who has transformed himself into the dignified patron priest of the High Arts, monumentalizing himself via the David Geffen Hall at Lincoln Center? My guess would be yes!

33. This is the essential insight implied in Stanley Cavell's understanding of the significance of the comedy of remarriage for America (see his *Pursuits of Happiness*). Here, the question of romance and the romantic conversation are both internal to the legal framework of marriage and exceed it, providing the foundation for the new American community.

34. The last song of the movie, "A Boy Like That / I Have a Love," is staged as another aspect of this feminine doubling/mirroring between Maria and Anita.

35. Jacques Demy makes a similar point in his musical *Donkey Skin (Peau d'âne)*. The daughter whose father, as a result of incestuous desire, wants to marry, requests from him, as a condition, a series of magical dresses, each of which, especially the last one (the dress with the color of time), is made to look like a cinematic screen.

Chapter 2

1. See Joseph McBride, *Searching for John Ford: A Life* (Faber and Faber, 2004).
2. Hegel, *Aesthetics*, pt. 3, sec. 3. (Oxford University Press, 1998).
3. It is the contention in my book on the paintings of Leonardo, for example, that Leonardo attempted to create an art belonging neither to the logic of the sacred nor to that of modern aesthetics, an art that has a claim on truth and reality, even if differently understood.
4. Joseph Beuys often spoke of his artistic enterprise as implying an extended concept of art, thus something beyond art, yet in relation to what it was.
5. There is of course another line of thought (or perhaps several others) within the Germanic attempt to reconceive an originary, thus post-aesthetic, art, an art in which the origination of a new reality and way of life will be inscribed, which is not the line of thought leading from the *Gesamtkunstwerk* to the fascistic work. I have mentioned the name of Beuys as a figure who possibly tried to think differently about the question. Heidegger, in his work from the 1930s onward, has posited Hölderlin as the exemplary figure in such an attempt, trying to originate a new Germany, and through it a new Europe, and probably the entire West with them. We cannot enter into these complex questions here, but needless to say the question of America, and the originary art that is called in relation to it, will have a different logic than either the *Gesamtkunstwerk* or the Hölderlinian prophetic project, as conceived by Heidegger. Nevertheless, it will be of great interest to put these various

projects in a more detailed conversation with one another, though I will not attempt this here.

6. Ford's *The Searchers* investigates the place where the Indians become fully uncanny, in the manner of the German Jews, simultaneously without and within, through the figure of the mixed Indian-white Martin and that of Debbie, the girl kidnapped by the Indians. The full danger of every outside is of course its coming to contaminate the inside.

7. Thus, for example, Spike Lee can say, in a reductive manner, adopted, I assume (to give him the benefit of the doubt) for the sake of provocation: "Those people have done a lot of damage. I've never been a fan of John Wayne and John Ford and that cowboy bullshit. I hate them: Native Americans depicted as savages and animals ... F*** John Wayne and John Ford" (David Lean lecture, Bafta, 2018).

8. As Freud's book was in many ways a response to the onset of the Second World War, so Ford's film was a response to the Vietnam War.

9. Though the directions of my inquiry are somewhat different, I would like to refer in this context to Robert Pippin's important book on the question of the western. See *Hollywood Westerns and American Myth: The Importance of Howard Hawks and John Ford for Political Philosophy* (Yale University Press, 2010).

10. I will elaborate on the adverbial phrase "more-than" a bit later.

11. Ford's third film of 1939, his first one in color, *Drums Along the Mohawk*, is probably not as fundamental.

12. In a similar way, Kubrick will highlight the similarity of *2001*'s monolith to the shape of the screen.

13. In the manner of a dead twin sister who left her scar on the one who is living, as in Brian de Palma's *Sisters*.

14. Perhaps the most beautiful moment in Ford exemplifying this, though there are many, is the scene in *She Wore a Yellow Ribbon* where John Wayne speaks to the tombstone of his dead beloved as an almost ghostly someone appearing from the off-screen casts its shadow upon him and the grave.

15. Both the black people who originally were brought by force and the Indians who have been displaced by force have also, if differently from the at-first European and later global immigrants, acquired the condition of a constitutive migrancy, a new, foundational migrancy that, as it comes to the Indians, Ford deals with very beautifully in one of his last films, *Cheyenne Autumn*.

16. We have dealt with the question of the "more" under the question of the expression "more-than-one" in the previous chapter.

17. The loss of actuality can be understood either as something actual that has been lost or, more profoundly, as the exposure to a dimension beyond actuality, that of the potentiality to, or the medium. To be inscribed by the medium is to suffer the loss of actuality in the sense that we are forced to remember something that never actually was.

18. Which also means, as we will see in our discussion of *Liberty Valance*, that every actual thing that returns to us from the past, thus as something we remember, appears in the manner of a ghost, that is, appears as inscribed by the dimension of absolute memory, which is to say, the ghostly dimension that exists only as memory.

19. An "off" whose logic is anticipatory of, yet different from, film. For an elaboration of these points, see my book *The Off-Screen*.

20. This address to the as-yet-unconstituted public is to be juxtaposed with a later scene where Lincoln will address a public that has constituted itself as a mob, finding a scapegoat figure around which it can gather in a classic mythological manner, a mode of gathering that Lincoln manages to disperse, speaking as he does in the name of a logic beyond the mythical, even if at that moment Lincoln is perhaps not yet fully conscious of the message in the name of which he is to finally speak.

21. The most complete development of the question of the dispossessed family on its way to . . . in Ford will come a year later, in his film *The Grapes of Wrath*.

22. It is thus not accidental that Leonardo, the painter of what is often considered the first landscape in modern European painting, is also the painter of the great *Saint Jerome*, a sort of desert landscape between ruin and habitation.

23. Interestingly, in Spielberg's fairy tale about going home, *E.T.*, *The Quiet Man* is the film that the nostalgic extraterrestrial watches on TV, as he unconsciously transmits his vision to the child Elliott.

24. A "Somewhere," in the terms of *West Side Story*. In Leonardo, thus at the origin of the Western pictorial reflection on the landscape, such a complex paradisiacal fairy tale vision is suggested in *The Virgin and Child with Saint Anne*.

25. We can say that paradise is where the quietude of the man of the American desert—John Wayne, who has been transposed to Ireland in *The Quiet Man*—has finally been reached.

26. Or, in the words of Gilles Deleuze, the Whole is now the open.

27. Or even, though this is a topic too large for us in this context, from the point of view of modernity's concept of self-legislating Reason. The Law (whose most basic tenet is "thou shall not possess infinity") can only be received as a gift, the gift of the medium (from the dimension of the off inscribed in the invisible height of a mountain, as in the Mosaic example). The Law cannot be grounded in human will or determination.

28. We can say that with Renaissance painting the Christian image that was the inscription of eternity has been transformed, perhaps most paradigmatically with and through the paintings of Leonardo, into the modern image understood as an inscription of a new infinity, an infinity in which the modern landscape is also born. With film the image has fully opened up to the implication of technological modernity vis-à-vis infinity.

29. It is also the gift of thinking, in Ford, though we will not get into this question here.

30. I am thinking here of the famous Deleuzian distinction between the movement-image, where we see, so to speak, time only through the mediation of something taking place in time, and the time-image, where we open up in a more direct way to time itself, a distinction that for Deleuze characterizes the transition between classical cinema and the modern, post–Second World War, one. We can easily see, though, that the direct time-image is already marked here, thus at the heart of classical cinema, in the experience of the cut arriving between the two states of the river.

31. In this sense we can perhaps distinguish between metamorphosis, the being inscribed by the empty force of the medium directly (the passage through annihilation), and movement, as passing through time in a less direct manner, that is, without having been annihilated, even if constantly being informed by the nothing.

32. As the beautiful opening of *How Green Was My Valley*, which in many ways summarizes Ford's poetics, says, uttered by a moving ghostly voiceover: "Memory. Strange that the mind will forget so much of what only this moment has passed and yet hold clear and bright the memory of what happened years ago, of men and women long since dead. Yet who shall say what is real and what is not? Can I believe my friends all gone when their voices are still a glory in my ears? No, and I will say no and no again, for they remain a living truth within my mind. There is no hedge nor fence around time that is gone. You can go back and have what you like of it if you can remember."

33. In psychoanalysis, such forbidding is associated with the Oedipal interdiction of possessing the mother. What psychoanalysis perhaps does not formulate is a law higher than the Oedipal, positing that the mother/feminine is the messenger of infinity/the medium, the one through whom one is to receive infinity. Lincoln's originary love, as the film indicates, is the mother he lost (with whose ghost the film opens), and she operates as the ghostly voice marking the place in relation to which he receives infinity. Indeed, the entire trial that is the movie's central event circulates around Lincoln's relation to the accused murderer's mother, who reminds him of his own late mother and whose power of love is indicated—through a key scene where she refuses to choose between her two sons as to who might have been responsible for the murder (it turns out later neither of them was, which she didn't know)—as being higher than the legal law, which we can associate with the paternal Oedipal law (the law of right and wrong, and of forbidding the possession of what is not one's own, which is thus not the higher Law of the receptivity of infinity).

34. With the caveat that I would not see it exactly as a political movie but as a movie that brings into questioning visibility the relations between the artistic call inscribed in the being of the screen and the possibility of the formation of a community informed by the call, or that revolves around the reception of the call, even if it can never exhaust it, to the degree that the call is always also in excess of the political.

35. "Look at it," says Hallie to Ranse at the end of *The Man Who Shot Liberty Valance.* "It was once a wilderness; now it's a garden. Aren't you proud?" Yet it is clear, from Ranse's next question, through which he displays his realization that he never had Hallie's love, that in fact the wilderness/desert has never really turned into the garden. Indeed we can say, and this is a point to which we will return, that Hallie's statement in fact involves a rebuke, implying Ranse never understood what a true garden is—which has to do with his not understanding what a true flower is, the subject of an early discussion between them where he says condescendingly that she has never seen a real rose, when she is moved by having received the gift of a desert rose from her earlier, true beloved, Tom Doniphon (John Wayne).

36. See Jean-Luc Nancy, "Myth Interrupted," in *The Inoperative Community*, ed. Peter Connor (University of Minnesota Press, 1990) 43–70.

Chapter 3

1. Or, more accurately, nearly fully formed—for fully formed art, I claim, emerged only with the Renaissance, thus with the modern demise of the grounding in a religious order, a grounding to which tragedy still partially belongs.

2. See the brief remarks in the Introduction about this latest of Coppola's films, which we will not be discussing.

3. Brian De Palma's *Carrie*, another *monstre sacré* of cinema, is located as well in a logically similar place. Coppola in fact seems to have indicated in interviews that he dreams that *Megalopolis* will become "like *It's a Wonderful Life*, a movie everyone goes to see, once a year, forever."

4. And of course, for Coppola, of a corrupt Rome that has betrayed its republican origins.

5. It is thus that in the tragic age of the Greeks, a moment of transition between the age of sacrifice and what I called the emergence of the image in its stead, the very functioning of the mechanism allowing the medium and the world to communicate is interrupted, as if blocked in the way that it hitherto functioned. This blockage, the fact that we no longer know how to communicate with the medium, is what tragedy emerges from, for the medium now comes to penetrate as an incomprehensible stain (which we can understand in psychoanalytic terms as a phobic object) threatening the very intelligibility of existence. It is this stain that comes to be expressed in the plague of the city around which *Oedipus King* revolves, an incomprehensible stain coming to haunt from inside the paternal figure that gave consistency to existence as standing at the center of a sacrificially comprehensible world. If *Oedipus King*, in this sense, expresses an anxiety internal to the democratic city, a city no longer grounded in the order of existence characterizing the age of gods and of sacrifice, then we can say that democracy is always (or at least still) haunted by the stain emerging at the place of blockage between sacrifice and image, and until we have figured out what the images are that can make the stain as phobic object—a

shadow of the age of sacrifice that as such, at the moment of its demise and disappearance, leaves a trace even if no longer operative—disappear or be transformed, we will not manage to emerge fully into democracy nor truly have art in the full sense of the term.

6. We can think of a painting like Bosch's *The Haywain Triptych*, with its double-sided images, at the edges of the frame, of damning annihilation and beatific birth as emerging out of this logic.

7. Thus, for example, a menacing, exposing camera movement such as we find at the beginning of *Psycho* can be figured as a murderous agent taking one's life, a murderous agent then shown to be guided by a fantasy, transforming an uncontrollable inner excess (the erotic, the mother) into a dominating act of control and sacrificial destruction.

8. In fact, we can say that the appearance of the image of the Godfather in relation to the father's failure indicates, among many other things, most fundamentally, that the truth, the essence, of being the traditional father, the one who is to serve as master and regulator of meaning, blocking all unwilled excess, is revealed to be sacrifice, in the sense that the father can be a father, can hold on to the position of the father, only because he is the figure, or relies on a figure, who holds a power over the limit between death and life, a power expressed in actual sacrifices meant to display the simultaneous appearance of excess (of the medium-world-as-such over the content of the world) and the coming to take possession of this excess. In many ways it is the son and daughter (in the Judeo-Christian tradition the son seems to take precedence here), the ones whose coming into the world, thus whose appearance in the world, expresses an excessive power over the world, over any of its contents—the power expressed as birth and tied to the figures of Eros, the feminine, and the maternal—who are the sacrificial site par excellence for establishing the father as father. This is the case since the son, especially (perhaps because a proto-paternal figure and a site from which maternal excess needs to be eliminated) is a site of excess (of the inscription of Eros and the power of the maternal/feminine, and most fundamentally the medium of coming into the world in general) that needs to be dominated and brought under control in order for the father to really establish itself, in a bringing under control whose ultimate figure is the sacrifice of the son as the sign of the ultimate domination of excess. Yet a son, like the *Godfather*'s Sonny, who dies a death not controlled by the father (and Sonny dies when the Godfather is in fact wounded and helpless in his own bed) becomes (precisely because the son is supposed to be the ultimate inscription of paternal control) the father's ultimate failure, and with it the failure of the whole mechanism and logic of sacrifice.

9. There is another tragic death that is as if mysteriously, prophetically, inscribed in this scene, that of Coppola's son, Gian-Carlo Coppola, who was killed in a boating accident in 1986, thus at a much later date than *The Godfather*'s filming.

10. And it is a question, how far back we want to stretch this modernity. In many

ways, we said, the stain appears at the very heart of Greek tragedy, even if its appearance increasingly comes to the forefront in full force upon the demise of Christian Europe at the dawn of the modern age proper. This fully modern appearance of the stain perhaps reaches its culmination in the nineteenth and twentieth centuries, under the concept of the death of God and of nihilism, but of course it shows itself with the return of tragedy in Shakespeare or Racine.

11. In Greek tragedy the gods are not yet fully absent but become an opaque, enigmatic force haunting a human will that is powerless in front of it.

12. Or, more precisely, a murderous force entangled with a desire to return to a sacrificial regime in a tragic age, thus an age in which the logic of ancient sacrifice is no longer in full effect.

13. Who, on the one hand, stands for the question of the Law in general but, on the other, stands for a specific concept of the Law of the state, the latter standing in tension with the Law of the sacrificial Godfather and of the family.

14. Which, in our terms, has to do with the question of potentiality and the nothing, yet traditionally it has not been interpreted in these terms.

15. And of course, the Godfather, coming from Italy, is a late representative of this Roman figure.

16. If a rose is a rose is a rose, it is because its cut nature (the cutting of which out of any context the tautological sentence performs), its shine in/as beauty, disconnects it from any continuity and makes it nothing but the possibility of repetition of its cut, of its inscription of the nothing of the medium of which it is a messenger. The repetition signifies the empty power of the medium to constantly reopen the world in excess of any content and context. The same goes for Angelus Silesius's celebrated rose without a why, thus without any causal and contextual explanation of its beautiful shine. Needless to say, the beautiful rose does not literally need to be cut; rather, the act of its cutting is called for as the activation of what is implied in its shining beauty (i.e., the announcement of its singularly appearing out of the nothing, which is the pure medium as such, not in relation to anything else), a beauty that in this sense is to be understood as the inscription of the mediumistic cut—that is, of the withdrawal that is the medium in excess of any content—shining in it. The cutting of the rose is always in a sense a cutting for the purpose of a gift (which can be the gift of oneself on a wedding day, as in the case of the Godfather wearing the rose before he exits to the wedding), that is, of the transmission of what cannot be possessed.

17. The origin of the force of Law is thus not, as is often said, especially within the context of Kantianism, the demand of the universal—a dimension demanding that we act according to the fact that there is what we have called a medium, that which opens us to the Whole (the universe) precisely because it is beyond any specific thing—but rather the cut of the inappropriable, which signifies an absolute cut, a prohibition against knowing or possessing the medium. At the origin of the Law

there is a force of cutting dispossession, paradigmatically announced to Moses as he approaches the burning bush: "Take thy shoes off" של נעליך מעל רגליך (Is that a defining difference between Christianity's and Judaism's understanding of the Law, which is also at the source of the Judaic circumcision, thus in a cut to the flesh ordered at the site perhaps most invested in the possessive desire of sacred power, namely, the Phallus?)

18. To a degree this already indicates that no sacrificial killing—i.e., the willed elimination of any human life so as to bring about the presencing of the medium, and thus its Law—of any sort is allowed, and thus that every such killing (as, for example, in the carrying out of a death sentence) is a murder. This is the case since any human existence is that which opens in the light of the medium, and as such its life is forbidden from being eliminated willingly, being possessed, with the aim of bringing about the shining of the Law.

19. Jacques Lacan famously says that desire is the desire of the Other (in both senses of the "of"), and we can now see that the Other is what we have been calling the medium.

20. We can understand logic here as being synonymous with Law (which is why Greek Logos and Jewish Law can be seen as two fundamental historical discoveries at the heart of what came to be known as the West and developed roughly at the same historical moment), which articulates the manner of inscription of the medium in the realm it opens, namely, the world. Since the image as we define it revolves around sites of the shining inscription of the medium, we are entitled to speak, as we are doing here, about the logic of the image.

21. In fact, it is in this smelling of the beautiful rose, a moment of passive reception, in which there is inscribed, in the most powerful way, the future demise of the Godfather, for this smelling gesture announces a future scene where, just after smelling in pleasure the oranges that he is stopping to buy, the Godfather will be shot. In fact, these oranges will themselves come back, thus connecting even more powerfully this initial scene and his final demise, in the Godfather's great death scene, where he inserts orange peels into his mouth as he is playing monster with his young grandchild. Through this play the Godfather in fact will have become an image, fully shedding his position as paterfamilias (connecting to the question of corpse and image we discussed in relation to the undertaker), having transferred the power and position of the Godfather (as paterfamilias agent of sacrifice) to his son Michael. Thus, it is at the point we can call the King Lear moment—as the Godfather transitions, beyond being the sacrificial paterfamilias agent to that realm beyond sovereign power, and is transformed into a childlike, playful jester submitting to an ungovernable pleasure—that the image is liberated from, and comes to shine beyond, the logic of sacrifice.

22. For an interesting discussion of an originary Yes in our relation to the medium (in this case, language), see Jacques Derrida's "Ulysses Gramophone," in

Derrida and Joyce: Texts and Contexts, ed. Andrew J. Mitchell and Sam Slote (SUNY Press, 2013).

23. It is thus essential that the marriage with which the film opens, of the Godfather's daughter, Connie, is doomed to failure, a failure at the source of the death of Sonny, the godfather's firstborn son and thus the key element in the continuation of the sacrificial family.

24. This barring itself of course also increases our desire, since desire is that which emerges in relation to encountering what one cannot have, most fundamentally the inappropriable as such, the medium that, we saw, is in many ways inscribed in the wall. The cinematic image, as inscription of the medium, is also always from the get-go, as *Citizen Kane*'s celebrated opening emphasized, a No Trespassing zone, the encounter with the command forbidding the possession (of the medium).

25. It's important to indicate that as part of the new logic of "marriage" these two sides of the Law should not be understood as being neatly divided across sexual difference, where the man stands for the Law of forbidding and the woman for the higher Law of the Yes to desire, and shining as beauty in its reception of the opening of the world. Even if there might be a certain precedence to either of the two sexes (already a somewhat problematic formulation within the new logic) in relation to the two sides of the Law, respectively, they are in fact each split by the two sides of the Law, living the Law's internal tension, if perhaps slightly differently, though we can't get into this question at greater length here. In any case, perhaps more than as a division between two sexes, sexuality (which is the index of our being inscribed by the medium, the nothing "beyond" or more-than appearance, as the inappropriable—which is thus inaccessible to us, haunting us as the unconscious, that erotic netherworld) needs to be thought along the lines of the infinite number of ways one lives the relation between the two sides of the Law, all of them probably, in post-sacred human history so far, tainted by tragedy, that is, not fully managing to open to the Law beyond sacrifice.

26. Which is the reason *One from the Heart* ends in a festive street scene where all the people gather in a sort of marriage in the open, no longer within the walled family compound.

27. In the following pages I collapse for the sake of convenience the distinction I have pointed to in the Introduction between what I called the Medium writ large—by which I understood the very Being of the world as a no-thing, a non-actual openness with the means of which or through which we open to any actual thing—and what I called the poetic medium, in our case film, which is a specific way of actualizing the general power of the Medium qua openness, which is more-than any actual content, a specific way that is moreover, qua poetic, fascinated by the Medium writ large and functioning as its embodied emissary. The poetic medium is a messenger of the Medium, I argued.

28. This forbidding was already articulated for modern art in an age slightly pre-

ceding the birth of the camera, that of Diderot and his famous interdiction of any reciprocal relation between the audience and the gaze of the actors onstage, known as the theory of the fourth wall: "Imagine a huge wall across the front of the stage, separating you from the audience, and behave exactly as if the curtain has never risen." The imaginary wall separating the audience from the actors has exactly the same function as the inhuman quality of the camera, that of preventing any appropriation of the gaze through which a view is given us (here, the world opened onstage). As such, the view depends on our dispossession and constitutive alienation.

29. And we can remember here the famous ending of *The Godfather* where the door, the parallel to the wall, closes, leaving the new Godfather, Michael, inside a defensive realm, and the wife, Kay, outside. The principle of the wall, the task of which was to defend the family as a sacred realm beyond intrusion, has now finally entered the family itself, cutting it, irretrievably, from within, in a defensive attempt to control the cut of sexuality in an age where it can no longer be appropriated via the sacred marriage. We can also add that, much like the gun in *The Man Who Shot Liberty Valance* discussed earlier, the border wall here becomes a paradigmatic figure within the problem of America, at the threshold between horrifying exposure and the attempt at possession.

30. The other way to bring the alien gaze under the power of the world of the Godfather in this scene is through the actual destruction of the camera—and Sonny indeed soon destroys a camera, when he sees someone outside the compound filming. Elsewhere in the scene another Mafia boss sees his image being taken, and he demands the film be destroyed.

31. Which is the reason for the fall of the filmmaker, his loss of control over the fact that the singer Johnny Fontaine, the godson of Vito Corleone, has "stolen" a woman he saw himself entitled to own.

32. Nor within the diegetic content of the entire tragic *Godfather* trilogy.

33. The way that Vito's grandson, Anthony—it is as if he becomes the heir to Vito's poetic song, through the intercut of that song of freedom with Anthony's communion in these opening scenes of the second *Godfather*—will activate this poetic inheritance of freedom by becoming an opera singer in the third *Godfather*, a familial inheritance that nevertheless opens the family to a principle in excess of the sacred, the poetic principle. Thus it is as if the family will have crossed in its own destiny the history of a humanity from its sacred age to the tragic epoch and beyond it to the poetic era (though which will still revolve around tragic opera, as the ending of the third *Godfather* demonstrates).

Chapter 4

1. It seems to me that her first film, *The Virgin Suicides*, though remarkable, does not yet announce a fully developed system (i.e., the being guided of each part by a conception of a whole) for the creation of cinematic images, similar to the way in

which Bresson, in his first two films, had not yet hit upon the fully rigorous and systematic way of creating cinematic images that would guide him for the rest of his trajectory. I'm mentioning the case of Bresson since it seems to me that Coppola, perhaps to an even greater degree than the previous auteurs we have been discussing, aims to be a truly systematic thinker of the cinematic medium.

2. The case of sound recording offers here a certain parallel, but since the realm of sound does not provide an experience of continuity akin to that of the visual realm, there is a fundamental difference.

3. In the understanding of this book, we can distinguish between a specific artistic medium and what I'm calling an existential medium or, perhaps more accurately, existence as a medium, which I called in the Introduction the Medium writ large. This means that "existence" is the term for that empty openness beyond any content characterizing human life, which is what makes possible the specific opening to any content whatsoever. An artistic or poetic medium, within this thinking, is what activates pure existence, the Medium that is existence, with specific means, say, by having a new form of image making such as cinema revolving around the experience of a cut creating a unique decontextualized surface. The cinematic cut thus becomes a specific way of activating pure existence, and the relations between the cut and the screen content become a way of activating the way that existence as medium relates to the content to which we open through it or with the means of it. See my remarks on this question at the opening of the chapter about Spielberg, as well as in the Introduction.

4. Where the feminine becomes an enigma to the masculine, an enigma at whose heart is a knowledge of love and death, a knowledge remaining, in a way, inaccessible to the men.

5. As formulated within the context of modern philosophy from Heidegger onward.

6. The unconscious is the particular dimension that registers the shock (the surprising reception of what cannot be willed) of our passivity to existence; comes to circulate around this shock in various ways (including through an assortment of phantasmic scenarios of mastering this passivity); and serves as an archive of the numerous moments in our lives when we powerfully suffered such passivity.

7. The phallus, though, is not to be understood only as the site of defensiveness against the passion of existence through the imaginary transformation of our passivity into power. As we have seen in the previous chapters, it is also to be grasped as a site from which the dimension of the Law, thus of the experience of passivity not as passion but as prohibition, comes to utter its command. The interest in Coppola's films in this dimension of the Law (as prohibition) seems limited, however, so I will not elaborate upon it here. I will just mention that in its aspect as a messenger of the Law the phallus, as a magical object through which the medium can be possessed, is—and here the relevant psychoanalytic term would be "castration"—forbidden

from being possessed, which means, and this is the Law, "you cannot have or possess a magical object through which to gain power over the medium" (it is this aspect of prohibitory command that Jewish circumcision was perhaps the first to have discovered, going beyond magical thinking). Castration, from this perspective, is the Law of existence. Yet, as we have seen so often in our previous chapters, there is a more profound dimension than this forbidding, a dimension we can understand either as a higher Law (which comes with the imperative "must") or as something beyond the Law, and this is the passive and passionate receptivity of the surprising gift (that which cannot be anticipated or controlled) of existence, the welcoming of this excess that overwhelms us and that we cannot possess, yet we nevertheless can, indeed must, receive it. "You must passionately receive existence," says the higher Law, or, in the case where this is understood as beyond the Law, "though you cannot possess existence, you can receive it, and (only) passionately so." We might say that the artist, perhaps neither man nor woman (though probably closer to woman given women's dimension of being beyond, in excess of, the phallus), is neither the one who simply suffers passivity to existence, nor one who tries to imaginarily have power over it, nor one who transmits the Law forbidding the possession of it, but is the one who transmits the higher Law—"you must welcome existence passionately"—as well as creates events whose task is to enable such reception. Since artists are also women or men, the various pressures and relations to Eros inscribed bodily in them also come to expression, of course, in their art (in this sense works of art created by men, for example, but also by women, can at times contain imaginary phallic tendencies). Nevertheless, I suggest, works of art at their most essential level express a higher law that can no longer be associated with man or woman in their differences, and they do so through serving as sites, such as the screen, that can be described as non-phallic zones, zones through which the cut of existence can be passionately welcomed.

8. The first in the case of Louis; the second, Elvis; the third, Bob Harris (Bill Murray). Interestingly, in the case of Louis there is another object in which is inscribed what we might call the phallic crisis characterizing Coppola's artistic male protagonists, and this object is the lock, which grips Louis in fascination to a far greater extent, it seems, than the sword does. It is as if these protagonists have been exposed to an enigmatic dimension beyond the structuration of male eroticism by the phallus, an enigma coming to have for Louis an objective correlative as a lock, that which seemingly contains the promise of unlocking an enigma in excess of the phallus and prevents him from exercising his phallic potency in bed. In the case of the gay adolescent of *The Bling Ring*, the pink women's shoes come to serve as an objective correlative for the enigmatic feminine Eros beyond the domination of the phallus.

9. As I repeat-watch the movie on Amazon Prime, the side comments (which one can access on-screen) quite frequently point to various supposed mistakes in the

film's continuity: For example, a space within a specific scene is no longer continuous with an earlier part of the scene, or something talked about that was supposed to have happened earlier actually occurs later in the movie. Granted, Coppola may have been less than fully alert to every continuity detail in the film; yet it seems to me no less possible that these subtle discontinuities are part of the film's general poetics, which is the relation between the foreign land explored by the screen and the aspect of discontinuity, which subtly introduces almost unnoticeable effects of disorientation. Perhaps the funniest, and often mentioned, instance of such strange, disorienting, almost unnoticeable details in Coppola's cinema can be found in *Marie Antoinette*, in the scene where Marie, having become obsessed with shoes, tries on dozens of them. Among the many pairs of eighteenth- or pseudo-eighteenth-century shoes are a pair of Converse sneakers!

10. Or, a dream not far from this, such as the Heideggerian vision of Greek and German as languages closer to the speech of Being. We will come back to the question of a natural language, and of Rousseau, when we discuss *Marie Antoinette*.

11. The term "haunting" is warranted to the degree that pure language has no actual place but is that through which all actual languages emerge, even as it keeps insisting, invisibly, at the heart of all.

12. From this perspective we can say, as Deleuze seems to have intuited, if for different reasons, it would be wrong to speak of film as a language, in parallel to a natural language, which has its own grammar, rules, etc., precisely to the degree that what motivates the transition between the images is the engagement with pure language as such, or the medium as such, in excess of the logic governing the organizations of actual languages.

13. The concept of energy, denoting an excess beyond actualization, marks the fact of the becoming present and active of what we called the medium, that excess over any specific actual meaning and content, out of which all meanings and contents emerge.

14. *Moby-Dick*'s multilingual *Pequod*, a displaced, cut-off surface, is of course a paradigmatic allegorical site for America understood in such a way, and it also stages the encounter with enigmatic marks—not the Japanese letters of Tokyo but Queequeg's tattoos.

15. A feeling, we might add, characterizing much of Coppola's cinema.

16. In the films of Tarkovsky and Christopher Nolan such cinematic movement often occurs, though, through the dimension of time and is understood as time travel.

17. At its extreme limit such distraction results in an accident, as in *The Bling Ring*, when the car accident is due to the distracted adolescents singing along to music.

18. I discussed more thoroughly the question of the "to be" in the opening chapter dealing with Spielberg.

19. David Cronenberg's *eXistenZ*, for example, is a film revolving around this dual nature of the fundamental human questions we have called the existential and the unconscious-erotic. As does all of Cronenberg's cinema.

20. It is no accident that Freud discovered the unconscious by listening to female hysterics (i.e., those haunted most powerfully perhaps by the question of unconscious Eros).

21. This is another aspect of the reasons for which, briefly mentioned earlier, the art of film cannot be understood according to the model of a language, since the principle guiding the enchainment between its images is the communication between meaningless erotic marks

22. This image of the elegant man at ease with himself and with the world (even if contemplative and melancholic) while holding a glass of alcohol, also defines the other character Bill Murray has played for Coppola, the art dealer and father of the protagonist writer in *On the Rocks* (where the question of his assured being, linked to the drink, is part of the title's meaning). Speaking of Bill Murray, who seems to be the paradigmatic Coppola actor, it is clearly the relation he embodies, perhaps better than any other actor, of seeming to be, with the means of his eyes always looking half closed, perched between sleep and waking, even as he possesses at the same time the capacity to be cool and suave (related in one scene of *Lost in Translation* to the Rat Pack of Sinatra, Martin, etc.) but also always on the verge of existential anxiety and lostness, qualities that make him ideal for Coppola's cinema. In fact, she has said that she wrote *Lost in Translation* with him in mind and could not conceive of it without him. The film that, before *Lost in Translation*, activated these qualities of Murray in the most paradigmatic and existentially profound manner is *Groundhog Day*, clearly an important touchstone for Coppola's cinema. In a way *Lost in Translation*, with its habitation, much of it taking place in a hotel, of a seemingly endless zone between day and night from which one feels the need to escape, and to a degree *Marie Antoinette*, with its scenes of repetitive waking up every morning to the same day and feeling trapped thereby, are rewritings and reworking of the problematic of *Groundhog Day*.

23. To reiterate a point mentioned earlier, the phallus does not have only a fantasy function; it can also become that through which an experience of the Law emerges (Lacan, for example, distinguishes between the imaginary and the symbolic phallus). Yet in this context and that of the commercial, the phallus only emerges in its fantasy function, as the possession of "feminine" cutting exposure. But to reiterate another point, the task of the artistic image, which is the image of interest to Coppola, will not have to do with the phallus in its capacity as the messenger of a Law either but rather will involve a dimension beyond the Law (at least the phallic Law, for we might talk of a higher Law as well), which we have been calling the passionate receptivity of existence.

24. Perhaps not unrelated to a famous image by Picasso, *The Glass of Beer (Portrait of the Poet Sabartés)* (1901).

25. A relation perhaps not unlike the one depicted in another beautiful Picasso image, *Sleeping Woman (Meditation)* (1904).

26. As Priscilla will be the dream Elvis has pursued on his way to Germany, as it were, in Coppola's interpretation.

27. For a discussion of the relations between the cut and the call, see also the Spielberg chapter.

28. The actor of her *Somewhere* being a close second, in his hesitation between the phallic race car (the attempt to become the dominator of the passive ride) and his daughter. Notably, he abandons the race car at the end.

29. And all of Coppola's films are escape films: some ending in failure, some in success, and some, like *Marie Antoinette*, blurring the line between the two.

30. This is true even in the case of Coppola's Priscilla, who finally manages to escape Graceland into, in her words, a life of her own. Yet this escape would not have been possible without her pregnancy, which, though it happened some years before, allowed her to discover a passion that exceeds the entrapment in Elvis's phallic prison (a prison Elvis himself failed to escape, seemingly doomed to forever wander the corridors of a heartbreak hotel, thus of a transitional space that is neither an imprisoning patriarchal domain nor the life of erotic freedom). A life of one's own is not a property but the reception of an existence that cannot be possessed by anyone; it can only be received as a gift. One's own life is that excess in oneself that no one can own.

31. Perhaps with the exceptions of Nicole Kidman's character in *The Beguiled*, the empress Maria Theresa in *Marie Antoinette*, and some minor characters here and there, for example, the adolescent girl playing with the gun in *The Bling Ring*.

32. That which is supposed to ground and regulate everything in advance and of which everything that arrives is seen as a manifestation.

33. It is interesting to note that Hitler, the modern fascistic leader par excellence, thus the one aiming to fully take possession of the medium in the age of the modern exposure to it, suffered from debilitating insomnia. For an analysis of Hitler as attempting to position himself as a figure able to take possession of the medium, in the literal figure of the movie camera, see my analysis of Leni Riefenstahl's *Triumph of the Will*, in *The Off-Screen*.

34. Shakespeare, *Othello*, act 3, scene 3.

35. Thus, for many of Coppola's heroines, most recently Priscilla, the sexual frustration that they at first experience is not meant to be overcome to experience greater sexual fulfillment. Rather, they are aiming at something beyond the actual sexual act itself, something that in Priscilla's case allows her to embark on a life of her own, though this is not to be understood as possession or domination but as the welcoming of an existence that is one's "own" to the degree that no one can possess it, since it is unpossessable.

36. Jacques Lacan famously made a similar point in his accusation of the Paris 68 revolutionaries as hysterics looking for a new master.

37. We have seen in our discussions of *The Godfather* how a main question of Coppola père is how to exit the sacrificial compound. In many ways this is Sofia Coppola's question as well, albeit from a different perspective. Many of her heroines—from the sisters of *The Virgin Suicides* to Marie Antoinette and her Versailles, to Priscilla and her Graceland—dream of an escape from the sacrificial, namely, phallic and metaphysical enclosures, which take the form of a family compound that traps them. What Sofia Coppola understands, which perhaps the father does not fully, is that it is the woman, perhaps the daughter of a sacrificial, or even more accurately a non-fully-phallic, poetic father, who possesses the revolutionary means to escape. A whole fascinating work can be written about the relations between the father Coppola—who is a male artist and as such already activating an excess over phallic domination, even if never fully, as the tragedy of the *Godfather* trilogy demonstrates—and the daughter Coppola (the Coppola family with its numerous artistic members being perhaps the most allegorically remarkable poetic family—in the sense that the various family members inscribe various perspectives within the general logic of the question of the poetic medium—in American life), who aims to move beyond tragedy. Perhaps a key film in this regard is Sofia Coppola's *Somewhere*, where the father, an actor, thus an artist in a partial excess over the phallus, lives in a hotel, that transitional realm that is no longer a family compound but not yet a liberated site of habitation, and needs his poetic daughter to escape the hotel, as if it is only she who can supply the resources for the escape beyond sacrifice and tragedy.

38. Hence also the adventure she sympathetically depicts in *The Bling Ring* of abandoned adolescents (thus adolescents not really ordered by the traditional family structure, nor are they having sex) breaking into celebrity homes not exactly to steal but to go shopping (as well as to take selfies—that is, misguided attempts at the direction of the image), thus connecting the strange pleasure taken in shopping characterizing her protagonists and an excess over the (phallic) Law.

39. Unless a concept like Jean-François Lyotard's libidinal economy is useful, which is not clear.

40. See also the discussion of the question of the landscape in the chapter dealing with John Ford.

41. Again, "one's own" here—as in the case of Priscilla, and that of "my own" with which Marie refers to her newborn daughter—should be understood not as possession but as being inscribed by the freedom, the openness, of that which cannot be possessed by anyone.

42. See my earlier remarks concerning why the engagement with the pure medium that guides cinematic progression cannot be conceived on the model of a language, precisely because it is the activation of that which is in excess of any actual language guided by a specific grammar, an excess we called pure language, or here we can call, after Rousseau, but differently, natural language.

43. A beautiful scene hinting at this takes place while the angry revolutionaries are standing outside the palace with torchlights and pitchforks. Marie, exiting the palace through curtain-covered doors, comes onto the terrace, looks at them, and without saying a word, takes a very theatrical bow. First they remain silent for a moment, then start to shout, upon which she leaves the terrace. Is she apologizing to them for having occupied the corrupt palace? Is she trying to use her dramatic powers to invoke a sympathy that will save her life? Or is she implicitly saying, via a display of her theatricality, the cutting revolutionary power of repetition, to them, "You want the palace? Take it, it's yours, for I, a more profound revolutionary, always wanted to escape it."

44. I have refrained from discussing Louis as the movie portrays him due to wanting this chapter not to be inordinately long, yet there are many indications that Louis plays a somewhat similar part to that of Bob Harris in *Lost in Translation* vis-à-vis Marie in that, not being a fully phallic husband, and thus himself in many ways trying to escape the palace (he's constantly going out to hunt, which is the supreme sacrificial/metaphysical activity, yet, since we never actually see him hunting, it seems clear that his real desire is to be away from the palace), he helps Marie to escape it, the two of them being in many ways accomplices (I have mentioned he gifts her the Petit Trianon, as if he himself were dreaming of an outside that can be lived vicariously through her) in the attempt to leave.

Conclusion

1. The call, we saw, being that emptiness that opens us to anything whatsoever implies the dimension of the whole, understood as that in which everything is "included." See the Introduction for a more elaborate discussion of the question of the Whole.

2. For a more elaborate reflection on the question of cinematic genre, see my chapter "Howard Hawks's Idea of Genre" in *The Off-Screen*.

3. In the romantic comedy *The Quiet Man* Ford achieves his most successful exit from the Western, and with it releasing John Wayne from his desert solitude.

4. Perhaps most famously associated with the musical *Oklahoma*.

Index

Aeschylus, 209
A.I. Artificial Intelligence, 27–29, 35, 207, 209
Always, 210
Apocalypse Now, 107, 112, 117, 119, 123, 142, 143
Aristotle, 106
L'Atalante, 129

Beguiled, The, 165, 173, 225
Benjamin, Walter, 158, 161, 193
Beuys, Joseph, 59, 211
BFG, The, 209
Blanchot, Maurice, 158
Bling Ring, The, 165, 202–226
Bosch, Hieronymus, 216
Bram's Stoker's Dracula, 140
Brecht, Bertolt, 185
Bresson, Robert, 152, 221
Brooks, Peter, 205
Bruegel the Elder, Pieter, 52

Călinescu, Matei, 205
Cavell, Stanley, 14, 15, 16, 129, 206, 211

Citizen Kane, 29, 79, 107, 119
Close Encounters of the Third Kind, 27, 32, 206, 210
Conversation, The, 139
Coppola, Francis Ford, 18–20, 105–150, 215, 216, 226
Coppola, Sofia, 20, 21, 150–195, 204, 221–226
Cronenberg, David, 224

Day for Night, 174
Deleuze, Gilles, 14, 16, 152, 206, 213, 214, 223
Demy, Jacques, 211
Derrida, Jacques, 23, 218, 219
Diderot, Denis, 207, 220
Donkey Skin, 211
Drums Along the Mohawk, 212
Dunst, Kirsten, 179–182

Eisenstein, Sergei, 14
E.T. The Extra-Terrestrial, 27, 28, 33, 209, 213
eXistenZ, 224

Felman, Shoshana, 207
Ford, John, 18, 19, 22, 57–104, 202, 203, 208, 211–214, 216, 217
Freud, Sigmund, 34, 63, 224

Germany, Year Zero, 35
Godfather, The, 28, 105–149
Godfather Part II, The, 19, 133, 135, 143, 147
Griffith, D.W., 15, 22, 69, 205

Hamlet, 4, 6, 70, 168, 169
Hawks, Howard, 208
Hegel, GWF, 58, 59, 211
Heidegger, Martin, 10–12, 23, 41, 44, 161, 206, 211, 221, 223
Hitchcock, Alfred, 100, 152, 209
Hitler, Adolf, 117, 207, 225
Hölderlin, Friedrich, 41, 211

It's a Wonderful Life, 117, 215

Jaws, 27

Kafka, Franz, 33
Kant, Immanuel, 217
Kiarostami, Abbas, 206
Klein, Melanie, 159
Kubrick, Stanley, 209, 212

Lacan, Jacques, 154, 167, 209, 218, 225
Lacoue-labarthe, Philippe, 60, 61
Lee, Spike, 212
Leone, Sergio, 208
Lost in Translation, 21, 150–179, 182, 188, 189, 194, 224, 227
Lyotard, Jean-François, 226
Lumière brothers, 163
Lynch, David, 117

Malick, Terrence, 193
Man Who Shot Liberty Valance, 57, 62, 78–104, 215, 220
Marie Antoinette, 179–195, 223–226
Marx brothers, 211
Mcbride, Joseph, 211
Megalopolis, 19, 20, 107, 149, 215
Méliès, Georges, 163
Melville, Herman, 206
Morricone, Ennio, 208, 209
Moses (Biblical), 126, 207, 213, 218
Murray, Bill, 169, 170, 224

Nancy, Jean-Luc, 4, 10, 60, 61, 215
Nietzsche, Friedrich, 11

Oedipus King, 19, 91, 107, 110, 114, 215
On the Rocks, 165, 224
One from the Heart, 134, 219
Oresteia, 19, 107
Ozu, Yasujirō, 206

De Palma, Brian, 212, 215
Picasso, Pablo, 224, 225
Pippin, Robert, 212
Plato, 105
Porgy and Bess, 208
Priscilla, 21, 164, 173, 174, 189, 191
Psycho, 107, 216

Quiet Man, The, 61, 77, 213, 227

Racine, Jean, 217
Ray, Satyajit, 206
Riefenstahl, Leni, 59, 207, 225
Rossellini, Roberto, 35
Rousseau, Jean-Jacques, 32, 34, 192, 208, 223

Saving Private Ryan, 27
Schiller, Friedrich, 106
Schindler's List, 27, 28, 207, 208
Shakespeare, William, 9, 19, 81, 217, 225
She Wore a Yellow Ribbon, 96, 102
Somewhere, 162, 225, 226
Spielberg, Steven, 18, 22–56, 69, 154, 201, 203, 206–213, 221, 223, 225
Stagecoach, 63, 64, 87, 88
Stendahl, 207

Terminal, The, 28, 33
Truffaut, François, 174

Vertigo, 107, 152
Vigo, Jean, 129
Da Vinci, Leonardo, 211, 213
Virgin Suicides, The, 21, 154, 220

Wagner, Richard, 57, 59
Wayne, John, 63, 64, 87–89, 94–96, 99–102, 212, 213, 215, 227
War of the Worlds, 27
Welles, Orson, 14, 206, 209
West Side Story, 22–56

Young Mr. Lincoln, 57, 63–88, 103

Stefanos Geroulanos, *Transparency in Postwar France: A Critical History of the Present*
Sari Nusseibeh, *The Story of Reason in Islam*
Olivia C. Harrison, *Transcolonial Maghreb: Imagining Palestine in the Era of Decolonialization*
Barbara Vinken, *Flaubert Postsecular: Modernity Crossed Out*
Aishwary Kumar, *Radical Equality: Ambedkar, Gandhi, and the Problem of Democracy*
Simona Forti, *New Demons: Rethinking Power and Evil Today*
Joseph Vogl, *The Specter of Capital*
Hans Joas, *Faith as an Option*
Michael Gubser, *The Far Reaches: Ethics, Phenomenology, and the Call for Social Renewal in Twentieth-Century Central Europe*
Françoise Davoine, *Mother Folly: A Tale*
Knox Peden, *Spinoza Contra Phenomenology: French Rationalism from Cavaillès to Deleuze*
Elizabeth A. Pritchard, *Locke's Political Theology: Public Religion and Sacred Rights*
Ankhi Mukherjee, *What Is a Classic? Postcolonial Rewriting and Invention of the Canon*
Jean-Pierre Dupuy, *The Mark of the Sacred*
Henri Atlan, *Fraud: The World of Ona'ah*
Niklas Luhmann, *Theory of Society, Volume 2*
Ilit Ferber, *Philosophy and Melancholy: Benjamin's Early Reflections on Theater and Language*
Alexandre Lefebvre, *Human Rights as a Way of Life: On Bergson's Political Philosophy*
Theodore W. Jennings, Jr., *Outlaw Justice: The Messianic Politics of Paul*
Alexander Etkind, *Warped Mourning: Stories of the Undead in the Land of the Unburied*
Denis Guénoun, *About Europe: Philosophical Hypotheses*
Maria Boletsi, *Barbarism and Its Discontents*
Sigrid Weigel, *Walter Benjamin: Images, the Creaturely, and the Holy*
Roberto Esposito, *Living Thought: The Origins and Actuality of Italian Philosophy*
Henri Atlan, *The Sparks of Randomness, Volume 2: The Atheism of Scripture*
Rüdiger Campe, *The Game of Probability: Literature and Calculation from Pascal to Kleist*
Niklas Luhmann, *A Systems Theory of Religion*
Jean-Luc Marion, *In the Self's Place: The Approach of Saint Augustine*
Rodolphe Gasché, *Georges Bataille: Phenomenology and Phantasmatology*
Niklas Luhmann, *Theory of Society, Volume 1*
Alessia Ricciardi, *After La Dolce Vita: A Cultural Prehistory of Berlusconi's Italy*
Daniel Innerarity, *The Future and Its Enemies: In Defense of Political Hope*
Patricia Pisters, *The Neuro-Image: A Deleuzian Film-Philosophy of Digital Screen Culture*
François-David Sebbah, *Testing the Limit: Derrida, Henry, Levinas, and the Phenomenological Tradition*

For a complete listing of titles in this series, visit the Stanford University Press website, www.sup.org.

Cultural Memory in the Present

Jensen Suther, *True Materialism: Hegelian Marxism and the Modernist Struggle for Freedom*

Jean-Luc Marion, *Cartesian Questions III: Descartes Beneath the Mask of Cartesianism*

Walter Benjamin, *On Goethe*

Elliot R. Wolfson, *Nocturnal Seeing: Hopelessness of Hope and Philosophical Gnosis in Susan Taubes, Gillian Rose, and Edith Wyschogrod*

Severo Sarduy, *Barroco and Other Writings*

David D. Kim, *Arendt's Solidarity: Anti-Semitism and Racism in the Atlantic World*

Hans Joas, *Why the Church?: Self-Optimization or Community of Faith*

Jean-Luc Marion, *Revelation Comes from Elsewhere*

Peter Sloterdijk, *Out of the World*

Christopher J. Wild, *Descartes' Meditative Turn: Cartesian Thought as Spiritual Practice*

Eli Friedlander, *Walter Benjamin and the Idea of Natural History*

Helmut Puff, *The Antechamber: Toward a History of Waiting*

Raúl E. Zegarra, *A Revolutionary Faith: Liberation Theology Between Public Religion and Public Reason*

David Simpson, *Engaging Violence: Civility and the Reach of Literature*

Michael Steinberg, *The Afterlife of Moses: Exile, Democracy, Renewal*

Alain Badiou, *Badiou by Badiou*, translated by Bruno Bosteels

Eric Song, *Love against Substitution: Seventeenth-Century English Literature and the Meaning of Marriage*

Niklaus Largier, *Figures of Possibility: Aesthetic Experience, Mysticism, and the Play of the Senses*

Mihaela Mihai, *Political Memory and the Aesthetics of Care: The Art of Complicity and Resistance*

Ethan Kleinberg, *Emmanuel Levinas's Talmudic Turn: Philosophy and Jewish Thought*

Willemien Otten, *Thinking Nature and the Nature of Thinking: From Eriugena to Emerson*

Michael Rothberg, *The Implicated Subject: Beyond Victims and Perpetrators*

Hans Ruin, *Being with the Dead: Burial, Ancestral Politics, and the Roots of Historical Consciousness*

Eric Oberle, *Theodor Adorno and the Century of Negative Identity*

David Marriott, *Whither Fanon? Studies in the Blackness of Being*

Reinhart Koselleck, *Sediments of Time: On Possible Histories*, translated and edited by Sean Franzel and Stefan-Ludwig Hoffmann

Devin Singh, *Divine Currency: The Theological Power of Money in the West*